English Women Enter the Professions

BY

NELLIE ALDEN FRANZ, M.A.

CINCINNATI, OHIO

PRIVATELY PRINTED FOR THE AUTHOR

AUGUST 1965

cl

226631

Don.

Designed and printed by Columbia University Press,
Printing office, for Mrs. Nellie Alden Franz.

Contents

Nellie Alden Franz

An early Victorian home in Cincinnati, Ohio, where the writer lived and worked for close to half a century.

ELMSHADE

Heir of the past, the stately old house stands,
Shadowed by walnut, elm, and linden trees,
Where robin, thrush, or cardinal commands,
And pampered grey-squirrels frisk and frolic at ease.
Within are friendly treasures fondly cherished,
An ancient music box, a rosewood chair —
Mementoes of decorum long since perished —
And exotic objects gathered everywhere.
The rooms give evidence of days well spent
In family life or friendly gathering;
As myriad volumes witness minds intent
On dipping into wisdom's generous spring,
    It breathes an air of gracious dignity,
    Bequeathed by years to decades yet to be.

A GUEST

Acknowledgments

I wish to express my thanks to the authors, publishers, and editors who have generously allowed me to use copyright material—specific indebtedness is acknowledged in footnotes; to Professor Robert M. MacIver, Department of Sociology, Columbia University, New York, N. Y., who provided the title of this book for graduate study long ago; to official readers of Oxford University, Oxford, England, who made valuable suggestions as to the style and content of my book more recently. I am happy to acknowledge my debt to the Trustees of the Fawcett Library in London where the reference librarians have rendered efficient service at all times; and to the following English institutions for the use of their vast book-collections: the British Museum, Oxford and Cambridge Universities.

Here, too, I wish to express my thanks to Elfreda Graham, a student friend, who was ever-ready with helpful suggestions. For general assistance on seeing the book through the press, I am greatly indebted to my good friend, Muriel E. Kern, and to Melvin Loos, Manager of the Printing Office, Columbia University Press, New York, N. Y.

NELLIE ALDEN FRANZ

3300 Observatory Road
Cincinnati, Ohio
January 1964

Introduction

Much ought women to be held dear;
By her is everybody clothed.
Well know I that woman spins and makes
The cloths with which we dress ourselves,

And gold tissues, and cloth of silk;
And therefore say I, wherever I may be,
To all those who shall hear this story
That they may say no ill of womankind.[1]

THE courageous effort put forth by English women in their struggle for social and economic independence must stand as one of the most remarkable events of modern times. The movement was of course a symptom of change in a society that had weakened, then crumbled beyond repair. There were indications of unrest by the end of the nineteenth century, and a few "intelligent ladies" had begun to agitate over living conditions—making speeches, and having parades. These women resented their subordinate position in life, and make no mistake, they had been classed beneath men for centuries. How a situation of this kind could exist is a mystery, for women were important cogs in the wheels of industry, to say nothing of domestic pursuits: they did the spinning, weaving, brewing, salting, cooking, tailoring—even nursing the sick, and caring for children. But half-grown girls were given a poor deal as far as scholarly pursuits were concerned. Education infiltrated French understanding fifty years before it took root in England. Possibly the English people are a little slow about taking up new ideas, not especially from fear, but as James the psychologist liked to explain, from "seeing a bear," and judging it best to run.

[1] *Elevated Thoughts* (undated).

The first textbooks for girls reached England about 1550; they were strongly religious in character, emphasis being placed upon Biblical material. Unfortunately, Protestant reformers showed little interest in the affairs of women. Indeed, what could be worse than the gibes of John Knox (1513–1572), who said:

> I affirme the empire of a woman to be a thing repugnant to Nature, I mean not onlie that God, by the order of his creation, hath spoiled women of authoritie and dominion, but also that men hath seen, proved, and pronounced just causes why that it should be. . . . Nature, I say, doth paynt them furthe to be meake, fraile, impacient, feeble, and foolishe; and experience hath declared them to be unconstant, variable, cruell, and lacking the spirit of counsel and regiment.[2]

However, the majority of girls and boys turned out very well, despite the "feeble" influence at home. Such a display of prejudice is amusing today, but it was no laughing matter in the long ago. Yet there was nothing for women to do but accept these unpleasant conditions as a part of life.

To get ahead in any undertaking was almost impossible. For women were obliged to overcome not only economic obstacles, but those of a legal, moral, religious, and intellectual nature. How to proceed was the question. An important point to consider is this: opposition on the home-front was intense, even bitter, so difficult it was for the English people to realize that thousands of women were in dire distress because they had not been trained for any kind of useful work. But there is no standing still in matters of this kind, for as people change their ways of thinking, they will most likely change their ways of life.

The position of women in family life is a fair indication of the state of society at a given time. Up to the fifteenth century, English wives and daughters were subjected to strict discipline; they never questioned the right of father or husband to rule over them. Under this

---

[2] Laing, David. Editor. *The Works of John Knox*. Volume Fourth. Printed for THE BANNATYNE CLUB. Edinburgh. MDCCCLV. pp. 373–374.

domestic system, women were at a disadvantage—having little or no social standing. Yet they had grave responsibilities thrust upon them —that is, a housewife in upper-class social circles was expected to keep plenty of food on her pantry shelves, to entertain friends and relatives at any time—even to care for strangers who happened to be in the neighborhood. Really, hospitality at that time was obligatory, almost legally binding, if the wayfarer were ill or the roads washed out. In short, the work of these women took on the character of inn-keeping. Further,

> The Lord of the household was no constant dweller in his own castle or manor-house. He was away fighting, or hawking, or looking after his law-suits in London; and the lady had the rule of his retainers . . . the management of his farms, the sharp bargaining with his tenants. When she gave her hand she obeyed as well as loved with a fidelity and serious devotion to her duties that could dispense with romance; and the father of her children was always to her 'worshipful.'[3]

This was a time when housekeeping was a special calling, as many necessary, even luxurious articles[4] were made in the home. But at best, it was a dull life for the countless women who lived from childhood to old age under the restrictive influence of family life (this would be true whether the women were single or married). To make matters worse, it was the general custom to build houses in remote locations, more often than not in a thickly-wooded district. So it was that little news could come in from the outside world. Then too, both men and women had to be cautious in communicating with strangers, for this was an age of intrigue and suspicion.

To add to the difficulty, the status of women was definitely lowered when the Roman Catholic Church lost control of its various centers of activity. Whatever may be said for or against Catholicism, no one can deny the very obvious truth that women have long occu-

---

[3] Knight, Charles. *The Popular History of England.* Vol. ii. Frederick Warne and Co. London. c. 1867. p. 123.

[4] The housewife relied upon native skill for the making of laces, ribbons, twisted silk, purses, and embroidery patterns.

pied an exalted position under its creed. For is not the highest rank-
ing symbol the Mother and Child? The most serious result of the religious upheaval was the closing of the convent schools. Heretofore,
a girl well-placed in life could obtain training in any one of the church
institutions. She might give some thought to the study of religion,
and in this way find a life-interest—even becoming a nun. With
work of this kind, a clever girl would in many cases develop talents
of a rewarding character. There was always hope.

Another disturbing situation was this: English girls could no
longer turn to the French nuns (most of whom were well-educated)
for advice or solace in situations charged with difficulty. Marriage
there was of course, but this was a matter of expedience, affection
playing almost no part in the arrangement. In some cases, girls and
boys were betrothed in babyhood by strong-minded parents. Under
this arrangement, a woman would have no place as wife-companion
in the home; she would be more or less an upper-servant working to
a set schedule. Then too, it was the custom to value brides according
to the size of their dowries. What amounted to a life-association was
forced upon almost all women; happiness in wedlock was a chance
affair in England.

During the seventeenth century, the Society of Friends (later
called the Quakers) began active social work throughout England.
They visited people who were ill or in distress of any kind. From the
beginning, their innate sense of justice led them to give women a
highly-placed position in society. The Quaker movement stands as
one of the strangest social phenomena of the times. What was it that
caused these men and women to suffer persecution and imprisonment
with such strength and quiet dignity? For many years the Friends
traveled about preaching that pure truth comes only by direct in-
spiration; they fell under the hand of the law more or less regularly,
even serving prison sentences. But hardships, whatever they hap-

pened to be, did not dampen their desire for social work. In Fox's *Journal* of September, 1662, he speaks of riding with his fellow-prisoners in a cart, on the way to Leicester:

> So we rid through the Country—being five of us in number; fome carried their Bibles open in their hands, declaring the Truth to the People, as we rode, in the Fields and through the Towns, and telling them: 'We were the Prisoners of the Lord Jefus Chryst, going to fuffer Bonds for his Name and Truth-fake': and one Woman's Friend carried her Wheel on her lap, to fpin on in Prifon: and the People were mightily affected.[5]

Without doubt, the Quakers advanced the cause of social justice, not only for women, but for society in general.

There was, however, a counter force at work in the second half of the eighteenth century. Sir William Blackstone, a distinguished judge (1723–1780) was responsible for what might be called a "social interruption," for according to old records, he wrote and lectured in a forcible way on matters of great concern to the country. Indeed, the present constitutional sentiment of England is to a great extent the outgrowth of his theories. In discussing the status of married women, Sir William said:

> The hufband and wife are one person in law: that is, the very being or legal exiftence of the woman if fufpended during the marriage, or at leaft is incorporated and confolidated into that of the hufband; under whofe wing, protection, and cover, fhe performs every thing; and is therefore called in our law—french a femme—covert . . .[6] [Continuing he said] The hufband alfo, . . . might give his wife moderate correction. For, as he is to anfwer for her mifbehaviour, the law thought it reafonable to intruft him with this power of reftraining her, by domeftic chaftifement, in the fame moderation that a man is allowed to correct his fervants or children; . . . Thefe are the chief legal effects of marriage during the coverture; upon which we may obferve, that even the difabilities, which the wife lies under,

[5] Fox, George. *A Journal*. The First Volume. Printed for Thomas Northcott, London. MDCCXLIV. p. 256.

[6] Blackstone, William. *Commentaries on the Laws of England*. Book the First. Printed at The Clarendon Press. Oxford. MDCCLXVI. p. 442.

are for the most part intended for her protection and benefit. So great a favourite is the female fex of England.[7]

This was the type of antagonism women had to face, not only from ignorant people, but from the learned as well.

Just what middle-class housewives thought about social problems in the last years of the eighteenth century is open to question. Most certainly, the unrest across the Channel—France to be exact—must have made some imprint on the minds of women in England. It stands to reason that they did not confine their thinking to "the exact proportions of eggs and butter" that went into their cakes, or "the different shades of wool" that went into their samplers.[8]

Whatever happened, Mary Woolstonecraft was inspired to write, *A Vindication of the Rights of Women*, in 1792. This book was the first general protest against the subjection of women; it shocked many readers, especially those who had given little thought to social conditions. This publication greatly strengthened the movement for sex equality. It certainly roused the entire country from its hard-set way of keeping spinsters in the background. Consider this excerpt from a letter: "The Vincent birthday party went off very well. Amelia stood in the drawing room with her mother, while the older sisters—all up in age—watched everything from a vantage-point on the second floor."[9]

It was a social revolt which helped to emancipate English women, and the movement worked in a peculiar manner. For one thing, factory owners in England could not produce enough hand-made goods to supply the growing export trade. There was only one thing to do—increase production in every way possible. All kinds of crude contrivances were put in use at first. Then as various machines were

---

[7] Blackstone, William. *Commentaries on the Laws of England*. Book the First. Printed at The Clarendon Press. Oxford. MDCCLXVI. pp. 444–445.

[8] Blease, W. Lyon. *The Emancipation of English Women*. David Nutt. London. 1913. p. 92.

[9] *Letter* (from the writer's family). November 2, 1830.

invented and installed in the factories, production was speeded up and eventually, by improved methods, England took the lead over other countries in the making of finished goods. This general activity in business provided work for large groups of men and women, many of whom had been unemployed for a long time. This was the first time that women had been able to get out into the world *en masse*. At last, half-grown girls—if poverty-stricken—could earn their own living in a self-respecting manner.

In considering the conditions of factory workers in the first half of the nineteenth century, it should be remembered that the poor working arrangements were set up by merchant companies, and not by the newly-rich employers of England. Members of the nobility, tucked away in their country homes, with tenant-grown food coming in ever so often, and tax-bills coming in only now and then (in one case, the tax of a great estate being merely the gift of a flag to the ruling house), could not possibly understand the problems of people living in poverty down the side streets of London. This ignorance of general conditions was one reason why Parliament always moved so slowly with social legislation. It followed that the ill-treatment of workers, especially in large manufacturing plants, continued year after year.

As previously mentioned, women were a part of this vast army of day-workers. Consider this fact: they labored in the mills from fourteen to sixteen hours a day, some women in advanced stages of pregnancy. Children also suffered under this "make-shift" industrial system. Some of these little folks were paupers who had been transported to the factories in large wagons; they were very happy at the thought of leaving a public institution. What happened after these children settled down to the daily grind of work brings out a pathetic story. The following is the testimony of Elizabeth Bentley, whose evidence was taken before the Committee on the Factories Bill, on June 4, 1832:

What age are you? Twenty-three.

Where do you live? At Leeds.

What time did you begin work in a factory? When I was six years old.

At whose factory did you work? Mr. Busk's.

What kind of a mill is it? Flax-mill.

What was your business in that mill? I was a little doffer.

What were your hours of labour in that mill? From 5 in the morning till 9 at night, when they were thronged.

For how long a time together have you worked that excessive length of time? For about half a year.

What were your usual hours of labour when you were not so thronged? From 6 in the morning till 7 at night.

What time was allowed for your meals? Forty minutes at noon.

Had you any time to get your breakfast or drinking? No, we got it as we could. . . .

Suppose you flagged a little, or were too late, what would they do? Strap us.

Are they in the habit of strapping those who are last in doffing? Yes.

Constantly? Yes.

Girls as well as boys? Yes.

Have you ever been strapped? Yes.

Severly? Yes. . . .[10]

In giving further evidence, the witness said that it was "very common to have weak ankles and crooked knees." Other workers gave even more harrowing details of life in the factories. A procedure of this kind was open to question, as it savored very strongly of interference in labor disputes.

In the midst of this confusion, Queen Victoria ascended the throne. The country was in dire financial straits, many families living in abject poverty. It all came indirectly from farm conditions; the harvests had been bad two years in succession (1836–1837). Fortunately, the people kept up their courage by seeking solace in religion; they finally experienced a kind of mental and moral regeneration which was to light a torch of reform. That is, men and women without

[10] *Reports* from Committees. "Labour of Children in Factories." Vol. xv. Preserved in the British Museum, 1831–1832. p. 195.

means of support were helped as never before in the history of England.

As far as women were concerned, this was a period of definite frustration. For the new ruler was not only stubborn, but extremely self-centered. It was no secret that she disliked the idea of women in politics. When the movement for sex equality began to gain ground, news made its way out of Buckingham Palace—hardly by chance—that,

> The Queen is most anxious to enlist every one who can speak or write to join in checking this mad, wicked folly of 'Woman's Rights', with all its attendant horrors, on which her poor feeble sex is bent, forgetting every sense of womanly feeling and propriety. . . . It is a subject which makes the Queen so furious that she cannot contain herself. . . . Woman would become the most hateful, heartless, and disgusting of human beings were she allowed to unsex herself; and where would be the protection which man was intended to give the weaker sex?[11]

The attitude of Queen Victoria probably reflected the thinking of her ministers, whose business it was to keep the Queen posted on what was desirable, and what was not desirable in social matters. As this young woman could think clearly, she must have been conscious at times that her remarks were inconsistent with her own behaviour, for she wrote to her uncle, the King of the Belgians as follows: "I do regular, hard, but to *me delightful work*. . . . It is to me the *greatest pleasure* to do my duty for my country and my people. . . ."[12] How true it is that human conduct is well-nigh unpredictable!

By 1860, the newly-developed, wealthy middle-class had become firmly established in business. As a consequence, they began to exert great influence on the little niceties of daily life. It was in this group that education for girls made notable advances. Heretofore, the daughters of prosperous families had occupied themselves with a ceaseless round of routine activities—paying calls, reading books,

[11] Martin, Sir Theodore. *Queen Victoria as I Knew Her*. William Blackwood and Sons. London. MCMVIII. pp. 69–70.

[12] *The Letters of Queen Victoria*. Vol. I. 1837–1843. John Murray. London. 1907. p. 103.

and perhaps doing odd bits of fancy work. Few schools existed—to try and trace them is a hopeless task. For they were often temporary undertakings in the hands of untrained mistresses. The curriculum of all girls' schools at this time was very limited: French, music, dancing, and flower-painting. Outdoor exercise according to present-day standards was unknown. As a rule, there would be a formal promenade each afternoon down some main street—a sensible custom that is still followed by many of the older institutions.[13] Individuality was a quality which bordered on singularity; and most certainly, odd behavior was frowned upon during the Victorian period.

Regardless of the type of education a girl received, it was generally understood that she must prepare herself for marriage. For all young women were expected to follow the social pattern set by their mothers. But a "goodly" daughter who helped with the duties of the household usually secured a husband without difficulty. It often happened, however, that girls did not care to marry. Society had advanced to the stage where it was realized

> That marriage should not be the lot of all,—that there might be purpose and interest in a woman's life even when she could not be married, and that to use marriage merely as an escape from an empty, impoverished existence was an act unworthy of a good woman. Women were now willing to fit themselves for life independently of marriage, and to this end were seeking intellectual development.[14]

Social change is not a speedy process. The uncertainty of the situation is reflected in *The Wives of England*, a book written by Mrs. Sarah Ellis in the eighteen-forties:

> It is here, the privilege of a married woman to be able to show, by the most delicate attentions, how much she feels her husband's superiority to herself, not by mere personal services officiously rendered, as if for the purpose of display, but by a respectful deference to his opinion, a willingly imposed silence when he speaks,

---

[13] A group of school girls marching along two-by-two will always attract attention—everybody from the butcher-boy to the hurried shopper stepping aside to let them pass.

[14] Raikes, Elizabeth. *Dorothea Beale of Cheltenham*. Archibald Constable and Company, Ltd. London. 1908. p. 19.

and, if he be an enlightened man, by a judicious turn sometimes given to the conversation, so that his information and intelligence may be drawn forth for the benefit of others.[15]

Mrs. Ellis goes on to say that a wife should not lower the train of her husband's thoughts:

In the case of a highly gifted woman, even where there is an equal or superior degree of talent possessed by her husband, nothing can be more injudicious, or more fatal to her happiness, than an exhibition even of the least disposition to presume upon such gifts. Let her husband be once subjected to a feeling of jealousy of her importance, which without the strictest watchfulness, will be liable to arise, and her peace of mind and her free agency are alike destroyed for the remainder of her life; or at any rate, until she can convince him afresh, by a long continuance of the most scrupulous conduct, that the injury committed against him was purely accidental, and foreign alike to her feelings and her inclinations.[16]

The question arises as to how English women took all of these slurs and innuendoes. It is almost certain that those who were well-placed in life *smiled*, and that those who were down-trodden in life *sighed*—the great majority would be in the last category. Quite likely, a vital part of the bondage scheme escaped both groups: women were living under social conditions which denied them co-operation. Thus, they were denied self-expression. Under such conditions the woman bears the same relationship to man as does a pipe, a book, or any other object. Domination implies force, and pressure is likely to breed resistance. "Mary, Mary, quite contrary" was the natural outgrowth of England's woman-control system. As history has repeatedly shown, force is always in a tottering position, and falls under its own weight.

While these discussions were going on, Charlotte Mary Yonge (1823–1901) was a school girl absorbing facts and ideas of her day. Charlotte must have been an ambitious student, for early in life she

[15] Ellis, Mrs. (Sarah Stickney). *The Wives of England, Their Relative Duties, Domestic Influence, and Social Obligations.* (Dedicated by especial permission to Her Majesty the Queen.) J. & H. G. Langley. London. 1843. pp. 95–96.

[16] *Ibid.* p. 107.

began to write—producing altogether one hundred volumes of creative work. These books indicate quite clearly that the author had a broad field of interest—short stories, novels, histories, and school books. But it was in the recording of history that Miss Yonge showed special ability, going into details about what people were thinking and saying in those days of unrest and social change. It was natural then for Charlotte Yonge to take up questions concerning her own sex. But she treated the subject with a total lack of sympathy, and a display of prejudice almost unequaled in the accounts of suffrage. Following is an example of what this woman wrote in all seriousness (or was she trying to sell copy?):

> I have no hesitation in declaring my full belief in the inferiority of woman, nor that she brought it upon herself . . . woman was created as a help meet to man. How far she was then on an equality with him, no one can pretend to guess; but when the test came, whether the two human beings would pay allegiance to God or to the Tempter, it was the woman who was the first to fall, . . . Thence her punishment of physical weakness and subordination, mitigated by the promise that she should be the means of bringing the Redeemer to renovate the world, and break the dominion of Satan. . . . A woman of the highest faculties is of course superior to a man of the lowest; but she never attains to anything like the powers of a man of the highest ability.[17]

Apparently, these writers had no conception that ability, considered in the abstract, bears no fixed relation to sex.

Among the lower classes, the belief in woman's inferiority was equally well-established. Men were not expected to shoulder the burdens of family life, for the earlier years of cottage work[18] had instilled in their minds the idea that wives and children should support themselves. Therefore, as the factory system developed, it was taken for granted that women would work along with men. Now and then—

---

[17] Yonge, Charlotte Mary. *Womankind*. Walter Smith. London. 1881. pp. 1–2.

[18] Prior to the Industrial Revolution a great deal of textile manufacturing was carried on in the home—each member of the family performing some part of the work, be it the carding and spinning of wool, the tending of the dye vats, or the handling of the looms.

usually through hard work—a married couple would start in business for themselves. That is, they might produce specialties of some kind. A few of these enterprises grew into famous establishments patronized by the Royal family. In England, patronage is given as a reward for merit, not as a special scheme to boost sales. The English people have their own way of doing things—a very good way as a rule.

There was pronounced dissatisfaction among the working people along in the eighteen-sixties. Groups of men got together—just as they do today on the docks and in the parks—and talked in loud voices about low wages, and long hours of work. The consensus was this: the great mass of citizens needed immediate help from the Government. This was an old idea with a forward looking slant. Many well-to-do families were also having financial difficulties at this time; they could not pay-off everyday obligations with tradesmen.

It was at this time that "ladies" began to give more than a passing thought to the idea of employment. Unfortunately, the wives and daughters involved in this crisis were totally unprepared for the change; they had not received sufficient education to enter the teaching profession, and custom did not sanction work in shops or in domestic service. The only employment open to these women, without loss of caste, was that of governess; but the best posts were filled by French, German, Italian, or Swiss teachers, who had come to England armed with diplomas. Therefore, the average English governess was forced to accept a position which combined sewing, teaching, and light household duties. It is clear that reforms were long overdue in every section of the work-a-day world—the time having come for knowledge to be substituted for widespread ignorance.

Briefly, English women had met opposition of a general character over a long period of time; they were opposed by the "weaker sex"; they were opposed by the "sterner sex"; they were opposed by all the authority of Church and State. Yet in the face of these deep-rooted barriers, the notion that wives and daughters should have a more important place in social and business life gradually gained strength. This awakening—or clear thinking if you like—led to a demand that women should be given the rights and privileges enjoyed by men. So it came about that a radical idea overcame certain firmly established social forces that had persisted through the years as a part of the national heritage.

I. The Development of Education

WITH the decline and fall of the Roman Empire, England fell into the hands of migratory groups who concerned themselves chiefly with agriculture. The breakup of an orderly system of State, which may be placed with some degree of accuracy in the fifth century, changed the entire mode of social life: a centralized government becoming a loosely-knit organization of little or no consequence. The schools which had flourished under Romano-British schoolmasters either fell into decay or were destroyed by warfare. Hundreds of years passed before Christianity and other cultural forces brought about a revival of learning, and the development of a native literature.

There is very little to be said about girls' schools in those far-away days. Now and then a glimmer of light comes from what is *not* said rather than what *is* said about the education of girls. For instance, a Latin primer which was in use about 75 A.D., cautioned the little *puer* to be brave and honest, but made no mention of how the little *puella* was to become a good girl and true woman. Under the feudal system with its set customs, girls were closely confined at home, while boys were sent to fairs and markets, experiences which led to a better understanding of people and everyday happenings. It is clear that few opportunities were open to girls.

The Roman Catholic Church controlled the first important schools; it educated a limited number of young men for the priesthood or for clerical posts of one kind or another.

In the course of time, schools for girls were started in the different nunneries. A great deal has been written about Romsey Abbey, an institution founded in the early part of the tenth century on what was probably the site of a Roman settlement. About the year 1090, the daughter of Edmund Ironside (and a sister of St. Margaret of Scotland) became the Abbess of Romsey. The Abbess, being of royal blood, quite naturally attracted the daughters of kings and nobles to the convent-school. It was not long before

The Abbey of Romsey became famed as an educational centre, and probably the prosperity of the convent, and much of the wealth in its possession, which was partly devoted to the extension and beautifying of the church, came from those of the nobility whose daughters were pupils here.[1]

Romsey Abbey is today one of the finest examples of Norman architecture in England; it was preserved by the foresight of the townspeople who paid the Crown one hundred pounds for the entire church property. This transaction took place during the period when many notable buildings were being turned into stone quarries.

Beginning in the twelfth century a limited number of schools were started for boys. These institutions were financed by wealthy families, by religious groups, or by various City Companies. Many of these secondary schools[2] achieved eminence through inheritance or the great competence of a headmaster—even today, "the old school tie"[3] carries considerable weight in both social and business circles. It is of course bare supposition as to what advantages were offered girls in the twelfth and thirteenth centuries.

Fortunately, Chaucer throws some light on the character and ability of the well-born woman one hundred years later, the Lady Prioress appearing in the *Canterbury Tales* as a church-worker, the only profession then open to women. The Prioress must have been a very learned lady, for she could speak English, French, and sing songs through "hir nose ful semely." After being neglected for centuries, it is amusing to find that musical training is again considered a necessary adjunct to education. After all, this is a natural develop-

---

[1] *The Story of Romsey Abbey* told by Robert M. Fanstone. Designed and published by the British Publishing Company, Limited. Gloucester. c. 1937. p. 29.

[2] Primary instruction was given in the home.

[3] In *The Star* (Sheffield) of August 4, 1937, Professor John Hilton was quoted as saying that 52 of our 56 Bishops and 20 of our 21 Cabinet Ministers had been to Public Schools.

ment, for melodious sounds have long expressed a deep-bosomed instinct in human nature.

With the passing of years, the Church lost considerable prestige. The change was due in part to the Lollards,[4] a body of religious men who were directed by John Wycliffe. This group had attacked the corruption of religious orders, and to some extent had encouraged the Peasant Revolt against Church and State. Because of their activities, the Lollards were forced to close the schools which they had so generously provided for children of indigent parents. When the strong arm of the law fell, the unlicensed schoolmaster and the unorthodox schoolmaster were banished from society by popular feeling. A dark period in cultural activities followed. Indeed, ". . . by the end of the eighteenth century England was peopled by illiterates."[5] Letter-writing agencies flourished in London, as entire families used this service in communicating with relatives or friends who had made their homes in far-away countries. Strangely enough, all through this period of mental darkness the National Universities did very little to hold aloft the torch of learning.

As late as 1827—ten years before Queen Victoria came to the throne—schools in England were anything but a "bed of roses" for little people. Girls and boys actually suffered from the daily grind of classroom work. A different type of school developed during the next twenty-five years, not only in cities, but in small villages. Instruction was given in housework for girls, and fieldwork for boys; but many of these schools became homes where each group was guarded rather than taught. The main issue at hand was not how to educate young people, but how to keep a large part of the population from starving. Then too, the officials who handled public funds during this period

---

[4] The Lollards were a group of early reformers who settled in Oxford, England (c. 1387). They preached simplicity in religion, and denounced all complicated forms of worship—such as saying prayers in a foreign language. Probably, the Lollards paved the way for Protestant teaching.

[5] Stone, Gilbert. *A History of Labour*. (The Yorkshire Chantry Surveys). George G. Harrap & Co., Ltd. London. 1921. p. 161.

had to face problems for which there was no well-grounded precedent. The growing interest in pauperism and education came indirectly as seeds of the Renaissance.[6] For with the revival of art and
letters, a human being was no longer passed over as an organism requiring less care than a highly-prized head of stock.

Then the man-in-the-street began to show uncommon interest in
the way his children were being educated. This awakening came no
doubt from accounts of various teaching experiments then being
carried on in France, and other European countries. However, English education remained out of gear with social needs for years, as the
Government refused to co-operate with parents in the matter of expenditure. There was a very good reason for this hesitation: English
statesmen recognized the fact that forward-looking legislation would
more than likely stop donations from public-spirited citizens. Speakers and writers sensing the true state-of-affairs kept up a steady appeal for mass education.

The Reform Bill of 1832 was needed in no uncertain way. For one
thing, workers had long been mistreated, suffering indignities of a
serious nature. The Bill extended the right to vote, and also gave
considerable power to the growing middle class. The House of Commons was thereafter elected on a wider franchise, and its policies
were shaped more or less by wealthy traders or manufacturers. This
new element in political affairs was a godsend to the poor and lowly.
It was not long before the Government was contributing small
amounts of money to the principal educational associations—the
British and Foreign Bible School Society, and the National Society
for the Education of the Poor. The nineteenth century was well on its
way before any attempt was made to recast the curriculum of English elementary schools on scientific principles. Educators were aim-
ing at a working plan by which individuals could, (1) develop mind

[6] The Renaissance represented an escape from traditional ideas.

and body through exercise; (2) receive instruction in the sciences, especially those dealing with natural phenomena, and human relationships; both sides of the process, though logically distinct, were actually inseparable.

Most certainly, the professional men of England have long been culture-conscious. For example, the parson of a small community would often single out a cottager's child—usually a boy—and give him lessons in Greek and Latin. Under such circumstances, word would get abroad that an individual who was poor might become learned. But there was one stumbling block: the chosen few would have to show exceptional ability in giving undivided attention to one subject.

On the whole, however, educators paid scant attention to adolescents. Some American children have felt sorry for boys and girls in England. The idea came no doubt from stories, both true and fictional, as to how pupils in English schools were punished for petty pranks: they were turned over a whipping-block at Eton College, or like Traddles at Salem, caned every day, except one holiday Monday when he was "only rulere'd on both hands."

The educational system functioned in this way for many decades. Then a group of scholarly men decided to form a trust for the sole purpose of training young women. The founders had two objects in view:

(1) To promote the establishment of good and cheap day Schools, for all classes above those attending the elementary schools, with boarding houses in connection with them, when necessary, for pupils from a distance. (2) To raise the social status of female teachers by encouraging women to make teaching a profession, and to qualify themselves for it by a sound and liberal education, and by thorough training in the art of teaching, and to secure a test of the efficiency of the teachers by examinations of recognized authority and subsequent registration.[7]

[7] Roberts, R. D. (Editor). *Education in the Nineteenth Century*. At The University Press. Cambridge. 1901. pp. 90–91.

The schools were no sooner opened when hundreds of girls made their way through the doors—so great was the desire for a more formal type of education. In due time, similar institutions were started in Chelsea, Croyden, Notting Hill, Norwich, and Oxford. By 1900, the Company had authority over seven thousand school girls, the majority of whom lived in and around London. The men and women who sponsored this revolutionary movement in education possessed the courage and ability to carry out reforms on a broad front.

A great improvement in school programs came about with the passing of the Education Act of 1902.[8] This legislation was especially helpful to the schools that were trying to keep step with the Board's requirements, but were not financially able to spend money for equipment.[9] By this Act the County Councils and the County Borough Councils were henceforth to exert considerable control over education; however, these bodies were always careful to keep in close touch with the local education authorities.

The enactment of these revolutionary measures was a blow to the religious schools, for the Boards were non-denominational and could recommend changes and improvements which might easily impoverish the proprietary school owners. The question of religious observances among the student-groups was settled by a ruling that any girl or boy could be excused from religious exercises through the application of an order known as the "conscience clause." Thus, a delicate situation was handled with tact and uncanny foresight.

The secondary schools now offer a good education, but not in any way specialized; they do conform to certain standards which have been set up by the Local Education Authority. The pupil material in England ranks very high; this level of excellence springs no doubt

[8] This Act brought the primary and secondary schools under the control of the County Council in whichever district they were located.

[9] In one school, so the story goes, the teacher made a globe stuffed with cotton, and outlined the different countries with fancy stitches.

from the careful instruction given in early life. The secondary school provides a full four-year course which includes mathematics, science, geography, history, English, drawing, and one foreign language. It is a splendid program, subject to change of course, as the face of society undergoes the usual transformations.

All through her days of gloom and weakened hopes, England has managed to keep the educational system running at fair speed. It was a matter of habit, for good schooling is so firmly established on the island that "all the King's horses, and all the King's men" could not stop the usual routine—World War II offered proof of this fact.

Some mention should be made of the private and independent schools which serve an exclusive class of people, quite able and willing to pay their way. It is a deplorable fact that many of these schools set their own standards as to health and education—out of approximately 10,000 such schools in England and Wales, less than 800 were recognized as passable in the nineteen-thirties. However, these makeshift schools have always filled a real need in education, for they cared for children who had been retarded by illness, or other handicaps. These institutions are usually pressed to pay expenses—few of them having endowments, and they are not in a position to employ competent teachers. Taking everything together, this peculiar type of school is held together by loose reins.

The majority of residential schools have been patterned after the ancient institutions organized for boys, but there is said to be a slight laxity in methods of discipline. Each girl is supposed to get up promptly in the morning; she must make her bed, smoothing the covers with great care; she is expected to clear all rubbish from her special desk; she must above everything else keep her clothing in good repair; and she is expected to be prompt for classes. It is altogether a happy life, with milk and biscuits in the rest periods, extra servings at lunch and perhaps dinner, a complete let-down at tea-time, various games at odd moments of freedom—with sleeping hours coming all too soon by age groups.[10] Foreigners are apt to agree that these English girls have no peer as far as health and good looks are concerned —with Norway a close second.

For the past half-century, the inapt, along with the able child has been a serious topic of conversation among educators; but now the ordinary pupil, none too bright, none too stupid, comes into the limelight. Boys and girls as a group are to be given special consideration in the new teaching programs. And it will please parents to hear that these revised schedules have not only been widened, but slanted in the direction of practicability. The gap between the standard of work in older schools, and that of the modern secondary schools becomes less pronounced year by year. This change in policy is being welcomed by the authorities of many schools. For the selection of pupil material is a serious moral obligation. This step is a move in the right direction—remembering always that children differ.

In times past, even up to sixty or seventy years ago, girls and boys learned to read while leaning on their mother's knee. The lessons were usually taken from the Bible, for practically every family,[11] rich or poor, kept a copy of the Good Book in the living room. The writer is familiar with this custom, for she learned to read her first sentence in this way: "Blessed is every one that feareth the Lord;" (Psalm 128). Now that inventions have lessened home duties, women are working in shops and factories, leaving a goodly part of their personal obligations to teachers, men and women who have no particular interest in helping one child any more than another. The surprising fact is not that girls and boys fail in different subjects, but that they actually absorb enough information to pass on to higher grades year after year.

[10] Exercise of all kinds plays a large part in the school programs of England.

[11] The smallest Negro cabin in the United States was apt to have a Bible, often kept open, as a show of devotion to the Scriptures.

During the years that followed World War I, the movement to improve the educational system in England was given serious consideration and progress in this direction was made rapidly. There was an exciting scene in the House of Commons when a member—mentioned only as "Mr. Fisher"—introduced a Bill compelling children to attend school until the fourteenth birthday. Consider this news item: After the ". . . speaker had finished there was a scene of indescribable enthusiasm . . . and some members threw their hats into the air."[12]

It was the old story of hardship, uncertainty, and good tidings bringing the people of a country closer together. But the Act of 1918 was not carried out in full. It had been hoped that all employers of labor would "release boys and girls up to sixteen, and seven years later, up to eighteen, to attend continuation classes for 320 hours, or in certain cases for 280 hours per annum."[13] This legislation was unpopular. The ruling failed because it ran counter to public feeling, an all-important factor in social change.

Along in the nineteen-thirties, England faced a serious unemployment problem. Indeed, the general outlook in world affairs was far from promising. In 1931, Parliament and the Board of Education were forced to adopt a program of stringent economy. It was then that the House of Lords killed the Education Bill designed to raise the school-leaving age to fifteen. Many projects for new school buildings were given up entirely. For a number of years England had struggled along with a "black list" of schools which were marked for reconstruction or permanent closing. In one county alone . . .

Fifty-seven proposals for new schools or enlargements of schools have been deferred, but of those only 17 are stated to have been deferred on account of the

[12] Davies, E. Salter. "The Reorganization of Education in England." *New Educational Fellowship.* No. 3. London. 1933. p. 4.

[13] Ward, Herbert. *The Educational System of England and Wales and its Recent History.* At The University Press. Cambridge. 1935. p. 139.

financial crisis, the remaining 40 having been deferred owing to the abandonment of the proposal to raise the school-leaving age to 15.[14]

Interest in the new school buildings had by no means lessened. In the House of Commons, Lady Astor asked Mr. Kenneth Lindsay, the Parliamentary Secretary to the Board of Education, how many schools were on the "Black List." Mr. Lindsay gave this explanation:

> There were 999 schools on the Board of Education's list of schools with defective premises. Plans for the reconstruction, improvement, or replacement of 129 of them had been approved by the Board, and he expected further progress as reorganization proceeded.[15]

The estimate of the Board of Education for the year ending March 31, 1939 was £51,002,330, an increase of £1,463,371 over the amount voted for 1937.

Without doubt, the educational system was showing definite signs of weakness. Something had to be done to correct the situation. Dr. Alfred Richardson, Chairman of the Education Committee of the British Chamber of Commerce, made a study of methods used in the training schools in Belgium, France, Germany, and other countries, with the idea of improving general education in England. He was impressed with the fact that workers and artisans in these countries gain their education

> In a trade school rather than in the works. There are a variety of institutions of different grades. Some few students (those who will become the executives of large undertakings) will pass through colleges of a university type after completing a course of secondary education longer and fuller than is customary here [in England].
>
> There seems no doubt that technical education abroad assumes a greater importance than it does at home. . . . The trade school buildings and equipment are on a much more lavish scale than are considered necessary here. More trouble is taken in the matter of securing highly qualified teachers. These are recruited from groups which are still in close touch with industry. Many firms allow members of

---

[14] *The Year Book of Education*, 1933. Evans Brothers, Limited. London. p. xii.
[15] *The Times Educational Supplement*. London. July 24, 1937.

their staff to teach in the daytime, and in other cases a technical teacher spends part of his time in industry as a consultant. In the schools there is much closer approximation to workshop conditions than in this country.[16]

It is fully realized abroad that a man or woman must be well enough trained to shift from one job to another. This general preparation benefits both the employer and the employee, for it means that a manager can find work for a well-qualified person throughout the year.

Reports such as this bring to mind the valiant efforts of England's half-grown girls and boys as they hurry along at night in the wind and rain to pass a few hours in some training center. Thus, investing their leisure time in self-improvement—hoping for a brighter future. England has never provided enough trade schools and junior technical schools to care for young people under sixteen years of age, and very little stress is placed on crafts requiring expensive equipment. In *The Times Educational Supplement* of April 2, 1939, it was reported that more than 7,000 of the trade schools "are devoted to commercial or domestic service." This arrangement would have fitted very well into a nineteenth century culture-pattern, but it falls far short of requirements in this fast-moving age of technical development.

At this time, there was no such thing as training in domestic science. On the whole, the public elementary schools have always done fairly well, for they provided a complete lower-grade education, with emphasis on reading, writing, arithmetic, and drawing. The teachers then, as today, did everything possible to stimulate interest in first-class literature, history, and geography. In recent years, children have been adopting ships,[17] and writing letters to the officers asking all kinds of questions: "What color is your ship?" or, "Has an engine eternal combustion?" or, "When does your ship go starboard?" The educational authorities have an extraordinary responsibility in framing a program for girls and boys in the elementary

[16] *The Times Educational Supplement.* London. April 2, 1938.

[17] The British Ship Adoption Society had its origin in a trial correspondence arranged between four London schools and four cargo ships.

grades, for they must provide a course of study quite general enough for half-grown children who must go on to adulthood with a very little store of knowledge. Unfortunately, this group has been somewhat neglected in past years; they were neither young enough for infant care, nor old enough to care for themselves.

Many children in England are absorbed into industry at an early age. They can find plenty of work at a low wage. The rush to make armaments in recent years has added to the need for extra helpers. In some cases, employers have actually provided free lunches, and free transportation to pupils who impressed school visitors as being especially bright. A young English girl—the writer's secretary—said that she "quaked in her shoes" when the employment officer made the rounds of her school in London for the purpose of selecting the more apt pupils for office or factory. The serious drawback to this wholesale employment of young people is that some will draw what is known as a "blind-alley job," a fate which has proved a pitfall for many a half-grown child, especially in the poorer districts of large cities.

Surprisingly enough, there is some discontent among people in the prosperous middle-class, or lower middle-class. It is difficult to pinpoint the reason. For the average citizen is well-placed in life— plenty of work, plenty of creature comforts. But apparently, all is not perfect. For there is a feeling of inferiority which develops with advancement in living standards. A carpenter in London (1953) who was making more money than he had ever dreamed about in youth, said to a housewife in Chelsea, "Your home has a look that mine will never have, your friends have a manner that mine will never have." Back of this wishful comment could have been social stratification. For how can a boy or girl on the way to adulthood say the right thing or do the right thing if all that he or she knows of good manners is learned on the street? So it is that business men and state officials hand out coveted posts to applicants who have enjoyed social and educational advantages from childhood. If snobbishness plays a part—and who can doubt that it does—then social reformers have a knotty problem before them.

Loss of markets and post-war difficulties have caused serious economic and social problems for England at the present time. Business and industry in general have felt the strain. To complicate matters further, labor unions keep demanding higher wages. Inflation is holding a menacing hand over the educational system. In such times of stress, educational institutions are among the first to suffer:

Between 1939 and 1954, masters' salaries rose by 55 per cent; employees' wages by 114 per cent; and the cost of catering by over 110 per cent . . . Fuel, light, repairs, replacements—all these cost more, and hardly any schools have any reserves left.[18]

To meet emergencies, many schools have turned to former students for help, and centenary appeals have brought most satisfactory results. The Government would no doubt welcome assistance for education, be it from wealthy individuals or from prosperous groups in industry.

The school authorities try to hold children in school as long as possible.[19] But there are real loop-holes, many of which are provided by parents anxious to place boys and girls in good-paying positions. It must be recognized that some of the pupils consigned to an escape-group are hopeless in a scholarly sense, and yet they might do well in a job in some market. It is a real tragedy when a bright student must leave school while keen for study, and in the best of health. The following table throws some light on

The percentage of school-leavers from secondary grammar, secondary technical, and secondary modern schools, respectively, who were 15 years of age or

[18] *The Times Educational Supplement*. London. December 14, 1956.
[19] The school-leaving age was raised to 15 by Section 35 of the Education Act of 1944.

under, and who were 16 years of age or under, giving figures for boys and girls together and for boys and girls separately:

Type of School	Sex of pupils	Aged 15 yrs. and under	Aged 16 yrs. and under (includes those in Column 1)	Total at all ages	Column 1 as percentage of Column 3	Column 2 as percentage of Column 3
		1	2	3	4	5
Modern (including Primary All-age)	Boys	170,457	174,871	175,305	97.2	99.8
	Girls	167,090	172,260	172,849	96.7	99.7
	Boys & Girls	337,547	347,131	348,154	97.0	99.7
Grammar	Boys	6,786	26,834	44,170	15.4	60.8
	Girls	8,419	28,470	45,654	18.4	62.4
	Boys & Girls	15,205	55,304	89,824	16.9	61.6
Technical	Boys	7,710	14,863	15,816	48.7	94.0
	Girls	4,292	8,352	9,403	45.6	88.8
	Boys & Girls	12,002	23,215	25,219	47.6	92.1[20]

In 1944, Parliament set up what may be called an ambitious educational program. The reforms could not be carried out all at once, but at least they did provide a goal for all academic procedure. Classrooms had long been too crowded—one idea being to reduce the number of children in each study group to fewer than thirty. The articles listed below offer further suggestions for an improved school system:

(a) A large increase in the number of Nursery Schools for children between two and five years of age.

[20] *The Times Educational Supplement.* London. December 21, 1956.

(b) The raising of the age of compulsory school attendance from fourteen to fifteen and later sixteen.

(c) The abolition of the term "elementary" and the definition of children's education in two stages—"primary" for children up to about eleven years of age, followed by "secondary" education of different types for all children, up to a minimum age of fifteen and later sixteen.

(d) A requirement that boys and girls after ceasing full-time schooling shall continue their education part-time up to eighteen years of age in County Colleges normally for one full day a week or its equivalent.

(e) A wider provision of technical, commercial, and art education, full-time and part-time, for people of all ages, and also of classes of a cultural or recreative kind.

(f) Wider and better provision for the medical inspection and treatment, where necessary, of all boys and girls at school and for the expansion of the School Meals Service.

(g) The abolition of the practice which has hitherto operated in some parts of the country whereby women teachers are required to resign their posts on marriage.[21]

Examinations leading to the General Certificate of Education have helped to formalize all teaching in secondary schools; they cover a definite line of work for students wishing to go on to a university, or a training college. Small wonder these awards are so highly prized, paving the way as they do for countless girls and boys anxious to enter one of the professions.

From 1920 onwards there has been a substantial rise in the preparation of candidates offering English and History, the sciences and modern languages, and a corresponding decrease in the numbers offering classics, . . . There have been introductions of new subjects in the last twenty years, and there is at present a considerable body of opinion which wishes to introduce into the General Certificate of Education, at the ordinary and advanced levels, a general paper which would insure preparation over a wide field of cultural activity.[22]

[21] *Teaching as a Career*. London. His Majesty's Stationery Office. 1945.

[22] *The Year Book of Education 1958*. Published by Evans Brothers, Ltd. Russell Square. London. pp. 74–75.

There was some revision made in 1950 in the material set up for the comprehensive examination, the pupil being allowed more freedom-of-choice in subject matter. The schools of today are operating under a firm, rather than a strict framework of requirements.

If England has one special claim to distinction it is this: higher education is something for which a student must be fitted, not only by nature, but by an inborn desire to get ahead in life. As a consequence, school principals have fought vigorously to keep from "watering" the daily programs just to satisfy the less capable groups clamoring each year for passing marks. It is unfortunate that pressure of any kind should threaten a well-established training system, for after all some one must be left in the various communities to dig the ditches, and pile up the bricks. Consider also the matter of frustration: even the youngest pupil cannot be pushed beyond what he or she can do or wants to do. The writer recalls a woman-operator on a lift in London who said, "My boy will pass his examination to-day, or I will beat him up." So it is that temper sometimes rules over common sense.

The Labor Party was the first well-organized body to favor a comprehensive school-plan as a means of promoting understanding, and minimizing cultural differences. The start was made with young children, individuals without natural prejudices of any kind—color of skin, texture of hair, shape of features, having little or no significance for this group. Then to broaden the proposal, students who were especially bright might be sent on to a county college where a full-time or part-time schedule could be set up to satisfy any number of requirements. It all took on the aspect of a simple operation: primary education, right through the secondary stages, could be carried on in common schools. However, there was one point in the program which was given little or no consideration: "Shall pretty Sandra (in a co-educational institution) go out with smutty Bill, a foundry apprentice who only attends college one day a week . . ."[23] Such a problem would have to be solved by a group of half-grown boys and girls, for, after all, it is they who must accept the burden— for better or worse—as responsibility raises its problems in later life.

The experimental schools have not been wholly successful, whatever their champions may say to the contrary. As might be expected, the whole procedure has been watched with interest, and to some extent with sympathy. If England must educate her children *en masse*, perhaps this is the only practical way to mould the dull-witted, and the keen-witted all together under one educational system. The people were warned against the new teaching arrangements, but there was nothing for them to do but stand on the side-lines, and await results, be they good or bad. There have been arguments a plenty, but no one can say that ". . . the comprehensive have been triumphantly confounded and that the institution has won success on every count. Nothing could be further from the truth . . . it cannot be emphasized too strongly that nothing has yet been proved."[24] It is well to point out that people today, many of them at least, are so anxious to "be progressive" that they snatch at anything, the untried having a strange, almost hypnotic appeal.

Public school fees in England have increased at an alarming rate since 1950. The question arises as to educational preference: will girls be held in the background, and boys moved ahead regardless of ability? More than likely, people in the prosperous upper-class will favor the son, while those in the hard-pressed middle-class will give preference to the brightest child—girl or boy—the idea being to improve family status in a shifting social order. The sums which were actually paid by parents and guardians for one year's matriculation in different public schools are listed as follows:

[23] *The Times Educational Supplement.* London. September 14, 1956.
[24] *The Times Educational Supplement.* London. November 23, 1956.

ANNUAL FEES: Board + Tuition (£)

School	Jan. 1957	Jan. 1956	1950	1939	percent rise 1939–1957
Eton	413	370	318	250	65
Rugby	411	351	270	201	104
Harrow	400	360	315	250	60
Winchester	387	354	276	210	84
Clifton	384	345	236	186	106
Stowe	384	351	270	189	103
Cheltenham	378	328	236	174	117
Marlborough (out-college fees)	375	321	250	185	102
Marlborough (in-college fees)	336	288	225	155	114
Oundle	375	315	220	180	108
Wellington College (out-college fees)	375	336	231	175	114
Wellington College (in-college fees)	354	309	216	140	114
Charterhouse	360	315	264	180	100
Uppingham	360	327	246	186	93
Shrewsbury	360	320	251	180	100

At some schools fees have more than doubled since 1939, with the most rapid increases since 1950.[25]

To speak further of costs as related to education, it is found that substantial citizens make every effort to provide good schooling for their sons and daughters. But this is a different matter now that the Government demands such an enormous slice of earned income, whether it be from the weekly pay-check or from the more indirect form of investments. Small wonder that the tramp of fiction goes to sleep under a tree, and lets the world-of-men pass him by. The following figures give a true estimate of how the average man and woman fare under the modern tax-load:

Fewer than 1,000 persons out of Britain's 26 million salary and wage earners received more than $16,800 after income tax in 1957, . . . and only 1,249,000 persons got more than $2,800 and 190,000 got more than $5,600. . . .[26]

[25] *The Times Educational Supplement.* London. December 14, 1956.

[26] The Cincinnati *Post and Times Star* (from a Government publication on national income and expenditure). Cincinnati, Ohio (U.S.A.). September 9, 1958.

With conditions so trying there is little that the average family can do but cut everyday expenses, and pray for wise counsel in affairs of State.

Another innovation threatens the school system: children may be paid for going to school—educators of the last century would have gasped for breath at this statement. And surprisingly enough, the proposition is gaining strength year by year, as young people are being taken from school, and sent into the work-a-day world totally unprepared for any worthwhile job. Of course, these employees can secure places, and earn good wages without much difficulty—the catch being that the work is temporary. So it is that many educators have ". . . come to believe that the State should buy later school-leaving by paying allowances which compete with the wage earning of the adolescent worker."[27] Vigorous protests would no doubt be heard if public funds were used for this purpose. As heretofore suggested, industry might come to the rescue and pay a low wage to pupils who stay on in grammar school as a step toward apprenticeship in some special field of employment. It all sounds plausible in this time of social change, to say nothing of social unrest in a world deranged to a state of confusion.

As for scientific training, English children had all the rules set down for them by way of a school technical certificate in 1957. The idea was put forth in order to meet the urgent requirements of a country sorely in need of technicians. There are hundreds, maybe thousands of children, who are technically inclined, and yet rank poorly in their everyday school work. For them, the additional certificate was made to order, as it really provides a bridgework between the secondary schools, and the technical colleges. However, this is not a plan designed for easy-going, as the following list of subjects will show: English, French, science, mechanics, metalwork, and technical drawing. The average child should find this program quite within his or her intellectual reach. It is a move in the right direction.

[27] *The Times Educational Supplement.* London. July 12, 1957.

The most formidable hurdle for education in England is the general concern for safety and respectability. But the scientific revolution is here, and young people have got to 'brace up' for the necessary tasks, be they soil-handed or clean-handed. This snobbish attitude is unfortunate in that educators are faced with a two-way proposition: what the people want, and what the country needs. Industry has been forced to rely upon the less-gifted—that is, upon boys and girls who have done only mediocre work in the secondary schools. It is all very disheartening. Why not train the youth from childhood to think of machines as desirable implements in the wage-earning years ahead? As one writer has said, skill with the hands, and acquaintances with machines, should be looked upon as a part of education, "just like cricket."

In some schools and colleges an effort is being made to do away with class-consciousness—a somewhat dubious experiment. There are, for example, a number of well-bred girls who come down to London each year for advanced training. What they find is new, strange, and at times open to question. Consider this episode: a seminar was being held at the University of London—often called "a melting pot of ideas." A well-known professor was meeting a class in the late afternoon; he walked into the room with rapid steps, adjusted a chair and sat down. Then with piercing eyes and an accent bordering on a lisp, he began:

> Professor: 'Would any one like to talk?'
> Student: 'Yes Sir, I would.' (a tall youth in the back row was speaking).
> Professor: 'Well, go ahead.'
> Student: 'I think this civilization stuff has gone too far.'
> Professor: 'Yes, and just how?'
> Student: 'Well Sir, this bath business every Saturday night.'[28]

All was quiet—then a young woman giggled.

There is another problem: it has long been a question as to the

[28] The writer's diary. 1933.

value of specialization in the more formal period of schooling. The tendency to follow a narrow groove of thought prevails very definitely among men and women in the professions. This weakness—for such it is—can hardly be avoided when schedules are fitted to only one subject. Scholars have come to realize that the educational system should provide a wider field of interest for this particular group. Dr. Grayson Kirk, President of Columbia University, New York, had this to say:

> No professional school program can possibly teach any student everything he needs to know about medicine, law, engineering, or anything else. . . . Therefore, we must give up our past efforts to meet this problem by adding courses and requirements for our professional degrees. We must see to it that the student is given the most significant basic knowledge, that he is led to develop techniques of study, that he is made aware of the relationship of his field to others.[29]

This situation is laden with difficulty—so much ground to be covered in so short a time.

Only scant attention has been given to post-graduate work in England. There have been so many self-made scholars on the island that only a minimum of thought has been given to organized study—that is, research in history, science, and literature. The idea uppermost in the minds of parents and teachers was to train young people to speak correctly, and to converse in a manner which reflected a background of general knowledge. Under such conditions, the woman who married a college-trained man was at a disadvantage, becoming a silent partner when the conversation got beyond her depth —and the English wife does not take kindly to playing "second fiddle." But times are changing. For this reason the Government is doing more and more for men and women who wish to go on with graduate work.[30] The following table gives some idea of the benefits

[29] *Newsletter* (Graduate Faculties). Columbia University. New York 27, N. Y. February, 1959. p. 3.

[30] Queen Juliana of Holland is, at the present time (1963), the only woman-ruler who has earned a university degree.

provided for exceptional students—the group most likely to succeed
in the years to come:

Grants received in £.	Percentage of students in receipt of such grant
Nil	4.6
60 plus fees	0.6
160 plus fees	1.2
176 plus fees	2.8
200 no fees	0.6
220 plus fees	2.1
232 plus fees	2.1
240 plus fees	1.7
245 plus fees	12.5
250 no fees	1.7
260 no fees	0.6
260 plus fees	1.2
275 plus fees	1.2
285 plus fees	40.0
290 plus fees	0.6
300 no fees	1.7
320 no fees	1.7
300 plus fees	6.0
325 plus fees	4.5
350 plus fees	5.1
352 no fees	0.6
382 plus fees	0.6
400 no fees	1.1
425 no fees	1.1
400 plus fees	1.1
425 plus fees	0.6
475 plus fees	0.6
495 plus fees	0.6
500 plus fees	0.6
900 (salary)	0.6–100%[31]

The universities are in considerable difficulty at the present time,
for they, like the secondary schools, must carry on in the face of
rising costs. It is estimated that what the University of London got
for 1957–1958 was close to £500,000 short of actual needs, while in
the same year Oxford University carried a deficit of £89,000, and
Cambridge University struggled along with a shortage of £56,000.
Capital grants have thus been inadequate. Indeed, ". . . the Govern-

[31] *The Times Educational Supplement*. London. November 23, 1956.

ment's authorisation last February of a provisional building pro-gramme totalling £60 million over the four years 1960–63 can be criticised as too little and too late."[32]

As for growth, the number of persons seeking full-time training in the universities since World War II has just about doubled. Officials accept suggestions for expansive plans of one kind or another, but do not always follow these ideas with grants large enough to cover additional costs. It all adds up to a kind of economic merry-go-round at a time when England needs scholarly men and women as never be-fore in her history.

To a great extent, the educational system of England has stood as a model for all English-speaking countries. Yet, it is possible, even more than likely, that the teaching program has become too cut-and-dried for the needs of an ever-changing social pattern. There is too much emphasis on past events—the Roman occupation being a case in point. Small wonder that a boy from the United States started to Sunday School with a Latin grammar under his arm, because, as he explained to his mother, "All the boys over here carry them." No one would care to deny the value of the classics. But a school will always be a living organism; it cannot be held in check for any length of time. Then too, the human element must be considered—teachers reporting that many pupils who drag along in Latin often make great headway in other subjects. However, English children have very little choice in this matter, as foreign languages constitute 500 out of 1,000 marks in the entrance examinations to Public Schools (really private secondary schools which offer food and lodging). These in-stitutions *emphasize character training*. Further, there are the old, en-dowed Grammar Schools—partly supported by Government grants —which often care for gifted children in the lower income groups. All in all, England has clung to the past in educational matters. There may be some truth in the remark that sometimes an English boy

[32] *The Observer*. London. October 12, 1958.

leaves secondary school more of a "little Roman" than a "little Englishman."

This slant on educational procedure comes to the surface again in studying old records, for the teaching of history in England meant the teaching of English history, with only about ten per cent of the time-quotient being spent on general history. The average English child of thirteen knows nothing about the Constitution of the United States, while by comparison, almost any boy or girl from New York to San Francisco (U.S.A.) would understand the significance of the *Magna Charta*. Furthermore, the time given to the study of geography was evenly divided between the British Isles and the British Dominions, an arrangement out of all proportion to the value of the material—Ireland being a case in point. The hours spent on reading the Bible are open to question, as many parents feel that such work should be covered in the home. In composition, both the spelling and the sentence structure are criticised quite fully, while the *legibility* of the hand-writing is passed over without comment.

Another fault of the educational system rests on the months of time spent in the study of Shakespearean plays, many of which are memorized by students from beginning to end.[33] Such a method might be defended if it developed proper reading habits; however, statistics show that the books English children read in the classroom, and the books English adults take from the libraries have little or no connection. For, as indicated in library records, John Masefield, the Poet Laureate, has a very small following in England, but is widely read in other English-speaking countries. What to retain and what to cast off is a vital question in educational circles today. Since World War II, England has been plagued by alien ideas which would have disrupted a society less tolerant, less resistant to change. What amounted to a mild social upheaval did generate enough strength to disturb

---

[33] At any performance of Shakespeare, English children can be heard going on right along with the actors, word for word.

an old, well-established school system in a somewhat vital way.

The changes which have taken place in education during fifteen years were discussed in *Time* (April 21, 1961), an American magazine, as follows: though college enrollment in England "... is still only two-tenths of 1% of the population (v. 2% in the U.S.), it has more than doubled since 1948 to 103,000; in four years it may hit 175,000." Purists fear that *more* may mean *worse* in this struggle for learning. However, many Britains feel that actual survival depends upon the future of their educational institutions. So it is that more glass-and-steel buildings are going up at Leicester and Birmingham for chemistry; at Hull for physics; at Liverpool for engineering. Even Brighton, that peaceful sea-side resort, is moving into the picture with plans for a university whose main course will be technical in character.

School teachers in England have told the writer that the new colleges do excellent work in teaching American literature. These centres of learning have very capable staffs—men and women who have been trained in the best tradition, sometimes in England, sometimes abroad. People in the upper-classes still smile at any innovation in education. Indeed, to this day, commuters—that is, those who have had little time for tea and tutors—are addressed as Mister (never Doctor) after receiving a Ph.D. degree. The main thing is to have all avenues of opportunity left open. The small adjustments will come later.

Education must be tied in with military activities, unsavory as the suggestion may be. Retired warriors often move into posts of responsibility in civilian life. It has come to pass that there is need for intensive training, not only in subjects related to combative tactics, but in the wider field of general knowledge. To complicate the situation, modern inventions have come to play a large part in war maneuvers; the aeroplane, radar, satellites, and guided missiles, for instance, making the study of physics and chemistry almost imperative in all schools operating under the Ministries of War. The centres of learning conducted by agents of the State have always been more progressive than the ancient universities in England.

They were the first to introduce science, drawing, and 'life situations' into schools; they were the first to free the school from a deadening monopoly of religious dogma; and they were among the first to use national languages as the medium of instruction instead of medieval Latin.[34]

It is clear that the institutions devoted to military training have taken on the role of God-parent to progressive education. They do not fall under criticism very often—future benefits being far more important than immediate costs. But with the rapid changes now going on in society, the day may come when emotional interests will give way to scientific statesmanship, leaving the Armed Forces with but one duty: to guard a world dedicated to peace.

[34] *The Year Book of Education. 1938.* Published by Evans Brothers, Ltd. Russell Square. London. p. 413.

II. Education

In the long ago, education for girls was either a matter of evasion or thoughtless planning. It was an arrangement that went unchallenged for centuries. But women as a group had no feeling of incompleteness, for the sum total of their desires was to marry and bring up a family. Therefore, to secure a husband was to all intents and purposes, the main objective of life, with no time to waste. But it sometimes happened that an attractive maiden would grow up from childhood to womanhood without having had a proposal of marriage. Consider this lament:

> "Being foreteene and toward tother yeers,
> Good Lord, thought I, fifteen will nere be here."

To be a spinster was not altogether a personal problem, for the entire household shared in the embarrassment. To complicate the situation, daughters one, two, and three, were the rule, rather than the exception in large Victorian families.

With so many troublesome problems complicating social life, it is strange that no one thought about raising the standard of education for girls. This was a time when fresh streams of thought were making their way over the nation—Caxton and his printing press having produced a large quantity of books and other printed matter at low cost. It is worthy of note, that a few wealthy families began to employ tutors for their sons and daughters—that is, for the special arts—leaving the instruction of reading, writing, and counting, for the domestic chaplains. In the eighteen-sixties, there were thousands of families in the lower income brackets who lived well, but could not afford private instruction for their children. After a time, a kind of lecture program, known as "the virtues," was recommended for girls, and it was usually supervised by friends or relatives. The

subjects were listed in the copy books as "good music," "easy dancing," and "fine needle-work." Sometimes these class exercises were
carried out in a haphazard way, all studies being suspended if they
interfered with pleasures of any kind. But social movements sometimes take a devious course, and it is possible that a rational system
of instruction was even then in the process of development.

Families of all religious faiths suffered under the "spinster blight,"
but it was the Roman Catholics who handled the problem with some
degree of competence. It became the custom for prominent families
to announce with a show of pride that "our most saintly daughter" is
planning to give herself to the Church. The practice worked very
well, the custom being accepted without question by an easy-going
public. That is, until about 1850, when a few people began to make
adverse comments—actually calling the plan a "church device" to
recruit labor without payment of salaries.

An English woman relates the trials of a young girl, a neighbor,
who was living in Hampton Court. It was no secret that all forty-
five families—favored tenants of the Queen—were disturbed over
the fact that one of their group was being hustled off to a convent because she had passed her seventeenth birthday without securing a
husband. The nun-to-be, as reports had it, was very unhappy at the
thought of spending the rest of her life in seclusion. But all turned
out happily when a "charming Mr. Elwes came forward in time to
save another reluctant novice from taking the vows of the Church of
Rome."[1] It was indeed a symptom of social change—this time a
movement in defense of fair play.

With education, as with most everything else, complete submis-
sion was the lot of young people for centuries. Girls were kept under
strict supervision; they had almost no outside contacts, being more
or less confined in their own homes. Private entertainments were
given occasionally, occurring for the most part during the Christmas

---

[1] Barrington, Viscountess Charlotte. *Through Eighty Years* (*1855–1935*). John Murray.
Albemarle Street, W. London. 1938. p. 48.

holidays—a time when relatives were apt to get together for a few days of merry-making. As other writers have pointed out, there were benefits invisibly exercised in many homes—that is, a bracing atmosphere was provided for boys and girls in everyday life. Even small children were brought up with the idea that they must take a lively interest in history, and have definite opinions on current events. This approach to cultural training was carried over from century to century—English children often surprising foreigners with remarks far beyond their years.

Unfortunately, a number of girls were growing up without the benefit of mental cultivation of any kind. This was the group that suffered so severely when financial troubles beset family life in the nineteenth century. The only work a well-bred girl could do without losing the respect of family and friends would be to open a school, or seek a teaching position. The question of reference was a difficult hurdle; for what could friends say, when there was nothing to say. Mrs. Gaskell gives a clear picture of such a situation:

If Miss Matty could teach children anything, [she said] it would throw her among the little elves in whom her soul delighted. I ran over her accomplishments . . . She had . . . been able to trace out patterns very nicely for muslin embroidery, by dint of placing a piece of silver-paper over the design to be copied, and holding both against the window-pane while she marked the scollop and eyelet-holes. But that was her nearest approach to the accomplishment of drawing, and I did not think it would go very far. . . . I had come down to reading, writing, and arithmetic; and, in reading the chapter every morning, she always coughed before coming to long words. I doubted her power of getting through a genealogical chapter without any number of coughs. Writing she did well and delicately—but spelling! She seemed to think that the more out-of-the-way this was, and the more trouble it cost her, the greater the compliment she paid to her correspondent: . . .[2]

At this time a governess received a salary which barely covered living expenses; but she was spared the embarrassment of leading a parasitical existence in a large Victorian family. Eventually, eco-

[2] Gaskell, Mrs. *Cranford*. Printed and bound . . . by The Greycaine Book Manufacturing Company, Limited. Watford. c. 1853. pp. 258 & 260.

nomic pressure became so severe that hundreds of teachers found themselves in dire distress because they could not obtain positions of any kind. It was then that a small body of men and women, known as the "Christian Socialists,"[3] came to the rescue by forming the Governesses' Benevolent Institution. This organization still flourishes in England, giving annuities to women who are ill, and providing homes for women who are destitute. The idea was welcomed by hundreds of gentlewomen who were in difficulty because they had never been trained to do work of any kind.

Methods of education have long been a process of trial, error, and change. The general pattern of training has had to be re-examined from time to time. In England in the long ago, the farmer needed only a simple knowledge of arithmetic to manage his properties and cultivate his land; as head of the family, he alone shouldered the financial responsibilities. Modern youth gains knowledge of property through the family purchase of a bicycle, a washing machine, a television set, or a motor car. Methods of payments are freely discussed in the family circle: shall the money be taken from a savings account, or should the purchase be made by the installment plan—with members of the family contributing their share. Young people today are learning how to handle financial affairs not only through installment contracts, but by Government financial regulations which affect about every aspect of their school and work-a-day lives. Through the mass production of new books, through newspapers, periodicals, and the medium of radio and television, the public is being informed of the ever-changing demands of a changing society.

The function of educational institutions is to conserve, advance and disseminate knowledge. English children have always had to depend upon the head of the family for general information. It has been the fathers, rather than the mothers—ever busy in the nursery—

[3] The "Christian Socialists" represented a social and educational movement. It was an effort to apply the principles of Christianity to industry.

who have read extensively, and discussed freely the enlightening productions of human thought. An influence of some importance was, that girls who had brothers studying under a tutor were in a particularly good position to obtain some education for themselves. With the advantages of such a background, a few women were able to get ahead without the benefit of university training.

Consider astronomy: Caroline Herschell and Mary Somerville made outstanding progress in a day when names of women were seldom mentioned in educational circles. These two scientists were elected to honorary membership in the Astronomical Society in 1835. In the report which contained the recommendations, the society made the following observations:

> Your Council has no small pleasure in recommending that the names of two ladies, distinguished in different walks of astronomy, be placed on the list of honorary members. On the propriety of such a step, in an astronomical point of view, there can be but one voice: and your Council is of opinion that the time is gone by when either feeling or prejudice, by whichever name it may be proper to call it, should be allowed to interfere with the payment of a well-earned tribute of respect. . . . And your Council, therefore, recommends this meeting to add to the list of honorary members the names of Miss Caroline Herschell and Mrs. Mary Somerville, of whose astronomical knowledge, and of the utility of the ends to which it has been applied, it is not necessary to recount the proofs.[4]

The men who sat at that particular council-table were ahead of their day in deciding that the time had come when neither banter nor prejudice should be allowed to interfere with the payment of a well-earned tribute.

The time of awakening was at hand. In the early years of Queen Victoria's reign the idea got abroad that women as well as men should have the advantages of a good education. It was an impulse destined to mould the curriculum of the few girls' schools then in

[4] Hill, Georgiana. *Women in English Life*. Vol. II. Richard Bentley & Son. London. MDCCC-XCVI. pp. 139–140.

existence. In one institution afternoon walks were given up for the
practice of outdoor games. Croquet was the most popular exercise,
followed a decade or more later by lawn tennis. More modern methods of instruction had to be substituted for the trifling activities
which had hitherto been an integral part of school life. However, it
was not an intellectual force that was pushing women forward—the
women of Greece were never touched by the wisdom of their philos-
ophers—but it was an all-absorbing, world-wide interest in public
affairs. Women became students in the truest sense of the word;
they lost no time in reaching the highest ranks of scholarship in art,
science, and literature, to the surprise of many.

Educators in England were coming to realize at last that the economic problems of women could be overcome by way of special
training. To this end, a committee of professors from King's College,
London, formulated a plan by which women could qualify themselves for the teaching profession. "Lectures for Ladies" were begun
in 1847, the sessions attracting women of all ages. The movement to
spread "female knowledge" led to the establishment of Queen's College one year later. This institution offered "Certificates of Proficiency" to women who had finished the prescribed courses. However, the authorities had no power to grant university degrees. It was
up-hill work all the way, for the men who taught these women soon
discovered that they were woefully deficient in the rudiments of
grammar and arithmetic. Therefore, it was necessary to arrange a
curriculum which included both elementary and advanced subjects.

Two young girls attending Queen's College at this time were
destined to become well-known educators: Frances Mary Buss and
Dorothea Beale. They were both women of strong character. Miss
Buss was the daughter of R. W. Buss, the painter-etcher, who made
some of the original Pickwick illustrations. She entered Queen's
College in 1848, and apparently made more than average headway—
founding the North London Collegiate School for Ladies a few years

later. As a schoolmistress, Frances worked very hard, and gave not only time, but small sums of money to educational projects. Old residents have written accounts of the way in which discipline was handled. It is apparent that Miss Buss made rules that touched about everything in school-life. For instance,

Every book had to be covered (a different colour for each subject). No girl might bring a pen to school. We were forbidden to get wet on the way to school, to walk more than three in a row, to drop a pencil-box, leave a book at home, hang a boot-bag by only one loop, run down the stairs, speak in class. As for speaking, it would have been easier to enumerate the few places where we were permitted to speak than those where talking was forbidden.[5]

With all of this discipline, it was to be expected that the activities of the school would be conducted with a certain degree of mechanical precision.

In academic matters, there was less rigidity of procedure.

After every test done in class there would follow a cascade of questions as to whether some answer might 'count' or not. Thus: 'Please will it count if 1488 is put instead of 1588 for the Armada?' 'Well dear, give it a half-mark'.[6]

Unfortunately, the students were not very co-operative, for they felt themselves to be a part of an educational experiment. They did not realize how much opposition existed. Then too, considerable snobbishness was present in the school-body; it cropped up in the selection of both students and teachers. But this brave woman—and it took bravery to go against well-established customs—discouraged such foolish ideas, and tried to make every girl realize the importance of judging people by merit—and merit alone. Frances Buss showed good common sense in such matters. She had been motivated by a desire to help girls in middle-class society, understanding full-well that hundreds of women in this group were living with friends

[5] Hughes, M. Vivian. *A London Girl of the Eighties*. Oxford University Press. London. 1936. p. 26.
[6] *Ibid*. p. 36.

or relatives in the capacity of unpaid, upper-servants—for the simple reason that they had not been prepared for an independent way-of-life. Miss Buss was determined to raise the standard of education for women. This teacher never faltered in her purpose, even when faced by unfriendly parents, and an unsympathetic press.

Dorothea Beale conducted her school work along different lines. She had benefited from a home atmosphere that was more stimulating—stories from Shakespeare and other well-known writers being read at night after the half-hour-of-prayers. Upon reaching her sixteenth birthday, Dorothea had been sent to a fashionable boarding school in France and remained there until 1848. Then political troubles broke the calm of comfortable living. On returning to England, this young woman entered Queen's College, attending the inaugural lecture delivered by the Rev. F. D. Maurice, the Head Master. The following year she became the first woman mathematical tutor in the College. Dorothea was never content to stay in a rut; she promptly resigned teaching posts when conditions seemed to warrant the change. In keeping with her advanced ideas, Miss Beale's connection with Queen's College ended because

> There was a tendency for the whole administration of the College to get too much into the hands of one person; and . . . there was consequently not enough scope for that womanly influence which she felt to be so important where the education of young girls is concerned.[7]

Miss Beale then took up work in a School for Clergymen's Daughters at Casterton, but she was forced to resign on account of the many duties involved. She was expected to teach mathematics, ancient and modern history, geography, English literature, French, German, Latin and Italian. Miss Beale, who was now well-known in educational circles, did not remain long without a post. In 1856, she was appointed Principal of The Ladies College in Cheltenham.

[7] Raikes, Elizabeth. *Dorothea Beale of Cheltenham.* Archibald Constable and Company, Ltd. London. 1908. p. 33.

This was work for which Miss Beale was peculiarly fitted, both by nature and mental cultivation.

The College was in a deplorable condition; it had few pupils, little money, and was only half-furnished. Miss Beale refused to be discouraged and did the work of several people, even answering the door while meals were being served. She managed the problem of discipline in a really clever way. When one student asked about the *rule* for going home for weddings, she was told, "there was no rule, Miss Beale dealt with each case separately and on its own merits."[8] She controlled the teaching staff in much the same manner, using tact, along with understanding. A teacher who was sitting on a hard, backless bench with her legs crossed, saw a note traveling in her direction one day. It contained the following cryptic message: "PLS DNT + LGS." During her administration, Dorothea made many changes in the College; she extended the curriculum, and reduced the hours of classwork to some extent. The Ladies College reached a high state of efficiency under Miss Beale's control and it played a definite part in the reformation of girls' schools in England.

Looked upon as experts in educational work by 1865, Miss Buss and Miss Beale began to exert considerable influence in the training of immature girls. The first Schools Inquiry Commission (1864–1867) sought information from both women in an attempt to improve the general plan of study in girls' schools. The two schoolmistresses showed some signs of nervousness in testifying before the seven men on the Commission; but they acquitted themselves fairly well, and gave intelligent answers to all questions.

At the time when attention was being directed towards the innovations at Queen's College, a young girl, Emily Davies, who was destined to become the foremost leader in the movement for higher education for women, was herself a student. She was the daughter of

[8] *The Cheltenham Ladies' College Magazine.* Privately printed for The Ladies College. Cheltenham. 1931. p. 41.

a Vicar in Gateshead. From all accounts, she led a dull, restricted life. The insertion of an advertisement in a home-newspaper affords an amusing characterization of Emily at the age of eleven:

Wanted, a Governess in a gentleman's family. The lady who is to fill this situation must be a person of great firmness and determination, as the young lady who is to be the object of her care is rather inclined to be self-willed. Phrenologically speaking she has the organ of self-esteem rather largely developed, and it will require the utmost care on the part of her governess to prevent this organ from being unduly developed. The lady who is to fill this situation must be a person well skilled in the languages and sciences, as Miss D. is ambitious to excel all her contemporaries in these departments of knowledge. The salary proportioned to her success in the management of her pupil.
ADDRESS. M. D. GATESHEAD.[9]

This churchman did a great deal for his children as far as education was concerned—the sons of the family studying at Cambridge University, and the daughters acquiring knowledge by reading good books, and listening to worthwhile conversation. Dr. and Mrs. Davies took Emily and her younger sister on a trip to the Continent in 1851. They spent several months in Geneva, Switzerland, where the young ladies took lessons in French and Italian. This was the accepted pattern for educating large families in the mid-Victorian period. The death of Mr. Davies in 1861 brought about great changes. After having spent twenty-three years in the quiet atmosphere of a country parish, this young woman went to live in London, the city that was henceforth to be her home.

The break, severe though it was, brought new friends and new interests. Apparently, Miss Davies followed the ordinary course of social life. She continued to study Greek and Latin—the idea being to take up medical training later on, but fortune's wheel was turning in another direction. Elizabeth Garrett, one of Emily's close friends, had been refused admittance to the University of London on the

[9] Stephen, Barbara. *Emily Davies and Girton College*. (From *The Herald*. October 6, 1841.) Constable & Co., Ltd. London. 1927. p. 24.

ground of sex. This was really the incident which determined the career of Emily Davies. She took it upon herself to prove that sex had nothing to do with superior mental ability. The question was how to proceed.

The information had been spread abroad that the University of London did not care to be used as a laboratory for strange experiments. Therefore, Miss Davies turned her thoughts to Cambridge University, an even more distinguished seat of learning. It was through her efforts, with the help of a small committee, that a plan was devised by which young women could take a special test. The offer was quickly accepted. The Examiners co-operated in every way, even giving the Woman's Committee copies of papers previously used in boys' examinations.

Miss Davies canvassed the countryside and collected names of possible candidates. She must have been apprehensive of the idea of sponsoring such an odd assortment of student-material. English girls came from Queen's College, the North London Collegiate School for Ladies, and some from country districts. Eighty-three hopeful students took the examination on December 14, 1863. They did fairly well in most subjects, but failed in simple problems of arithmetic.

The experimental test marked a step forward in the education of women, for it showed the need for a higher standard of teaching in the secondary schools of the country. Miss Davies and her committee decided that this "private examination" must be put on a more formal basis. Accordingly, she prepared a memorial asking Cambridge University to open the Local Examinations to girls; the signatories were university professors, "ladylike ladies," and other people friendly to the cause. The Senate confirmed the report of the delegates after much debate and opened the coveted examinations to young women.

It is remarkable what a grasp Emily Davies had on educational problems when she had never taught school. Her testimony before the Schools Inquiry Commission is so direct, so sensible, and more-over, so self-effacing that admiration for this woman increases with each reading of the report. Lord Taunton questioned her as to the training of girls on November 30, 1865:

> I believe you have devoted a great deal of time to the subject of education, especially the education of girls? Yes; I have paid some attention to it. . . .
>
> Have you specially attended to any particular schools or institutions connected with the education of girls? I have heard a great deal about them from school-mistresses in connection with the local examinations. My information is more from schoolmistresses than in any other way; it is what they have told me that I know.
>
> Still you have probably visited the schools themselves? Yes, I do not know much about the internal management of schools.
>
> I believe you took an active part in establishing a system of local examinations for girls? Yes; I was secretary to the committee which got up a memorial and made an application to Cambridge for the extension of the examination.
>
> That memorial was, I believe, successful, and a system of local examinations is now established for girls? Yes; it is coming into operation this year for the first time. It was decided upon last March.
>
> Of course you cannot speak of the effects which it is likely to produce by experience, but do you anticipate great good from it? Yes; it seems likely to work very well. . . .
>
> Can you favour us with any suggestions by which governesses might be better trained? I think if the education of girls were cheaper they might be able to go on with it longer. They usually stop at 18, and of course they cannot be completely educated by that time.
>
> I would like to ask you a general question; can you favour us with any suggestions, pointing out any modes by which, in your opinion, the legislature or the Government could assist in promoting the good education of your women in this country? I think the chief thing is by endowments.[10]

This was a radical suggestion, as in the past, only boys' schools or colleges had been the recipients of endowments.

It was while attending a schoolmistresses' convention in 1866 that

---

[10] *Schools Inquiry Commission.* Vol. V. George E. Eyre and William Spottiswoode. London. 1868. pp. 232–233, 235.

Miss Davies decided to found a college for women. She had a bro-
chure printed which presented, not only her own views, but the
opinions of other women interested in higher education. She organized groups for the purpose of raising money for the new college,
at the same time writing hundreds of letters in an effort to publicise
the movement. Funds for the undertaking came in small amounts,
but they came from well-known people in widely scattered districts.
It soon became apparent that a new building was out of the question,
consequently a house was rented at Hitchin, not many miles from
Cambridge.

The college opened in 1869, with five students in attendance, and
some visiting professors. Teaching during the first year is said to
have been "scanty but excellent." Many educators looked upon the
college as a trial arrangement, a laboratory, really, where original
methods in book-learning could be carried out. Miss Davies disregarded such ideas and insisted that the college work be set at the
standard required for young men. It is amusing to note that the students also had certain notions of what constituted a formal education;
they did not hesitate to criticise each and every thing that was undertaken by the college. One young woman entertained a member of the
Board by saying: "You see, nobody here knows anything." The
situation was awkward for all concerned. The women on the Committee knew very little about university work, and as far as the lecturers were concerned, they

Had never before had pupils quite like these, mature, intelligent, and eager to
learn, but wonderfully ignorant; and they found it difficult to enter seriously into
the plan of preparing them for the Honours examination.[11]

Miss Davies had exerted every effort to conciliate public opinion,
as she hoped some day to have her college included among those of
Cambridge University—a dream which became reality many years

[11] Stephens, Barbara. *Emily Davies and Girton College.* Constable & Co., Ltd. London. 1927.
p. 232.

later. There must be no ground for criticism. It was a delicate situation, for all along parents had hesitated to send their daughters to the new college, feeling that higher education was a kind of special training for unconventional girls. At the same time, it took a person with considerable courage to go against the wishes of family and friends in such a controversial matter. One student was allowed to attend the college at Hitchin for one year if she would promise not to get a degree, but just return home again as if "nothing had happened." Under no circumstances was she to consider school-teaching. To complicate matters, once a girl had entered college, she was almost sure to lose her place in society—being henceforth "a kind of outsider." Think of a girl studying Greek and Latin! Miss Davies was not the resident-head of the college, but her influence was felt in all departments, and strangely enough—this invisible moral power was noticeable almost one hundred years later.[12]

As an outgrowth of the college for women founded by Emily Davies in 1869, Girton College was established in Cambridge a few years later, with the assistance of a small body of Cambridge educators.

This group held different views as to what should constitute higher education for women. The Girton Committee made the Classics compulsory, and required students to reside at the College for the exact number of terms prescribed for undergraduates at Cambridge University. On the other hand, the authorities at Cambridge did not make the Classics binding in any way, and they more or less ignored the idea of forcing students to live in the residence halls for any specified length of time. Members of the University staff felt that

The important point was the Tripos itself, and that, in forming a judgment as to the intellectual capacity of women, the University should be influenced mainly by

[12] Late in the nineteen-fifties, the writer asked a student at Girton College if they ever mentioned Emily Davies at the College. "Oh yes," she said, "all day long we give the time *by Emily*, never by the clock." (Meaning the great clock-tower which stands at the entrance gate.)

the result of this test, and would not, . . . attach much weight to the preliminary conditions.[13]

Apart from subjects of study it might be thought that the standard required for a degree in honours was too high for women, or that the work to be done in the limited time allowed at Cambridge might be too much for them. The following analysis of classes obtained by men and women for the five years, 1896–1900 inclusive, affords a satisfactory answer to these questions:

	Men	Women	No. of women to 100 men under each head.
Class I.	496	58	11.6
Class II.	671	161	23.9
Class III.	570	142	24.9
Total classed.	1737	361	20.7
Ægrotant in Honours	12 ⎫	3 ⎫	⎫
Attained standard of Ordinary Degree	121 ⎬ 133	9 ⎬ 12	9 ⎬ 10.1
Excused the General Examination	44	6	13.6 ⎭
Failed completely.	No. of men unknown to me		

It will be seen that the ratio of women to men is less in the first class and very much less among the failures than it is in the whole number classed, the deficiency being made up in the second and third classes.

It should be noted that the true proportion of women among the failures is considerably less than appears in the last column, as all the women who failed completely are included and none of the men.[14]

While this table makes many points clear, it leaves far too much to guesswork. How did the grades of the men compare with those of the women? Surely, this is a question which deserved more than a stretch of blank space in a report. However, women had started a movement which was to double the ranks of skilled workers, not only in England, but in other countries as well.

[13] Clough, Blanch Athena. *A Memoir of Anne Jemima Clough.* Edward Arnold. London. 1897. p. 176.

[14] Roberts, R. D. (Editor). *Education in the Nineteenth Century.* At The University Press. Cambridge. 1901. pp. 207–208.

Girton College was granted a Royal Charter in 1924, and was incorporated as a college in Cambridge University in 1948.

Another woman worked quite independently for the education of women in the North of England. She was Anne Jemima Clough, who was born in the year 1820. Anne spent much of her childhood in the Southern part of the United States, where she no doubt absorbed many practical ideas. She did not attend the American schools, and therefore led a life somewhat apart from other children. At the age of twelve, Anne wrote: "As soon as it was cool enough in the afternoon, the neighbor's garden was alive with children and their mothers. I could see them playing—how I watched them—bonnie, sweet-looking girls and boys."[15] This period of semi-seclusion in another country may account to some extent for Miss Clough's extreme reserve and "hesitating manner," which seriously handicapped her in later years.

The Clough family represented what would be referred to as "upper middle-class." That is, they possessed sufficient means to give their children the advantages of education and travel; but they were not bound by beliefs and customs which had been handed down by their ancestors. Small wonder that so many of these families have left a lasting imprint on art, history, and literature. Mr. Clough took his family back to England in 1836; he was having financial reverses of a somewhat serious nature.

Anne Clough started a school at Liverpool sometime later. She must have done fairly well, for in 1852, another "teaching-room" was opened at Ambleside. Children of farmers and trades-people were drawn to this school. Anne's great interest in this group is evident in this straightforward observation:

The parents of these children especially need help; they are willing to pay moderately, as they do not like sending their children to charity schools; and I

15 Clough, Blanch Athena. *A Memoir of Anne Jemima Clough.* Edward Arnold. London. 1897. p. 11.

think this is a good feeling and one to be encouraged. The gentry and the clergy do not often help this class; they are occupied with the really poor. Besides that, in this class there are many dissenters, and they are as a whole often very independent about their children, . . . They have neither time nor knowledge enough themselves to set up schools for their sons, much less for their daughters, so it frequently happens that their whole families are neglected or ill-taught.[16]

Anne Clough turned the school at Ambleside over to a company in 1862. She passed the next nine years with relatives in different parts of England. This was a fruitful period, as she was constantly meeting people who were interested in her dedicated work for a good system of education for girls. While still under fifty years of age, this pioneer in the teaching profession wrote an article for *MacMillan's Magazine*. Needless to say, she amazed some people by suggesting: (1) That a special board be appointed for the purpose of supervising all branches of school work; (2) That lectures be given in different parts of England, not only for young girls, but for older women. Further, that university-trained men should hold key positions in case such a plan were undertaken. How clear it is that Miss Clough was ahead of her time as far as education was concerned.

A magazine article of this kind was always passed from friend to friend, a custom that insured a wide circulation. Within a short time, steps were taken to organize study groups along the lines that had been suggested by Miss Clough. A canvass for funds was made in Liverpool. A number of wealthy women became enthusiastic over the proposal, and an organization called the North of England Council was formed. A young don from Cambridge was secured as lecturer. As a result of these study groups, hundreds of women acquired intelligent reading habits and the lending libraries were unable to cope with the increased demand for books.

The new method of education grew into the University Extension system (1873). It was taken up in later years by men students de-

---

[16] *Schools Inquiry Commission.* Vol. XXIII. Part II. George E. Eyre and William Spottiswoode. London. 1868. p. 84.

siring special courses. Finally, the Council persuaded the officials of Cambridge University to give a Special Women's Examination, known as the Higher Local Examination. This progressive action was the forerunner of a movement to offer greater opportunity for a college education, not only in England, but in other countries as well.

One of the most consistent workers in the movement towards a formal system of education for women was Professor Henry Sidgwick of Cambridge University. In the Lent term of 1870, Professor Sidgwick started lectures at Cambridge for girls who wished to take the Special Women's Examination. He later rented a house on Regent Street as temporary living quarters for women students. Anne Clough was placed in charge of the building. Newnham College was founded when the first series of lectures was given to five resident students in 1871. It was not long until Newnham Hall (now called the "Old Hall") was erected to fill the need for a larger dormitory. Newnham was incorporated as a college in 1880. It was governed by the Board of Trade in Cambridge. The college was granted a Royal Charter in 1917, and was incorporated as a college in Cambridge University in 1948.

Although women were enjoying the same advantages as men, they were handicapped by social forces of varied character. For one thing, the public at large looked upon women students as queer eccentrics, however normal, however attractive they might be. It was yet the same; family demands often brought serious complications. Parents never hesitated to lean upon daughters for help, in the field, or in the home. Nor did they hesitate to take girls out of college if there were financial troubles of any kind.

Educators took it more or less for granted that girls who attended the first colleges for women would eventually take up teaching as a profession. Graduates, therefore, accepted posts and proceeded to teach what they knew. Then, the information got about that you could be taught "how to teach." Well-known people took up the challenge, and were instrumental in founding The Cambridge Training College for Women. The first principal of the college was Miss E. P. Hughes, a graduate of Newnham College. As there was no set method of training teachers, Miss Hughes developed a system of practice teaching work. She had difficulty in persuading schools to co-operate in this strange project. A former student wrote

It was customary during our first week or two for Miss Hughes and *all* of us to attend every lesson. In the halcyon week before any of these lessons were started we were rather light-hearted about them. Give a lesson! Pooh! Any one can do that. . . . The first ordeal was at hand, and an afternoon was fixed for two lessons to be given in an elementary school right accross the town. . . . The stage was set for the first pupil-teacher to give an object lesson. She produced a large piece of rock-salt, and held forth on its properties. She had become very hot with the walk, and still hotter with nervousness. I can see her now, perspiration streaming from her, as she talked ever faster and faster about this lump of stuff.[17]

The Training College for Women started without funds, and with only a few students. It has survived by means of grants and subscriptions. Fortunately, the college was situated in a town where citizens have always been friendly to educational institutions.

It has been said that in the past English girls who studied in co-educational institutions had to steel themselves against harsh treatment from men students, and indirect ridicule from men professors. This was said to be especially true of the older universities. The late Sir Walter Raleigh of Oxford addressed a group of men and over-zealous, note-taking women thus: "Two important items for today," (the girls' pencils flew across the pages), "When I give a talk I *sit down*, and when I give a lecture I *stand up*."[18] Undergraduates said that college girls also suffered from the rules of "spinsterish dons."

Oxford women are at the mercy of a spinster-autocracy. A girl is expected to look, behave, and dress as the spinster did when she was young. If she is alive and pretty and asked by young men to go to dances, she is docketed as an undesirable

[17] Hughes, M. Vivian. *A London Girl of the Eighties*. Oxford University Press. London. 1936. p. 131.
[18] The writer's diary. 1937.

influence in the college. The spinster-mind waits until she infringes on one of the thousand rules which clutter life in the women's colleges—then it pounces. It refuses to believe that the girl can be doing her work efficiently. The spinster-mind cannot appreciate the possibility of an existence maintaining an even balance in its activities. Because it often has a one-sided view of life it tries to impart the same vision to others.[19]

So much for a way-of-life in the past in an ancient centre of learning.

There are also financial complications in the field of education; because of the heavy burden of taxes, contributions from individuals for educational institutions have reached a low point in recent years. To meet this very pressing problem, business firms are contributing to what is known as an "Industrial Fund" to be used for the advancement of scientific study in both the grant and the independent schools. These grants are not made without a thorough investigation of the needs of the various institutions. The assessors have "visited 143 schools or the bulk of those entitled to first priority—defined as schools with at least 250 boys and girls over the age of 13 and with 10 per cent or more in the science and mathematics sixth form."[20] It was hoped that the fund would reach the total of £4M., and that a goodly part of it would have been contributed by 1958. These gifts help to pay for urgent requirements—classroom and laboratory equipment for the study of mathematics, chemistry and physics. Of the applications received from 500 schools, only one was rejected as below standard in all respects. England is preparing for a higher level of training in special branches of education.

A problem seldom mentioned in educational circles is this: there are still many men and women brought up in settled English communities who are poorly educated, the group having left school under sixteen years of age. Many individuals in this group are very able, but they have very decided views as to what is good, and what is bad in youth training—leaning heavily in favor of clerical work. But

[19] Briant, Keith. *Oxford News.* Published by Michael Joseph, Ltd. London. 1937. p. 126.
[20] *The Times Educational Supplement.* London. August 10, 1956.

why should students be bank-minded, or insurance-minded in a society short of skilled artisans? Training methods should be re-
examined and emphasis placed on skills more closely related to the
requirements of national life. Parents shudder at the mention of tool
work; they look upon such an occupation as perilous, quite unsuited
to a son or daughter bound for study at a university. This concern
can be both foolish and dangerous at a time when industry has come
to rely so heavily upon its trained personnel. Indeed, the day may not
be too far distant, when mechanical ability will rank ahead of many
other skills.

The first colleges for women have gained considerable prestige in
less than a century. They are now being besieged by hundreds of
girls anxious to work for diplomas and degrees of various kinds.
These institutions examine the credentials of each applicant, selecting the most promising candidates. It is not generally known that
young women still labor under a feeling of "difference." It is far
more difficult for a woman to gain entrance to Oxford University
than it is for a man. It is a well-known fact that "the standard which
she is required to attain in the college entrance examination would
win her an Exhibition in many of the men's colleges."[21] Indeed, the
first-year student is given to understand that she is very fortunate to
be in the college at all. For are not hundreds of girls "clamoring for
entrance" to old, well-established institutions.

Whatever may be said about the universities, they do set the
standard of academic achievement in England. They are connected
with the state system of education by association, but are more or
less independent units. As for work, some idlers will be found in all
schools and universities. But on the whole, students—even those
who have been pampered by too much attention at home—adopt the
spirit of their particular college and become oriented to the routine of
college life within a few months. The *esprit de corps* among students

[21] Briant, Keith. *Oxford News*. Published by Michael Joseph, Ltd. London. 1937. p. 125.

and faculty members develops character and responsibility, and constitutes an honor system worthy of the school.

In concluding this chapter on education, it must be emphasized that, the development of the intellect through university training, and the companionship of students of like interest as they pursue their fields of knowledge, is a vital and stimulating experience— even though it covers a short span of years. The Spanish philosopher, Ortega y Gasset, rightly said that a student takes on the spirit of his Al'ma Mat'er, and finds himself "thenceforward and forever a different person." Obviously, he was not referring to youths who go to college merely for social reasons, or at the insistence of ambitious parents.

The spirit of inquiry that is constantly asking the question of *why* the universal experience of mankind—not only in the environment of the classroom, but also in the informal gatherings of students and teachers—is not to imply ignorance, but intellectual curiosity of a high order. This characteristic persists into later life wherever educated men and women engage in the discussion of the topics of the times. In fact, when relieved of the confines of the classroom, scholars will travel to far distant centers of learning to seek new enlightenment and thus broaden their mental horizons. For there can be stalemates in the realm of the intellectual, as well as in the game of chess.

III. Teaching

SCHOLARS who enter the teaching profession are usually motivated by a compelling interest in education and their desire to communicate knowledge. By arousing in the mind that inner quickening of curiosity, the successful teacher can overcome pupil-resistance to study and so develop the first essential to all study, "the desire to learn." Further, the teacher should try to inculcate in the minds of the young the desire for the attainment of mastery that will enable them in later years to take part intelligently and responsibly in community life and public affairs, whether at home or abroad.

In England, well-known educators preside over the far-famed boarding schools. These educational institutions have gained recognition over the years by graduating "young gentlemen" of more than average competence. This is no chance affair, daily duties being regulated with business-like efficiency—long hours of intensive study, long hours of strenuous exercise—the strong succeed. In considering applications for entrance to these schools, which have considerable influence and prestige, preference is usually in favor of families that are not only wealthy, but highly placed in social and political circles.

Educators of an earlier day did very well for boys of high descent, but they showed no consideration at all for children in the lower classes. As late as the eighteenth century, there were men and women on the island who knew almost nothing about mental cultivation. Communities of this kind had no schools—boys and girls growing up with little or no idea of social responsibility. To aggravate matters, leading officials—usually large land-owners—passed over day-to-day abuses as necessary evils. Laws were made with the unspoken thought that they would be broken. It was a sorry situation.

Into this crude environment came Hannah More, a school teacher, whose interests lay primarily with the poor and neglected. This remarkable woman was born in Bristol in 1745. Her family must have been in prosperous circumstances, as the five More sisters were educated by way of the tutorial system, acquiring proficiency in French, Italian, and Spanish. Hannah had the benefit of long talks, not only with local teachers, but with learned scholars from the Continent. These were stimulating experiences enjoyed by few women in the long ago. She took up school-teaching while still very young—just seventeen years of age. This was a daring move at a time when "proper girls" seldom left home except for afternoon calls, or church services; and high-class ladies were not seen on the streets before noon. But this was preparatory work. Hannah More was acquiring self-assurance in a very practical way.

By middle age, Miss More had moved to London and was attracting some attention as a writer. Naturally, a woman of this type was welcomed into literary circles; she finally became a member of the famous blue-stocking society. But the demands of a large city were too exhausting for comfort and a new home was established at Cowslip Green (1786). Entertaining went on as usual—no doubt with a more limited group of friends. William Wilberforce was one of several guests who had dinner with Miss More on a Sunday. The great liberator held the company spellbound with his stories of people and places. He told of a boorish group living not far away at Cheddar—a driving experience over "washed-out roads on a moonless night." Hannah was fascinated, and made a journey to the region a few weeks later. How she fared on this pilgrimage is described in a letter to Mr. Wilberforce:

After the discoveries made of the deplorable state of that place, my sister and I went and took a lodging at a little public-house there, to see what we could do, for we were utterly at a loss how to begin. We found more than two thousand people in the parish, almost all very poor; no gentry, a dozen wealthy farmers, hard, brutal, and ignorant. We visited them all, picking up at one house (like fortune-tellers) the name and character of the next. We told them we intended to set up a school for their poor. They did not like it. We assured them we did not desire a shilling from them, but wished for their concurrence, as we knew they could influence their workmen. One of the farmers seemed pleased and civil; he was rich, but covetous, a hard drinker, and his wife a woman of loose morals, but good-natured sense; she became our friend, sooner than some of the decent and the formal, and let us a house, the only one in the parish that was vacant, at £7 per annum, with a good garden. Adjoining was a large ox-house; this we roofed and floored; and by putting in a couple of windows, it made a good school-room. While this was doing, we went to every house in the place, and found each a scene of the greatest ignorance and vice. We saw but one Bible in all the parish, and that was used to prop a flower-pot! No clergyman had resided in it for forty years.[1]

What method Hannah More used to subdue the people in and around Cheddar will always remain a mystery.[2] The school opened and prospered; within six years there were two hundred children in attendance. Miss More described her teaching methods as "simple and limited." The pupils learned to read from two tracts called *Questions for the Mendip Schools*, and *The Church Catechism*. They were also taught sewing, knitting, and spinning. After the school had gained recognition, small Bibles were distributed to pupils who had taken good care of their textbooks. Usually, a girl who had been trained in the school received a large, well-bound copy of the "Holy Book" on her wedding day. Encouraged by work at Cheddar, Miss More started schools at Shipham, Rowborrow, Congresbury, Yatton, Ambridge, and Nailsea. Without doubt, Hannah More was a born teacher, as well as a born missionary.

Another teacher of importance, Mary Woolstonecraft, worked with girls well-placed in life. In 1774, she opened private "teaching rooms" in Newington Green. More than likely, this was a typical

[1] Johnson, R. Brimley. *The Letters of Hannah More.* John Lane, The Bodley Head, Ltd. London. 1925. pp. 166–167.

[2] In some parts of the Mendip Hills, at that time, no constable dared execute a warrant for fear of being thrown down a pit.

"Dame School"—that is, girls of all ages were admitted. This young woman had advanced ideas on educational matters. There should be, she thought, schools for the different age groups established by the Government. In these institutions boys and girls would be

Educated together. The school for the younger children, from five to nine years of age, ought to be absolutely free and open to all classes . . . boys and girls, the rich and poor, should meet together. And to prevent any of the distinctions of vanity, they should be dressed alike, and all obliged to submit to the same discipline, or leave the school.[3]

Miss Woolstonecraft advocated specialized training after the age of nine; domesticity for the girls and mechanical trades for the boys. The school prospered; but because of her failing eye-sight, other plans became necessary.

Miss Woolstonecraft then obtained a post as governess in the home of Lord and Lady Kingsborough in Michelstown. The work was far from satisfactory, as she had to follow a supervised teaching program. She wrote from "The Castle" on November 5, 1787, as follows:

I have committed to my care three girls, the eldest fourteen, by no means handsome, yet a sweet girl. She has a wonderful capacity, but she has such a multiplicity of employments it has not room to expand itself, and in all probability will be lost in a heap of rubbish, miscalled accomplishments. I am grieved at being obliged to continue so wrong a system.[4]

In 1788, Mary gave up teaching and began literary work in London.

During the first quarter of the nineteenth century, men and women who taught school did little more than read questions from a book, and then stand by for answers. This was of course an unsatisfactory system, quite limited in value. Consider this recitation:

What is they duty towards God? My duty toads God is to blede in Him, to fering and to loaf withold your arts, withold my mine, withold my sold, and with

---

[3] Woolstonecraft, Mary. *A Vindication of the Rights of Women (1792)*. Walter Scott. London. 1891. pp. 241–242.

[4] Linford, Madeline. *Mary Woolstonecraft (1759–1797)*. Leonard Parsons, Ltd. London. 1924. pp. 54–55.

my sernth, to wirchp and give thanks, to put my old trash in Him, to call upon Him, to onner His old name and His world, and to save Him truly all the days of my life's end.[5]

It was a matter of guesswork, teachers doing the best they could under difficult circumstances. The standard textbook for children in the elementary grades was *Mangnalls' Questions*, which passed through many editions. English children either had to memorize the "Mangnall" or lag behind their class-mates. To aggravate the situation, lessons were sometimes carried on by way of group recitations. Each child would call out his or her version as follows:

Question: Name the most famous battles fought in ancient times in their order.
Answer: Marathon, Thermopylae, Artemesia, Salamian, Plataea, Eurymidon, Arginusae, Leuetra, Mantinea, Cheronaea, Granicus, Issus, Arbela, Ticinus, Trebia, Thrasymene, Cannae, Pharsalia, Phillipi, and Actium.[6]

In the early days, education was certainly a hit or miss affair.

As for teaching methods, modern educators do not look upon memory work as the proper kind of training. But what should take its place is not clear even today. For the abilities of children differ in different stages of development. Teachers in England have long had an advantage not enjoyed by fellow workers in the United States— that is, if a child is lazy, he or she hears the truth, not some glib statement about *inattention*. The "multiple chance" theory has never taken root in Great Britain. A study was made quite recently of children in Leyburn, England—how they lived, played, and worked. One of the differences "between Leyburn and a comparative American town was the degree of candor about difference in ability. In England, when a pupil gave a foolish answer the teacher was likely to respond with a candid appraisal, saying "Jonny sit down—you're not up to this.""[7] It is said that frankness acts as an incentive to hard

[5] Peel, Mrs. C. S. *A Hundred Wonderful Years: Social and Domestic Life of a Century, 1820–1920.* John Lane, The Bodley Head, Ltd. London. 1926. p. 23.

[6] *Historical and Miscellaneous Questions for the Use of Young People.* Printed by J. Clarke. London. 1800.

[7] *Reader's Digest.* "Can We Be Equal and Excellent Too?" Pleasantville, New York (U.S.A.). October, 1961.

work. The average child in England must make a choice: be studious or be humiliated.

Experiments in reading ability are conducted from time to time—the idea being to discover which procedure is most effective. Within the present century three basic methods have found their champions: (1) the method by which children learn the letters of the alphabet and sound equivalents; (2) the whole-word method by which pupils are taught to recognize words rather than letters; (3) the phonic word-method, so-called because although it "resembles the traditional phonic method, in using materials which are graded according to degree of phonic complexity, it also resembles word-methods in its insistence upon reading for meaning and in not teaching the sound values of letters in isolation from whole words."[8]

To test the effectiveness of two different theories, a study was conducted with two groups of children just learning to read.

Group A were taught for a year by the phonic word-method, Group B by mixed methods. At the end of the session six word-recognition tests were administered, two being sentence tests. The children's responses were recorded on a tape-recorder and from these records, played and replayed as often as required, the statistics and lists of errors were compiled.[9]

The following table will give some idea of results from the first four examinations:

PERCENTAGES OF RIGHT, WRONG, AND NO RESPONSE:

TEST	GROUP A			GROUP B		
	Right	Wrong	Nil	Right	Wrong	Nil
I	85.5	7.8	6.7	43.1	11.6	45.3
II	60.5	13.1	26.4	35.2	11.5	53.3
III	79.9	6.4	13.7	47.7	11.8	40.5
IV	73.5	8.0	18.5	44.9	10.4	44.7
I–IV combined	74.9	8.8	16.3	42.7	11.3	46.0[10]

[8] *The Times Educational Supplement*. London. November 16, 1956.
[9] *Ibid.*
[10] *Ibid.*

From these statistics, the following conclusions were drawn:

The group of children taught for a year by the phonic word-method was definitely superior in word-recognition in all . . . tests, to the group of children taught for one year by mixed methods. . . . There was a great difference in the number of nil-responses between the two experimental groups, the group taught by mixed methods being much inferior in word attack.[11]

Pioneers in the teaching profession lacked facilities for experiments of a worthwhile nature. Each educator was forced to move along by way of trial and error.

The next teacher—one who went ahead without financial backing of any kind—was Charlotte Brontë. She was born in 1816 at Thornton, in the parish of Bradford. Charlotte's mother died before reaching the age of forty. Patrick Brontë, Charlotte's father, was an alumnus of Cambridge University. He started out as a clerical assistant, and later received a perpetual curacy at Harworth. It was in the church-house that Charlotte grew up, and where she spent the important years of a short life. The Brontë children, six in number, received their early education at home. The father used very original methods of teaching. One day he stood the children in a row, and asked them questions. Each pupil was masked. Religious views as well as educational processes of the day, are reflected in the following lesson:

MR. BRONTË: Anne, what does a child like you most want?

ANNE (aged four): Age and experience.

MR. BRONTË: Emily, what had I best do with your brother Branwell, when he is a naughty boy?

EMILY (aged five): Reason with him, and when he won't listen to reason, whip him.

MR. BRONTË: Branwell, what is the best way of knowing the difference between the intellects of man and woman?

BRANWELL (aged six): By considering the difference between them as to their bodies.

MR. BRONTË: Charlotte, what is the best book in the world?

[11] *The Times Educational Supplement.* London. November 16, 1956.

CHARLOTTE (aged seven or eight): The Bible.

MR. BRONTË: And what is the next best, Charlotte?

CHARLOTTE: The Book of Nature.

MR. BRONTË: Elizabeth, what is the best mode of education for a woman?

ELIZABETH (aged eight or nine): That which would make her rule her house well.

MR. BRONTË: Maria, what is the best mode of spending time?

MARIA (aged ten or eleven): By laying it out in preparation for a happy eternity.[12]

Apparently, Charlotte was especially favored, for she attended three different boarding schools. Then, without any special training, and with little or no experience, this young woman accepted a position as governess in a large country home and made an independent living for herself. She wrote long letters to her sister Emily revealing intimate details of how she lived and worked in those early days. A few pertinent remarks follow:

I said in my last letter that Mrs. Sidgwick did not know me. I now begin to find that she does not intend to know me, that she cares nothing in the world about me except to contrive how the greatest possible quantity of labour may be squeezed out of me, and to that end she overwhelms me with oceans of needle-work, yards of cambric to hem, muslin nightcaps to make, and, above all things, dolls to dress. I do not think she likes me at all, because I can't help being shy in such an entirely novel scene, surrounded as I have hitherto been by strange and constantly changing faces. I see more clearly than I have ever done before that a private governess has no existence, is not considered as a living and rational being except as connected with the wearisome duties she has to fulfill. . . . One of the pleasantest afternoons I have spent here—indeed, the only one at all pleasant— was when Mr. Sidgwick walked out with his children, and I had orders to follow a little behind. As he strolled on through his fields with his magnificent Newfoundland dog at his side, he looked very like what a frank, wealthy Conservative gentleman ought to be. . . .[13]

[12] Benson, E. F. *Charlotte Brontë*. Longmans, Green and Co. London. 1932. pp. 19–20.

[13] Shorter, Clement. *The Brontës. Life and Letters*. Vol. 1. Hodder and Stoughton. London. MCMVIII pp. 158–159.

Under such circumstances, teaching must have been dull, but Charlotte Brontë may have felt very strongly that work outside the home was preferable to a state of dependence in the parsonage at Harworth. Women of this period had great difficulty in trying to support themselves.

Charlotte and Emily Brontë spent ten years as governesses and found the occupation altogether hateful. The two sisters then spent some time in Brussels, Belgium, studying French and German. They returned to Harworth in 1845 and tried their hand at writing. The manuscript of Emily's first novel, *Wuthering Heights,* found a publisher. Charlotte's first manuscript was returned with an encouraging letter. But the manuscript of her second novel, *Jane Eyre,* was accepted right away and the book became an immediate success. Three more of Charlotte's novels were published. She died in 1855—one year after her marriage.

The Head Mistress of a girls' boarding school also faced many awkward situations. She had to make her way with a small store of knowledge, and a very limited expense account; considerable tact was required. The main consideration was, how to please exacting patrons. The problem was usually solved by producing a curriculum that was elastic enough to satisfy both the studious and the not-so-studious pupil. It must not be forgotten that thousands of English women were still training their daughters for but one career: to become wives and mothers. This program meant that no time could be wasted before the twenty-fifth birthday. In fact, one Victorian mother settled the matter in her own way. "Why," she said, "you can't send a girl into the drawing-room repeating the multiplication table." And who would care to contradict that bit of reasoning? There was often a "figure head" in the schools—usually a voluntary worker from a well-known family. Even in the writer's day there were "helpers" of this type at Lady Margaret Hall, Oxford University.

Half-way along in the nineteenth century a few educators began to familiarize themselves with teaching methods in Holland, Switzerland, and Prussia. A Committee of Privy Council (originally the King's confidential advisers) was formed, and charged with the duty of investigating English schools. The Committee soon found that inefficiency in the classrooms resulted from general incompetence among the teachers. Therefore, they urged the Government to establish Normal Colleges where men and women could receive up-to-date training for the teaching profession.[14] But it was the old story: religious bodies took a stand against colleges regulated by the State. However, there was no turning back, and somewhat hurried plans were made to start classes for teachers in London (c.1860). After a time, textbooks were put together for mature students. The teachers of England understood their own shortcomings and flocked to the lectures in considerable numbers.

The next step taken by the Committee was this: candidates for teaching were required to take an examination at the end of each term. The official circular on this subject stated that from eight hundred to one thousand teachers

Will be assembled, by the invitation of the Government of this country as Candidates for the formal recognition of their capacity to instruct the humbler classes of Her Majesty's subjects, and as a consequence of such recognition to receive immediately from the State an annual stipend proportioned to their merits and exertions. Such a fact is in itself very significant of the continually increasing interest which the Civil power takes in the condition of the working classes, whose moral and religious state and whose intelligence are acknowledged to be objects of vital importance to the common weal.

It is important that the assembled candidates should be impressed with a conviction of the anxiety of Government by means of a higher description of moral and religious education to improve the condition of the poor, and of their determi-

---

[14] These were the years when the Pestalozzian theory was being tried out on the Continent. This educator believed that lessons taken from daily experiences were far more valuable than any number of "teacher talks."

nation, as an indispensable means to this end, to elevate the position of the elementary teacher. . . .[15]

Thus many schoolmistresses were raised to a position of dignity and comfort, for living expenses were low, and salaries quite liberal.

A few decades later, there was another development in the field of education: men and women who had taken up scientific studies found their services in great demand by industrial firms. By the last years of the nineteenth century, machinery had just about revolutionized industry. The few graduates[16] available were employed by industry and as this practice left the school authorities with but few science teachers, it was necessary to employ part-time lecturers from the factories. These men would travel from school to school giving lectures on general science and physics. The local teacher was invited to the student sessions and she was expected to give periodic examinations on the material covered by the visiting lecturer. It was a make-shift arrangement of uncertain value.

At this time, Charlotte Mason—a clever Victorian woman developed, or in her own words, "chanced to find" a system of education especially suited to children. Charlotte was born in Liverpool in 1842, the only child of Joshua Mason, a prosperous merchant. During the American Civil War (1861–1865), her father lost his fortune. As a little girl, she had received the usual home training and led what might be called a sheltered life. In later years, she was drawn to teaching and faced the choice of working in a crowded industrial area or going out as governess in a well-to-do family. In the light of events that followed, it is clear why this active North-country woman took up school work in preference to a do-as-you-are-told position in a private household.

[15] Roberts, R. D. *Education in the Nineteenth Century*. At The University Press. Cambridge. 1901. p. 44.

[16] Scientific training had long been available for adults, but English students had not cared much about the subject.

Charlotte began to teach, trying at the same time to study in a small college near at hand. This last experience was a great disappointment—the methods used to teach adults how to teach children being little more than a farce. From the first, she objected to the constant emphasis on "don't's" in nursery-school work; moreover, she was the first educator to reject the idea that children should be "seen-but-not-heard." So it was that an intelligent young woman with very little mental training was about to transform the system of elementary education in England and elsewhere.[17]

In 1866, Miss Mason found time to publish her views on education. These articles came under the notice of the Marquis and Marchioness of Aberdeen and Temain, both of whom recognized the value of supervised education for children. In the following year, a meeting was held for the purpose of arranging a study program for Home Schoolrooms. Miss Mason wrote later:

> There were only about a dozen present and of these all were not clear as to what was intended. Had the scheme anything to do with refuge work, or was it intended to better the teaching in elementary schools, or to supplement the good work done in the cause of secondary education, are questions that appeared to be simmering in the minds of some of those present. It was hazarded that the education of parents was the object of the society, a suggestion which did more than touch the truth, but which met with a disclaimer all the same; because a proposal to educate parents sounds a little like an offer to teach the doctors—to the non-parent, at any rate, who has a great respect for parents, *per-se*.[18]

It is clear that a group of parents who met quite informally started an educational movement that was to guide amateurs in the business of home-education. This somewhat novel organization became known as the Parents' National Educational Union.[19] It functions

---

[17] It is a noteworthy fact that none of the great women reformers of the nineteenth century had university degrees.

[18] *The Parents' Review.* Published by the Parents' National Educational Union. Murray House, Vandon Street, London, S.W. 1. May, 1938.

[19] The Parents' National Educational Union (P.N.E.U.) was founded in 1888 and incorporated in 1921.

year by year with increasing efficiency; this fact is shown by the sort of papers sent in today and those sent in twenty years ago.

It is generally assumed that common experiences bring young people together. Beyond doubt, a child who works under the super-vision of the Parents' National Educational Union has a distinct so-cial advantage over the child who works under a less well-knit sys-tem of training. For the P.N.E.U. prides itself on the fact that pupils read the same books, look at the same pictures, play the same games, and lastly, study the same lessons. Among the general principles laid down are these:

1. Children are born *persons*.

2. They are not born either good or bad, but with possibilities for good or for evil.

3. The principles of authority on the one hand, and of obedience on the other, are natural, necessary, and fundamental; but —

4. These principles are limited by the respect due to the personality of children, which must not be encroached upon, whether by the direct use of fear or love, suggestion or influence, or by undue play upon any one natural desire.

5. Therefore, we are limited to three educational instruments,—the atmos-phere of environment, the discipline of habit, and the presentation of living ideas . . .

6. When we say that *'education is an atmosphere,'* we do not mean that a child should be isolated in what may be called a 'child environment' especially adapted and prepared, but that we should take into account the educational value of his natural home atmosphere, both as regards persons and things, and should let him live freely among his proper conditions. It stultifies a child to bring down his world to the child's 'level.'

7. By *'education is a discipline,'* we mean the discipline of habits, formed defi-nitely and thoughtfully, whether of mind or body. Physiologists tell us of the adaptation of brain structures to habitual lines of thought, *i.e.*, to our habits.

8. In saying that *'education is a life,'* the need of intellectual and moral as well as of physical sustenance is implied. The mind feeds on ideas, and therefore children should have a generous curriculum.

9. We hold that the child's mind is no mere *sac* to hold ideas; but is rather, if the figure may be allowed, a spiritual *organism*, with an appetite for all knowledge.

This is its proper diet, with which it is prepared to deal; and which it can digest and assimilate as the body does foodstuffs.

10. Such a doctrine as *e.g.*, the Herbartian, that the mind is a receptacle, lays the stress of Education (the preparation of knowledge in enticing morsels duly ordered) upon the teacher. Children taught on this principle are in danger of receiving much teaching with little knowledge; and the teacher's axiom is 'what a child learns matters less than how he learns it.'

11. But we, believing that the normal child has powers of mind which fit him to deal with all knowledge proper to him, give him a full and generous curriculum, taking care only that all knowledge offered him is vital, that is, the facts are not presented without their informing ideas. Out of this conception comes our principle that, —

12. '*Education is the Science of Relations*,' that is, that a child has natural relations with a vast number of things and thoughts; so we train him upon physical exercises, nature lore, handicrafts, science and art, and upon many *living books*, for we know that our business is not to teach him all about anything, but to help him to make valid as many as may be of, —

'Those first-born affinities
That fit our new existence to existing things.'[20]

Charlotte Mason was a saving-wedge between the teacher and the pupil—always considering how one would affect the other. To carry out this experimental work, she established the now-famous House of Education,[21] at Ambleside. The college was started in a small way, and attracted only four students the first year. It differed from the majority of teachers' training colleges in that students were taught how to live, as well as how to teach. The question of discipline came up in Miss Mason's College, just as it did in many other institutions during the last century. And it is an old student who gives a picture of how an untrained School Mistress handled a group-problem:

Once, and once only in my student days, was she [Miss Mason] confronted with one of those examples of youth's foolish rebellion . . . her method of dealing

---

[20] A Short Synopsis of the Educational Philosophy Advanced by the Founder of the Parents' National Educational Union.

[21] This institution was founded in 1892, and is now known as, The Charlotte Mason College.

with the situation gave me a marvellous insight into what she meant by discipline
—nothing was 'done to' the offenders—we were all simply left to talk over the
situation and find a solution; the offenders having time to 'come to themselves'
bitterly repented, and found, I think greatly to their surprise, that public opinion
had been greatly against them.[22]

From year to year adjustments were made. Finally, Ambleside was
unable to satisfy the demand for teachers. Certainly, Miss Mason
had planned well in carrying out her revolutionary ideas in education.

Strangely enough, people in upper-class society were always more
or less indifferent to formal education for girls. Families were large,
and half-grown girls were often kept busy with household duties,
especially the care of the younger children. Even in the closing years
of the nineteenth century—and in this case there would be no
shortage of help—the granddaughters of a wealthy English Duke
were being taught by a governess who was known to be neither
"proficient" nor "erudite." This particular governess believed that
the peerage was second only to the Bible; she passed over the parsing
of sentences and the solving of problems as work unsuited to little
girls of noble birth. However, great stress was placed upon correct
behavior, and the proper way to write a letter—emphasis being
placed on how to decline an invitation. It is clear that education
meant teaching a great deal that was superficial, and very little that
was helpful in everyday life. But in the State Schools teachers were
not allowed to use such casual methods; they followed a more or less
set program, especially in the elementary grades.

For a long time the school teachers of England have been faced
with multiple duties. They were expected to make the child of average ability conscious of life's responsibilities, and to make the child
of unusual promise develop along lines of individual interest. This is
a difficult undertaking for the man or woman who has but thirty-five
hours of pupil-supervision each week (and no time at all during the

[22] *In Memoriam Charlotte M. Mason.* Parents' National Educational Union. London. 1923.
p. 74.

holiday periods). Yet the rules submitted to teachers after 1870 were very clear on the subject, stating that the purpose of the Public Elementary Schools was to fit children "practically as well as intellectually" for the business of life. The authorities were feeling their way in a complicated situation.

The custom of cramming has been under fire. Many educators feel that special tests should be held for the gifted, not the less gifted. One institution has taken a definite stand: the Burrough Education Committee of Northampton informed members of its staff in the nineteen-thirties that additional training for examinations would no longer be allowed. This was a move in the right direction as it is well-known that knowledge acquired in a hurry, takes wings in a hurry.

English students who plan to become teachers are given special consideration by school authorities—that is, boys and girls are allowed to stay in advanced classes until seventeen or eighteen years of age, and then enter training colleges by means of scholarships. The plan worked well for some time. Then, pupils who had no idea of becoming teachers began to accept grants as stepping stones to a university education. The Board has tried to guard against such strategy. Students in advanced grades are now asked to sign an undertaking that they will serve as teachers for a certain period of time after graduation. However, there can be no compulsion; and to those of frail character, a promise means little, or nothing at all. So far, the Board has not thought fit to make changes in the general plan of training.

Discipline in schools can become a serious problem. Some children get into difficulty because they have too much self-confidence and for this group, strong measures are necessary. Again England had to go back to the Continent for suggestions: whipping-blocks were established in many of the best schools. But English boys were never held down by classmates—old prints suggesting that this was a Roman custom. Punishment of this kind can have serious effects on a child and apparently it was not always administered with good judgement. In fact, it became necessary for the London County Council to draw up a set of regulations which would stay the hand of teachers with ungovernable tempers. Here are the rules:

The open hand shall be used on a child's arm or hand.

Corporal punishment must never be inflicted on the face or any other part of the head.

Children under five may be sent home instead of being caned.

All punishment must be entered in the punishment book.[23]

As a result of these regulations, the supply of canes to Britain's schools has gradually decreased during the past thirty years. The matter of correction in schools has long been a debatable subject. In the United States, six out of ten adults believe that play-boy Tom and willful Anne should be kept up to the mark in deportment. But few are willing to go "so far as to support a practice currently followed in some English communities. Under this system . . . young people who commit minor crimes are required to be whipped by their parents in the presence of a police officer."[24]

In the following lines entitled, "A Schoolmaster's Soliloquy," an unknown teacher ponders the question:

To whip or not to whip?
That is the question
Whether 'tis easier in the mind to suffer the
Deaf'ning clamor of some fifty urchins,
Or take birch and ferrule, 'gainst the rebels,
And by opposing end it?

Very little has been written about discipline in the schools in England. And really, a teacher's life can be made miserable by a few "roughnecks," as unruly children are sometimes called. One difficul-

[23] *The Sunday Express*. London. August 15, 1937.
[24] *Scholastic Teacher*. New York, N.Y. (U.S.A.). February 13, 1959.

ty is this: educators, usually men and women who have been brought up in good surroundings, frame laws for all schools, assuming that all types can be managed in the same way. But this procedure has many loop-holes. For often there are half-grown children from the poorer districts—some with court records—who take over class-time at the slightest provocation. A bored pupil can always find excuses for disturbing the quiet of a schoolroom. Unfortunately, teachers hesitate sometimes to report cases of bad behavior; they fear unfavorable criticism from the heads of departments. Consequently, many unpleasant disturbances that occur during the recitation periods never come to the attention of the school authorities. But apparently there are serious school problems far beyond the grasp of the teachers. Consider Brenda, an English girl,

> She was fourteen years of age, and . . . the youngest of a large family who shared a house with some lodgers. Brenda had been up before the Juvenile Court and was sent to a remand home for two weeks. This had the effect of making her a heroine when she arrived back at school. . . . Brenda had complete control of the class and one 'Shut yer old' from her meant a nicely disciplined class.[25]

A large number of schools were without junior and senior divisions up to a few decades ago. This was especially true of the sparsely populated districts. Consequently, children of all ages might be gathered in one room, much like the class-arrangements of Shakespeare's day. After World War I, there were great shifts in the population, and for this reason many long-established schools had to be closed. This meant that teachers who had every expectation of an earned income to the end of their working days, were thrown out of employment at an age when re-employment was next to impossible. This caused many hardship cases. To ease any awkward situations, the Council of Schools tried to have the time of closing of a school coincide with the best interest of an aggrieved group. The plan worked fairly well except at Easter, a variable date, when involved questions concerning rights were apt to arise. The authorities often

[25] *The Times Educational Supplement.* London. January 29, 1960.

found their hands tied with rules and regulations. Changes made at Christmas or in the summer sessions presented no difficulties. But the removal of a person from a post which has been a part of his or her existence for fifteen or twenty years can be a real tragedy.

In the long ago, little was ever heard about handicapped children—a group often kept out of sight. But in time, a few brave mothers established schools in isolated parts of the world for little people who were not quite normal. As for England, the Government finally took over this arduous task. The number of handicapped children had risen to 65,950 by January 1960. It is a remarkable fact that this type of work attracts a superior type of woman, not only in England, but in other countries as well. The following table indicates school conditions in England for the year 1960:

Category of handicapped pupil	New Schools			Closed Schools			Net changes in number of places		
	Day	Boarding	Total	Day	Boarding	Total	Day	Boarding	Total
Blind	—	1	1	—	1	1	—	+27	+27
Deaf	1	1	2	—	–	–	+70	+20	+90
Deaf and partially deaf	—	–	—	1	1	2	–40	–113	–153
Partially deaf	—	1	1	—	–	–	+34	+86	+120
Physically handicapped	—	–	—	1	–	1	–80	—	–80
Delicate	2	–	2	4	–	4	+90	–151	–61
Maladjusted	4	1	5	—	–	–	+175	+45	+220
Educationally subnormal	13	2	15	4	–	4	+1,125	+80	+1,205
	20	6	26	10	2	12	+1,374	–6	+1,368[26]

Most annoying to teachers are the unexpected calls made by Her Majesty's Inspectors—men who play an important role in the educational system. These visitors report what they see and hear to a governing body. It is felt in many quarters that school inspection is

[26] *Education in 1960.* Her Majesty's Stationery Office. London. 1961. p. 30.

unnecessary now that capable instructors are employed in most of the schools. Then too, strangers can completely upset a school program, to say nothing of pupils and teachers. The writer has known not one, but a number of teachers, who have suffered great distress over the poor showing made by a particular class on what proved to be an ill-fated day. In her book, *I'm Not Complaining*, Ruth Adam gives the following account of a school inspector's visit:

I began to question them about the siege of Troy, giving the children a lead wherever I could. . . .

Mr. Vick . . . strode into the middle of the floor and addressed Georgie Hunt with the threatening mildness of a prosecuting counsel.

'Will you go on with the story?'

Georgie looked bewildered. But his neighbors prompted him and he stood up, glancing pathetically at me as if imploring my help. I gave him a sickly smile, intended for encouragement.

'So they went,' he said, and sat down again.

'Who went where?' asked the inspector.

Georgie stood up with the pained expression of a Job.

'Miss — sir, the men what was friends of the man who the lady had been stolen off.' He paused, but there was no help from earth or heaven. . . . It was odd to think that the test by which we stand or fall was over for two or three years. I had put in three years of conscientious work, hour by hour, day by day, controlling my impatience, my weariness, swallowing quantities of aspirins to quiet my nerves when they rebelled against the wear and tear of fifty-six restless minds and bodies. And now twenty minutes of nervous embarrassment and His Majesty's Government had passed judgement on all I had done. It seemed a peculiar arrangement to me. I would not judge a child so lightly.[27]

From this account, it is evident that at least one school inspector lacked both tact and understanding.

The extended study-programs now being offered in many schools are steadily gaining in popular appeal. An official report states that,

Those who stay on longer at school do so because their parents think they are not yet ready to leave and meet the world, but need more time in which to develop maturity and self-confidence in the friendly atmosphere of the school. The number

[27] Adam, Ruth. *I'm Not Complaining*. Chapman and Hall, Ltd. London. 1938. pp. 170–174.

of these pupils is increasing as more parents come to realize how much a school can contribute in this way.[28]

This further study is time well-spent and students should be encouraged to profit by the extra supervised instruction. Also, it may provide the enterprising boy or girl with the incentive for further study in the years to come. Knowledge is the key to understanding and when the individual is faced with critical decisions, helps in the mastery of circumstances.

Then, as so often happens in government affairs—first things coming last—it was learned that thousands of English children were under-nourished. It took World War I with its emphasis on physical fitness to bring out this unfortunate fact. Members of Parliament were aroused and came forward with timely legislation. It followed that meals were served in many schools—at first, in the poorer districts of large cities. But by 1956, roughly one-half of the pupils were taking the school lunch. Under this arrangement good food is served in pleasant surroundings. However, some boys and girls—the group given to criticism—like to bring their lunch from home and obtain milk at the schools. A recent report

Gave a total of 5,832,270 pupils taking milk at school, representing 82.11 per cent of those on Roll in maintained schools, and 80.18 per cent at non-maintained schools. . . . The proportion of pasteurized milk increased to 99.15 per cent from 96.87 per cent in the previous year.[29]

As for payment, many children receive the school lunches free of charge—the number being less than 10 per cent.

There has been some concern over the large size of classes in the primary schools. Arguments were carried on in the nineteen-thirties, the nineteen-forties, and into the nineteen-fifties. But improvements were only made in isolated cases. In some committee meetings the whole subject was treated as a joke—laughter greeting any mention of a room built for thirty pupils, and crowded with "twenty extras." Today, great improvements have been made. For instance, 415

[28] *Education.* Her Majesty's Stationery Office. London. 1960. p. 14.
[29] *Ibid.* p. 36.

new buildings have been opened during the past few years, and additional school buildings are being erected. It is pleasing to report that priority rights go to schools needed in areas where there is an increase in the child population. The over-sized classes of seniors have also grown smaller—now 62.9 compared with 64.2 a few years ago. These improvements have been accomplished under trying conditions, as there are many more children in school now than in the years prior to World War II.

The placement of teachers will be considered at this point. For many years the groups were divided as, certified and uncertified. In addition, a large number of people were employed as supplementary teachers.[30] The men and women who wished to take up school work were not required to follow any special line of study before applying for classification. Passing over this weak point, the matter of status was brought up again and again in the House of Commons. Consider the following session: Mr. Chester questioned the Parliamentary Secretary to the Board of Education as to whether he could give "The number of uncertificated teachers employed in elementary schools in England and Wales,". . . Mr. Lindsay: "Following are the figures: Estimated number of uncertificated teachers employed in public elementary schools in England and Wales on March 31, 1937 . . . 25, 194."[31] A more detailed report follows:

	1924	1935
Certificated Teachers (Men)	36,925	43,675
Certificated Teachers (Women)	79,173	87,658
Uncertificated Teachers.	32,524	27,447
Special Subjects Teachers (other than certificated)	3,890	5,837
Supplementary Teachers	10,709	5,957
Total	163,221	170,574[32]

[30] The supplementary teacher cared for children under eight years of age.

[31] *The Times Educational Supplement.* London. July 10, 1937.

[32] *The Year Book of Education 1937.* Published in association with the University of London Institute of Education. Evans Brothers, Ltd. London. p. 137.

NOTE. For statistical tables of teachers in England and Wales for the ten-year period 1951–1961, see pp. 75–76.

Generally speaking, uncertificated teachers, even those with personal qualifications of a high order, were not expected to serve in responsible positions.

There was an under-current of discontent with school management. A longer period of training for teachers was even then under consideration. Opinions differed as to the wisdom of such a move, as it would create many new problems: (a) the extension of training would mean an immediate shortage of teachers at a time when classrooms were crowded; (b) the extension of training would mean a controversy over status, the newly employed teacher having covered subjects somewhat advanced in character; (c) the extension of training would mean that a three-year graduate might expect a salary more in line with the man or woman who had obtained a university degree. It was suggested that a degree in pedagogy might be offered for students who wished to take up a more formal program of study. But the training colleges could not compete with well-known institutions any more than they do now — the best academic training would still be offered at the universities.

Due to the complete mobilization of manpower during World War II, there was a large decrease in the number of men and women entering the teaching profession. During the emergency, the teaching staffs of schools and colleges were badly depleted. The Education Act of 1944 was passed at a critical time. The new regulations made the provision of schools the responsibility of authorities elected by the people. For the first time, all teachers were required to have training in general education. Teaching was to be no longer a hit or miss affair. But the elected school officer was responsible for selecting competent teachers in his district.

From that time on all instructors in the Primary and Secondary Schools were to be known as "qualified teachers" — the term signifying that an approved course of study had been completed in an approved educational institution. Some by-play was necessary in order to carry out this ambitious program. For example, "temporary teachers" were called in to take the place of "uncertified teachers." At least the authorities were showing some concern for raising the standard of instruction in the schools. The required course of study for teachers included two years in a training college, or, an additional year in a university training department for graduates of universities. New strength was evident in all branches of the educational system. Thus, the Ministry of Education set a higher standard for all teachers. In 1960, the required period of study was raised to three years.

The teacher who has received both a teaching certificate and one or more college degrees is still the target of petty jealousies. Local authorities frequently get letters from older teachers complaining about their younger, college-trained colleagues. Unfortunately, teachers under thirty years of age are judged by the discipline they maintain in the classrooms. It is quite true that a novice lacks the *savoir faire* of a skilled lecturer, and this is the basis of criticism used to disparage the recent university graduate—comparing her with those trained under the old pupil-teacher system. Time, and advances in methods of training will alleviate this situation.

At this point the importance of courtesy and good manners in the conduct of daily affairs should be stressed, especially in the teaching profession. Many capable young men and women, with little or no cultural background, are graduating from the universities with competent knowledge in their chosen fields, but without having learned the rudiments of polite social etiquette. Along this line of thought, a headmaster says,

A colleague of mine, who had served the authority for over 30 years, informed his director of education that his son was about to be married. In reply to his application for one day's leave, my colleague received a formal note informing him that leave was granted, but that the education committee would in due course decide whether the leave would be with or without pay. It was not until a fortnight after the wedding, and more than four weeks after the date of his application for leave, that my colleague received a further curt note informing him that he would be paid . . . it never occurred to the education chief to add a few words of congratulation to the formal note.[33]

In the class struggle for precedence in the development of our many specialized activities, it is sad to relate that the importance of courtesy is being deplorably overlooked.

Without doubt, England could use more teachers who have been brought up in better social surroundings. For mistake it not, young students are impressed by correctness of speech and refined gentle manners. They are inclined to copy the patterns of activity and thought of teachers they respect and admire. At present,

> The social prestige of teaching is by no means on a level with that of other professions, and consequently few recruits are attracted to it from the upper classes. The best men and women in the land, irrespective of class, should be able to feel it an honour to join the ranks of teachers and should also—human nature being what it is—be able to look forward to adequate public recognition of merit in that field as much as in any other.[34]

In this respect, the personnel of the average teaching staff in England differs from that in the United States, where young women from old and respected families feel it is a great privilege to become teachers. The private schools especially, consider cultural factors almost as much as educational background; the late Mrs. Franklin D. Roosevelt is possibly the outstanding example—she taught in a private school in New York City (U.S.A.)—later becoming mistress of the White House.[35]

In rural schools, there has been some complaint about the general policy of selecting teachers, and arranging the various school programs. It was felt that some few children should be taught by country-bred teachers, and that their programs of study should include some instruction in agricultural economics. There was no desire,

---

[33] *The Times Educational Supplement.* London. October 23, 1937.

[34] Paul, Charles Kegan. *The Head Mistress Speaks.* Trench, Trubner and Co., Ltd. London. 1935. p. 77.

[35] The White House in Washington, D.C. (U.S.A.) was once known as the "President's Palace."

however, to follow the example of Dotheboys Halls, where "spell dairy, now go and clean it" was considered practical education. On the other hand, all boys and girls living on farms could profit by a knowledge of such matters as crop rotation, milk production, and animal husbandry. This demand for a special type of teacher harks back to the nineteenth century when the school authorities in France were calling for "environment and experience" as a basis for education.

All through the nineteen-thirties, the depression in business and industry caused wide-spread unemployment in England. It was a common sight to see people, young and old, going from door to door asking for work. Perhaps women suffered more than men, for they were too proud to walk the streets with worn-out shoes and shabby clothing.

There was teaching of course, a profession which had helped many individuals overcome their financial difficulties. But strangely enough, the average man disliked the idea of classroom work—that is, as a permanent career. A family man in Chelsea said to the writer, "Oh, I might try the teaching stuff until something better comes along." But there was a total lack of enthusiasm in his voice. Possibly, it took national suffering to change mass thinking. Whatever happened, children in advanced grades began to find men along with women in the classrooms after World War II. It was an opportune time, for salaries were going up as never before. Indeed, by 1945, the Minister of Education had approved a revised scale which would operate for three years. It applied to schools maintained by Local Education Authorities and established salaries and increments for qualified assistant teachers in Primary and Secondary Schools as follows:

Men	300 rising by annual increments of £15 to £525
Women	270 rising by annual increments of £12 to £420

Various additions to these scales are provided for—*e.g.*:

Men	£15 to £45	For teachers who have spent three, four or five years
Women	£12 to £36	in approved study or training.
Men	£15 to £30	For teachers holding a University degree or a qualifi-
Women	£12 to £24	cation accepted as equivalent thereto.

Men	£50 to £100	For teachers holding special posts in the schools.[36]
Women	£40 to £80	

But financial returns do not always attract teachers, as the poor response to advertisements offering well-paid posts in non-advantageous districts indicate. The story might be different if some of the inducements were of an educational nature. There are probably hundreds of women in the under-thirty group who would welcome the opportunity of doing advanced work in some training school or university while teaching. A comment in *The Times Educational Supplement* (London) of October 19, 1956, argues this point:

> Might not some untrained graduates, for instance, go to teach in Birmingham if the university offered them the chance to take a course of training in their spare time? . . . there must be others. Might not the future education officer be tempted to a place if it gave him classroom experience, and the chance of administrative study besides? Might not the ambitious teacher be attracted because there were courses in the vicinity on how to be a head?

Financial advantages must be considered, but they are not the sole attraction for men and women in the teaching profession. In spite of drawbacks, women teachers outnumber their male colleagues. The following table will give some idea of conditions from January 1951 to January 1960:

	1951	1956	1957	1958	1959	1960
Men	82,200	92,900	95,700	98,600	102,900	106,500
Women . . .	132,900	153,900	158,100	159,600	160,900	162,700
Total . . .	215,100	246,800	253,800	258,200	263,800	269,200
Increase during year . . Men		2,800	2,900	4,300	3,600	3,700 (est.)
Women		4,200	1,500	1,300	1,800	1,500 (est.)
Total		7,000	4,400	5,600	5,400	5,200 (est.)[37]

[36] *Teaching as a Career.* Ministry of Education. London. His Majesty's Stationery Office. 1945. pp. 20–21.

[37] *Education.* Her Majesty's Stationery Office. London. 1960.

Following is a detailed classification of teachers for the year 1961:

Teachers in full-time service in maintained primary and secondary schools (excluding special schools) in England and Wales in 1961:

Qualified teachers:

	Men	Women
Graduates:		
Trained[1]	24,490	14,702
Not trained	9,147	5,709
Graduate equivalent:[2]		
Trained[1]	1,686	937
Not trained	685	953
Qualified by long service	281	5,170
Other:		
Trained[1]	66,381	123,999
Not trained	6,469	5,893
Total	109,139	157,363

Other teachers:

	Men	Women
Supplementary teachers	—	837
Former uncertificated teachers	10	2,529
Other (including temporary)	1,396	1,530
Total	1,406	4,896
Total	110,545	162,259[38]

[1] For the purpose of this table trained teachers are those trained in England and Wales under the Training of Teachers Regulations and awarded qualified teacher status by an area training organization.

[2] Teachers with special qualifications who are treated as graduates for salary purposes.

It is common knowledge that economic conditions influence the marriage rate in all classes of society. In England, business and industry prospered following World War II. As a result, many teachers gave up their positions to become wives and mothers, and this caused a serious upset in the teaching staffs of schools. The loss of women teachers was three times that of men. Fortunately at that time a number of well-educated married women sought jobs outside

[38] *Annual Abstract of Statistics*, No. 99. 1962. Ministry of Education. Her Majesty's Stationery Office. London. p. 87.

the home and they were often employed as part-time workers in the primary schools. They have relieved a complicated situation, especially in the lower grades. On occasion, parents neglect to call for small children at the end of a school day, and there are times when the head of a school has to take over child-care responsibilities—for teachers cannot handle all of these problems.

If there are complications this year, what about next year? The number of pupils in the infant and junior divisons is expected to increase more or less steadily—possibly reaching a total of four million by 1970. The population explosion is a serious world-wide problem and must be faced with mature judgement and expert planning.

The English people like to follow a set pattern. What might be called a "mental bias" comes to light in almost all job placement issues. The majority of the women dislike assignments which entail any rupture in their fixed way of life. Up to the present time, appointments have been made on a voluntary basis, but this practice will be abrogated if the teacher-placement problem becomes a real challenge to the Minister of Education. Remedial measures have been discussed, but ideas of this kind make little headway with a people long accustomed to personal liberty. Any attempt to transfer teachers from their posts to other locations would most likely produce a nation-wide controversy. How this problem is to be solved is uncertain, but there is need for an equitable adjustment.

School officials in England have another problem: how can scientific subjects be taught when there are not enough science teachers to carry on the work. Now and then, recommendations are put forward, but there still remains a serious shortage of these teachers. Possibly, students—both boys and girls—might be attracted by a work-study plan in operation at an American University.[39] This is

[39] More than fifty years ago, Herman Schneider, who was Dean of the College of Engineering at the University of Cincinnati (Cincinnati, Ohio, U.S.A.), went about the city asking heads of business firms to employ students as part-time workers. The movement was a success —27 students being enrolled the first year; the number had increased to approximately 1,700 by 1962.

an arrangement by which engineering students carry on in pairs—two workers alternating every eight weeks between a job in office or factory, and attendance at specified classes in the university. Full-time study is required during the last or fifth year. Industrialists have been very co-operative, and have always been willing to pay the prevailing wage. In looking back, it seems that England would have done well to have adopted such a work-study program. But no one anticipated the present era of sputniks and telstars, or exploration of outer space. The unprecedented advance in scientific achievement, and the complex machinery of automation in all branches of business and industry, demand expert knowledge of mathematics and science, and school officials are hard-pressed to find teachers of these important subjects.

Sir Lawrence Bragg, Director of the Royal Institute at the University of London, drew attention to this really urgent problem by saying that more women should be persuaded to study science and mathematics. The Director felt very strongly that there should be "... a better general understanding of science. An educated person should not regard a scientific achievement with about the same extent of understanding as an Australian Aborigine looking at an aeroplane."[40]

As for women in educational work, they still have a long way to go. The number of women readers and lecturers in English universities is still relatively small. It is only the exceptional individual who attains such an honor. In the nineteen-thirties, the University of London employed one woman professor to about seventeen men professors. But the "lady professors" have always been very popular with undergraduates of both sexes. The name of one woman will almost always appear on the list of "Worth-Your-Time Lecturers," which is handed to new students by stealth at the beginning of each term.[41]

[40] *The Times Educational Supplement*. London. June 7, 1957.
[41] The writer's diary. London. Autumn, 1933.

In 1936, the following subjects were taught by women at the University of London:

	Lecturers	Readers		Lecturers	Readers
Anatomy	1	1	Histology		1
Biology		1	Mathematics		1
Botany	1	1	Obstetrics &		
Chinese		1	Gynecology	1	
Classics		1	Pathology		1
English		4	Philosophy	1	
French	1	2	Physics		1
Geography	1	2	Physiology	1	1
German	1	1	Romance		
Greek	1		Philology		2
History	3	2	Zoölogy	1	1

Some of the buildings of the University of London were demolished by enemy action during the 1939–1945 war, and some were burnt out. But with the restoration of normal conditions of work and life, many new departments have been added to its curriculum, and there has been a substantial increase in the number of women lecturers, readers, and research assistants.

As no definite technique is required at advanced levels of teaching, the question arises: What qualifications are needed to become a competent teacher? Dedication of purpose and enthusiasm for a particular subject are perhaps important requisites—and the writer pauses in memory of Professor Richard Lodge, who taught English history at Oxford University in the nineteen-thirties. This lecturer—and teacher as well—always stood in the classroom, and was so well prepared that he never used notes of any kind. Unfortunately, many men in similar positions neglect their classroom duties, spending the major part of their time writing scholarly books, or articles for magazines. This approach to pedagogy will no doubt continue as long as some scholarly individuals "resent having to teach at all, . . . regarding research as their primary function, and teaching as an irritating interruption of it."[42] However, a large num-

---

[42] *The Observer.* London. October 12, 1958.

ber of universities make publication of scholarly research a prerequisite to promotion.

Great credit should go to mature individuals who go back to school or college for further study with the idea of becoming teachers, or advancing in their business or profession. It is not an easy undertaking and only the strong-willed accomplish their purpose.

In 1958, a movement was started in England to provide educational facilities for older people. During World War II, a large group of students in secondary schools was forced to give up study for economic reasons. It was, primarily, concern for this group that the plan was established. As scholarships are available, the movement has met with popular demand and applications have been received from people in various occupations,

> All of whom were able to show evidence of continued study since leaving school, some by attendance at Workers' Educational Association classes, others at university extra-mural tutorial classes or by correspondence courses. The main interests lay in the field of economics, English, politics, and history. 75 candidates were interviewed and scholarships awarded to 27 including an iron moulder, a factory worker, an aircraft fitter and a postman.[43]

The results of this educational movement have been astonishing: "Of the 252 scholars who have so far completed their courses, 238 gained honours degrees, 29 with first class honours."[44] The Committee on Grants to students intends to continue these supports indefinitely.

Common interests bring people to collective action. For this reason, the National Union of Teachers was organized. It is a closely-knit association and was founded for certificated teachers holding posts in the first-rate Public Schools (actually expensive private schools). In time, membership requirements were made more elastic, and "other than regular" teachers were admitted to the parent organization. It may be said that English school teachers have no com-

---

[43] *Education in 1960.* Her Majesty's Stationery Office. London. 1961. p. 98.
[44] *Ibid.*

mon purpose, and few common interests. How could they have common interests with dissimilar training and dissimilar backgrounds? The head master in a public elementary school is an example: he belongs

In a category which was instituted a century ago when it became necessary to recruit and train men and women for service in the newly established schools for the people.[45]

The first members of the National Union of Teachers were selected from an especially well-qualified body—that is, the majority were university graduates.

Group action has brought many benefits to the teaching profession. Most certainly, the teacher in the State-aided schools has many advantages over her predecessor, the humble governess, and she works under a well-managed pension plan. A teacher may now retire at the age of sixty on an income which provides a comfortable, even pleasant way of life. For to the writer's knowledge, three women pensioners managed to live quite well in London by sharing living quarters, and dividing household expenses.

Under England's pension arrangements, contributions are payable at the rate of 5 per cent of salary—the worker and the employer sharing the cost of payments. Awards are based on the average salary earned. The clause which concerns married women should be clarified: a teacher who has been married, and who has not been able to teach regularly will have the usual thirty year period reduced by the number of years of absence. However, the period of semi-retirement must not exceed ten years. This arrangement is manifestly fair, not only to the teacher, but to the school authorities. University teachers do not come under the teachers (Superannuation) Act. This group is protected by a federated policy with corresponding benefits.

With all of these provisions, school teachers still face difficulties

[45] *The Times Educational Supplement*. London. January 1, 1938.

at times. For example, pay checks are reckoned by a system of "unequal allowances"—officials excusing the arrangement by saying that many young children are taught by inexperienced helpers. Fortunately, fully qualified teachers are well-protected.

The National Union of Teachers can usually settle disputes with little or no delay. In the year 1959, twelve hundred London teachers turned down a salary proposal which was said to be inadequate for comfortable living in a day when living expenses were going up, and the value of the currency was going down. In due time, the executive committee of the National Union of Teachers decided the issue; they accepted a proposal which would raise the minimum starting salary from £475 to £520. Many people are disturbed over the constant wrangling of teachers—low salaries, and extra duties being the chief complaints. But teaching as a career offers many benefits. Why shouldn't a public statement be based on obligation—that is, "What can I do for a school system that has brought me both prestige, and financial independence?"

In 1909, a movement was started that was to have far-reaching consequences for teachers in England. It was then that "seventeen educated ladies" formed a society with the expressed intention of helping themselves. The organization expanded, and, in time, led to what is now known as the British Federation of University Women. From the beginning, this group pushed forward many worthy projects, often in the face of ridicule. An idea which attracted more than passing attention was "The Teacher's Exchange Program," an arrangement whereby teachers could be transferred from schools in their own country to institutions in other parts of the world. But this step brought complications. A few of the English girls who went to the United States could not make themselves understood in the classrooms, and a few of the American girls who went to England could not teach regularly because of colds, and other bronchial ailments. There was also an amusing side to this undertaking: a young woman from the State of Pennsylvania (U.S.A.), a somewhat nervous type, was completely upset the first day—stumbling over a door-stop—when thirty-five English pupils called out in voices loud and clear, "Good morning, teacher." But an exchange program has many advantages, and will no doubt be continued for many years to come.

Generally speaking, the English people look upon university training as the right of men, rather than women. They think nothing of sacrificing a daughter's education if perchance her services are needed in the home. As late as 1962, the number of students registered in the colleges for advanced work was in the ratio of three men to one woman. A situation of this kind is entirely out of line with educational surveys—the shortage of teachers being a case in point. The old idea propounded for a woman—establish yourself in a man-made society, or mark time with countless household duties—should have been discarded many years ago.

A debatable question is this: Will machines ever replace teachers? This is a timely problem, as the number of students is increasing at a faster rate than the number of teachers. Moving pictures, the most popular of all teaching aids, have made a poor showing in the primary grades, educators reporting that young children, the group with roving eyes, fail to grasp the meaning of screen productions. Most certainly, the *capacity* to learn depends upon the *ability* to apply the mind. Going on to higher levels, conditions change. Many advanced students find teaching machines very helpful; they remember what is seen far longer than what is heard. Film-strips and tape-recorders have a definite place in college programs. Possibly, the time may come when advanced students will register, not for class attendance, but for reading and listening courses. All things considered, it is safe to assume that electronic machinery will be an adjunct, rather than a replacement of teachers, in the educational system.

IV. Medicine

THE art of healing has gone a long way since the Babylonians made a bed of straw on the highway, and laid their patients down for observation and questioning. As time passed these people stored up an enormous treasury of information; they gave special attention to the patient who had received good, rather than a casual type of nursing. It was a period of trial and error. Just how medicine developed into a science might be likened to a small rivulet making its way to the sea—following an uncertain course from one country to another, and then emerging as a mighty waterfall in Greece. It is worthy of note that the Greeks deified Æsculapius in exactly the same way that the Egyptians deified their physician Imhotep. By the seventh century B.C., a philosophical system of medicine had become a part of Hellenic culture.

On the island of Cos lived Hippocrates.[1] Unfortunately, it is only through his writings that the great physician is known—even the most familiar portrait of him is the mind-creation of a Greek artist. Yet this spiritual figure has infused into medicine a divineness of purpose quite unknown in other professions. In the Hippocratic Oath[2] is the whole essence of good medical service. It follows in part:

PAGAN OATH
(Translation from a fourteenth century manuscript)

I swear by Appolo Physician, by Æsculapius, by Health, by Herb-all, and by all the gods and goddesses, making them witnesses, that I will carry out, according to my ability and judgment, this oath and this indenture:

To regard my teacher in this art as equal to my parents; to make him partner

---

[1] Hippocrates was born about 460 B.C.

[2] Even today, the Hippocratic Oath is repeated by graduates of medical colleges in many parts of the world.

in my livelihood, and when he is in need of money to share mine with him; to consider his offspring equal to my brothers; to teach them this art, if they require to learn it, without fee or indenture; and to impart precept, oral instruction, and all the other learning, to my sons, to the sons of my teacher, and to pupils who have signed the indenture and sworn obedience to the physicians' Law, but to none other.

I will use treatment to help the sick according to my ability and judgment, but I will never use it to injure or wrong them. . . .

Whatsoever in the course of practice I see or hear (or even outside my practice in social intercourse) that ought never to be published abroad, I will not divulge, but consider such things to be holy secrets.

Now if I keep this oath and break it not, may I enjoy honour, in my life and art, among all men for all time; but if I transgress and forswear myself, may the opposite befall me.[3]

The society of physicians under Hippocrates was a very exclusive organization, for the members had to be either sons of physicians, or high-minded men who were willing to keep the Oath. The reason Hippocrates gained ground over his contempories was this: he cast aside irrational fear of the unknown, and studied manifestations in the body. He would sit long hours by the side of a patient noting his temperature, pulse, respiration, and facial expression. It is an amazing fact that Hippocrates described the facial appearance of a person near death so accurately that the condition is still called "facies Hippocrates." This great physician understood the limitations of knowledge, being ever ready to accept advice from other practitioners. He kept detailed records of examinations, even going so far as to start a filing system—very much like the card-index plan in general use today. Small wonder it is that the doctrine, Neo-Hippocraticism, sometimes called "Constitutional Medicine," is still making its way into everyday practice.

In the early Christian era, another physician came to public notice.

[3] Jones, W. H. S. *The Doctor's Oath. An Essay in the History of Medicine.* At The University Press. Cambridge. MCMXXIV. pp. 9 & 11.

This was Claudius Galen (A.D., 130–200), who was born in Pergamus, the capitol of Ione. Claudius attended the home-town schools as a boy, and then went on to a medical college in Alexandria, Egypt. Seeking a broader field, he settled in Rome, becoming a physician of great renown. He followed in the footsteps of Hippocrates to some extent. But critics say that Galen used drugs far more than was necessary. These two men have long been compared, to the disparagement of Galen. In truth, ". . . the noble vision of the lofty-minded, pure-souled physician has utterly passed away. In its place we have an astute, contentious fellow of prodigious industry."[4]

Galen was active in social life. His patients—persons like Marcus Aurelius—came almost exclusively from the leisure class. This doctor, when a young man of thirty years of age, liked to have his little jokes. He was called in to see

A lady for an ill-defined disability without symptoms, he suspected a purely mental trouble. With his fingers upon her pulse, he engaged her in general conversation, mentioning casually the name of the actor, Pylades; immediately, her pulse quickened. He repeated this on the following two days, but mentioned the names of different favourites—on each occasion the lady's equanimity was undisturbed. On the fourth day he again introduced the name of Pylades, the recollection of whom once more disturbed the rhythm of the patient's heart. Galen rightfully concluded that his patient was in love with Pylades, and that her condition was neuropathic.[5]

It is not difficult to picture this quick-witted physician entering the sick-room with a smile and a bow, then becoming just serious enough to satisfy the patient's self-esteem. Galen amassed a fortune, the amount of which had never before been equaled in the medical profession.

With the violent fall of the Mediterranean countries there was a trend towards stagnation in scientific thought; medicine stood ready to perish in the whirlpool of barbaric conquests. For it has always

[4] Singer, Charles. *A Short History of Medicine*. At The Clarendon Press. Oxford. 1928. p. 52.
[5] Dawson, Bernard. *The History of Medicine*. H. K. Lewis & Co., Ltd. London. 1931. p. 54.

been true that science and art, unlike religious undertakings, thrive best in an atmosphere of security.

The Arabs, carefree and courageous, carried on medical research in villages far away from the main routes of travel. These tribesmen understood, to some extent, that the natural was not the supernatural; they made no effort to tie up wind and rain with disease in its various forms. However, the acceptance of evil spirits persisted through the centuries—this being an easy make-shift for the diagnostician. Surgical operations were still carried on by means of crude instruments which left issues far more dangerous than the disease which they were supposed to cure.[6] Medicine, as a profession, was moving along by means of trial and error.

The Arabic version of Greek science made a deep impression on Arabic-speaking students. These men made valuable contributions to medical science by becoming acute clinical observers.

Thus Rhazes (860–932), a native of Basra on the Persian Gulf, wrote a pamphlet containing the first known description of measles, which he carefully distinguishes from smallpox. The Persian Avicenna (980–1036) composed a vast encyclopaedia of medical knowledge, the so-called *Canon*, which served as the main text-book of Medicine both among the Arabic-speaking peoples and in the Latin West until the seventeenth century. The Jew, Isaac of Kairouan (852–952), composed a treatise on fevers which was the best account of the subject available in Europe during the entire Middle Ages. The Moor, Albucasis (11th cent.), left a text-book of surgery which was an important element in the revival of the subject in Italy and France.[7]

This list of physicians and surgeons represents a scholarly group of men who lived and worked in the Arabic countries between the ninth and twelfth centuries. The translations of their books, many of them at least, reached England by way of Europe. During the early part of the sixteenth century the English universities[8] encouraged

[6] Headaches were treated by boring a hole in the skull.

[7] Singer, Charles. *A Short History of Medicine.* At The Clarendon Press. Oxford. 1928. p. 67.

[8] Thomas Linacre, a classical scholar at Oxford, translated the works of Galen.

students to copy accurately the works of the Greek authors, the Arabic-Latin scholars having sacrificed ideas for literary style in many instances. The Greek spirit of enquiry was persisting.

It was only natural, perhaps, that with a revival of learning should come a revival of art. Artists understood quite well that to produce the human form properly, they must have accurate knowledge of the bones and muscles of the body. Leonardo da Vinci was the first artist-scientist to question the theories of Greek physicians. He was especially interested in the heart and blood vessels, and ". . . reached the correct conclusion that, contrary to Galen, the branches of the air-tubes in the lungs do not come into relation with the heart, but, after branching and gradually diminishing in size, they finally end blindly."[9]

The great Leonardo left a wealth of material in note-books, which were accessible to scholars of a later period. It was a genuine craving for truth which enabled Leonardo da Vinci (1452–1519) to produce the "Last Supper," Michelangelo (1475–1564) to paint the ceiling of the Sistine Chapel, and Raphael (1483–1520) to shape those delicate frescoes in the Vatican.

Religious wars in the sixteenth and seventeenth centuries gave army surgeons experience in the treatment of wounds. The most prominent of these practitioners was Ambroise Paré,[10] who recognized the importance of anatomical knowledge, and applied his findings to the needs of surgery. Paré contributed something of his own personality to the medical profession—placing emphasis on the relief of suffering. As a "freshwater soldier" he gave the following description of a sad experience:

I watched the other surgeons going on with the old rules of treating gunshot wounds with boiling oil. The theory was that gunshot wounds contained a poison,

[9] Singer, Charles. *A Short History of Medicine*. At The Clarendon Press. Oxford. 1928. pp. 83–84.
[10] Paré, Ambroise. (1510–1590).

which the boiling oil was believed to drive out. Then one evening all supplies having run out, men had to be treated without the boiling oil. Next morning I was astonished to find that every man whose wounds had been treated only with a salve had rested fairly comfortably, while all who had undergone the customary treatment were, as we may well believe, in great pain. Then I resolved within myself never so cruelly to burn poor wounded men.[11]

Another saying of the shrewd old surgeon is the famous adage, "I dressed him and God cured him." The works of Paré were translated into many languages; they exerted wide influence among physicians of all countries.

The history of medicine in England may easily be associated with that of Rome.

There is nothing improbable in the supposition that men who had consulted Galen as to their health may have walked along the Roman causeway in Cheapside on which, fifteen hundred years later, Wren placed the foundations of the present tower of the Church of St. Mary-le-Bow, or may have watched the Britons bringing products of fishing or of the chase up Walbrook from the Thames in skin-covered wicker boats.[12]

London was long a city in which outside influence predominated; even the civil institutions of London have taken on a foreign complexion: the terms "communa" and "mayor" being introduced from the Continent.

It is clear that medicine had long been a mixture of mysticism, quackery and superstition. It may have been Kipling's journalistic experience in India—the land where almost anything is boiled down for medicinal purposes[13]—that brought him to the realization of unorthodox medical practices in the England of long ago. At any rate, he has left these admirable verses on what the "fathers" did to drive away disease:

[11] Singer, Charles. *A Short History of Medicine.* At The Clarendon Press. Oxford. 1928. p. 94.

[12] Moore, Norman. *The History of the Study of Medicine in the British Isles.* At The Clarendon Press. Oxford. 1908. p. 5.

[13] Samundar jahag is an Indian remedy for "suppurative lesions"; it is made either from powdered cuttlefish bone or dried scum taken from streams.

Excellent herbs had our fathers of old . .
   Excellent herbs to ease their pain . .
Alexanders and Marigold,
   Eyebright, Orris, and Elecampane,
Basil, Rocket, Valerian, Rue,
   (Almost singing themselves they run)
Vervain, Dittany, Call-me-to-you . .
   Cowslip, Melilot, Rose of the Sun.
     Anything green that grew out of the mould
     Was an excellant herb to our fathers of old. . . .

       .   .   .   .   .   ·

If it be certain, as Galen says,
   And sage Hippocrates holds as much . .
'That those afflicted by doubts and dismays
   Are mightily helped by a dead man's touch,'
Then, be good to us, stars above!
   Then, be good to us, herbs below!
We are afflicted by what we can prove;
   We are distracted by what we know —
     So—ah so!
   Down from your heaven or up from your mould,
   Send us the hearts of our fathers of old![14]

There had long been considerable illness among the English people—plagues developing century after century. The herb-doctors—
many of them women—never lacked patients.

Medical knowledge was to a great extent empirical. The universal system of
blood-letting twice a year was likely to produce more maladies than it averted.
Those who lived in detached cottages and small villages were subject to fevers,
from the ill-drained lands by which they were surrounded. Those who lived in
towns had to endure pestilent nuisances of the streets, which no magisterial power
was able to correct. The scarcity of fuel made the mud-hut cottages, in which
chimneys were still rare, miserably cold in winter. The thatched cottages of the

---

[14] Kipling, Rudyard. *Rewards and Fairies.* From "Our Fathers of Old" "A Doctor of Medicine." (Reprinted by permission of the poet's widow, Mrs. Elsie Kipling Bainbridge. June 3,
1938.) Macmillan and Co., Limited. London. 1910. pp. 275–276.

towns were often on fire; and the rapid destruction of whole streets produced the greatest misery. The protection of fire insurances was unknown. Such were some of the many causes that reduced the poor to helpless indigence, and which sometimes prostrated even the comparatively wealthy.[15]

It is evident that disease and unsanitary living conditions were more or less taken for granted.

Sometimes in diaries, sometimes by word of mouth, comes a story of women doctors. In 1336, a certain Nicholas Tyngewich, physician to King Edward I, ". . . related in his lecture theatre at Oxford that he rode forty miles to an old woman, who had cured innumerable men of jaundice, and gave her a sum of money for teaching him her method of treatment."[16] This physician stood high in the community, for his name is often mentioned in fourteenth century documents, including a charter at St. Paul's Cathedral. What an amazing commentary on the medical situation—the King's physician riding along the narrow paths of rural England in order to seek advice from a housewife who had made a name for herself in the treatment of disease.

There was plenty of medical work to be done—the question being, How to go about it? The authorities of both Church and State set the pace for women by constantly giving out statements of encouragement to girls who wished to become midwives. Writers of the period followed suit. Here is what Andrew Borde had to say:

In my tyme, as well here in Englande as in other regions, and of olde antiquitie, euery Midwyfe shulde be presented with honest women of great grauitie to the Byshop, and that they shulde testify, for her that they do present shulde be a sadde woman, wyse and discrete, hauynge experience, and worthy to haue the office of a Midwyfe. Than the Byshoppe, with the counsel of a doctor of Physick, ought to examine her, and to instructe her in that thynge that she is ignaurant; and thus

[15] Knight, Charles. *The Popular History of England.* Volume III. Frederick Warne and Co. London. c. 1857. p. 277.

[16] Moore, Norman. *The History of the Study of Medicine in the British Isles.* At The Clarendon Press. Oxford. 1908. p. 28.

proued and admitted, is a laudable thynge; for and this were vsed in Englande, there shulde not halfe so many women myscary, nor so many chyldren perish in euery place in Englande as there be. The Byshop ought to loke on this matter.[17]

Strangely enough, what happened in the realm of science did not impress the general public in England. It was a well-known fact that lower-class families would seek remedies from friends, relatives, even the milk-man, rather than pay a small sum of money to a doctor in the neighborhood. This was especially true of a population that was not only superstitious, but extremely antagonistic towards a system of treatment that was not bound up in some way with in-dividual experiences. Then too, thousands of families tucked away in tiny villages were unable to appreciate the difference between the qualified and the unqualified physician. At last, scientists gave serious consideration to the problem, and thought out a plan to protect the English people from themselves.

A Charter of Incorporation was drawn up by the President of the "Faculty of Physic" in London, and submitted to His Majesty, King Henry VIII, in 1518. A translation of this document follows:

Henry, by the Grace of God, King of England and France, and Lord of Ireland, TO ALL to whom these present letters shall come, Greetings.

Whereas, we consider it the duty of our Royal office by all means to consult the happiness of the people under our rule, we have thought it to be chiefly and before all things necessary to withstand in good time the attempts of the wicked, and to curb the audacity of those wicked men, who shall profess the assurance of any good conscience, whereby very many inconveniences may ensue to the rude and credulous populace: Therefore, partly imitating the example of well governed cities in Italy and many other nations, and partly inclining to the petition of the grave men, . . . We will and command to be instituted a perpetual College of learned and grave men who shall publicly exercise medicine in our City of London and the suburbs, and within seven miles from the City on every side: Whose care it will be, as we hope, both for their own honour and in the name of the public benefit, as well to discourage the unskilfulness and temerity of the knavish men

[17] *The fyrst Boke of the Introduction of Knowledge made by Andrew Borde of Physicke Doctor.* c. 1485. Edited by F. J. Furnivall. Published by N. Trubner & Co. London. M.D.C.C.C.L.X.X.

whom we have mentioned, by their own example and gravity, as to punish the same by our laws lately enacted, and by the constitutions to be ordained by the same College: . . . And that the same Commonalty or College every year for ever shall be able to elect and make out of that Commonalty some prudent man and expert in the Faculty of Medicine as President of the same College or Commonalty, to oversee, superintend, and govern for that year the College or Commonalty aforesaid, and all men of the same Faculty and their affairs: An that the same President and College or Commonalty shall have perpetual succession and a Common Seal to serve for the affairs of the said Commonalty and President for ever: And that they and their successors for ever shall be persons able and capable to acquire and possess in fee and perpetuity lands and tenements, rents, and other possessions whatsoever. . . .

We Have also granted to the same President and College or Commonalty, and their successors, that no one in the said City, or for seven miles in circuit of the same, shall exercise the said Faculty, unless he be admitted thereto by the said President and Commonalty, or their successors for the time being, by letters of the same President and Commonalty, sealed with their common seal, under pain of one hundred shillings for every month during which not having been admitted he has exercised the same Faculty; half thereof to be paid to us and our heirs, and half to the said President and College. . . .

We Will also and grant for us, our heirs and successors, as much as in us is, That neither the President nor any one of the College aforesaid of Physicians, nor their successors, nor any one of them exercising that Faculty shall in any manner in future within our City aforesaid, and the suburbs thereof, or elsewhere, be summoned or placed, in any assizes, juries, inquests, inquisitions, attaints, or other recognitions within the said City and the suburbs thereof, henceforth to be taken before the Mayor, or Sheriffs, or Coroners of our said City for the time being, or to be summoned by any of his or their officer or officers, or minister or ministers; Although the same juries, inquisitions, or recognitions shall have been summoned upon the writ or writs of right of us or our heirs: . . .

In Witness whereof we have caused these our letters to be made patent. *Witness* ourself at Westminster on the twenty-third day of September, in the tenth year of our reign.

TUNSTALL

By the King himself, and of the date
aforesaid, by authority of Parliament.[18]

[18] *The Charter of Incorporation* (Granted by Henry VIII). British Museum.

Up to this time, English women had played only a small part in the medical profession, although stories were going about that "feminine practitioners" were actively engaged in such work abroad. Quite possibly these shreds of information inspired the following comment:

> I meruayle gretely of the opynyon of fome men that saye that they wolde not in no wyfe that theyr doughters or wyues or kynnefwomen sholde lerne seyences and that it fholde payre theyr codycyos. This thynge is not to fay ne to fufteyne. That the woman apayreth by connynonge it is not well to believe. As the proverbs sayeth, 'that nature gyveth maye not be taken away.'[19]

Even in those early days certain group standards were being questioned—that is, shall a girl-child be a free agent, or shall she be a human chattel? The place of women in society was yet to be determined.

Some change in medicinal service had been in the minds of the people for a long time. Finally, a statute was passed which recognized women as well as men in the art of healing. These measures were intended to protect

> Divers honeft perfones as well men as women, whom god hath enduced with the knowledge of the nature kinde, & operacion of certein herbes, rootes, and waters, & the ufynge and miniftering of them, to fuche as ven peined with cuftomable difeafes: ... And yet the faid perfons hau not taken any thing for their peines or cunning, but haue miniftered the fame to the poore people only for neighbourhoode & goddes fake, & of pitie & charytie.[20]

The bill also states that the "company & fellowship of furgions" of London have thought only of their "owne lucres" and cared little about the suffering of patients.

Thus, it may be said that valuable contributions were made to medicine in the sixteenth century. But the country was not so fortunate in the decades which followed. For the Bubonic Plague, the

[19] Pisan, Christine de. *The boke of Cyte if Ladyes*. Imprynted at London in Poules Chyrchyarde at the syngne of the Trynyte be Henry Pepwell. M.C.C.C.C.X.X.I.

[20] Actes made in a fefsion of Parlyament. c. 1543. British Museum.

dreadful scourge of Europe, struck England with all of its fury, people falling on the streets with dizzy spells, and violent headaches.
It all started around the rat-infested areas, and spread quickly to the
more prosperous residential districts. This disease showed no
favoritism, striking children as well as adults. Home after home was
marked with a red cross, coupled with a simple passage from the
Scriptures. Private funerals were forbidden. Instead, great piles of
corpses were heaped into carts, and buried at night in communal
graves.

Little would be known about this period were it not for Samuel
Pepys (1633–1703), who wrote a somewhat remarkable diary. In
September, 1665, he gave this dark picture of life on the little island:
"What a sad time it is to see no boats upon the river; the grass grows
all up and down Whitehall Court, and nobody but poor wretches in
the streets." The great annalist was of course one of the 'poor
wretches' trying to make the best of a bad predicament. The physicians—and this comment would have pleased Hippocrates—stayed
in their offices giving sage, saffron, and snake-root to patients who
asked for help. Medicine, as a profession, had a long way to go.

Doctoring, as a profession, was at the cross-roads by the end of
the seventeenth century, logical thought having been replaced by
ideas that were to some extent guess-work. It was an unfortunate
situation. Then scientists began to think that theories were cumulative in character—that is, a new process was often an off-shoot of a
process previously developed. The trick might be in observation.

So it was that Dr. Edward Jenner (1749–1823), noticed ". . . in his
practice that dairy-maids who contracted cowpox from the udders of
infected cattle were apparently immune to smallpox,"[21] an illness
that was causing thousands of deaths, not only in England, but
throughout the world. The country doctor gave this fact some attention, finally deciding that the attacks of the two maladies were iden-

[21] Dawson, Bernard. *The History of Medicine.* H. K. Lewis & Co., Ltd. London. 1931. p. 137.

tical, but that they reacted on the body in a different manner—cowpox being less dangerous than smallpox.

These findings were put to work without further ado, and satisfactory results came within a matter of months. Over a period of ten years, 6,000 adults had been given immunity from the dread disease. The method was simple: matter from a cowpox patient being injected into the veins of a healthy human being. The more fanatic of opponents—and there were many—said that the treatment would give its victims "the features of a cow"; and they spread this idea by displaying pictures of bull-faced children who had received the vaccine. It was the old story: a miracle was being questioned! But Dr. Jenner continued his good work. His was a record of achievement that had never before been equaled in medicine.

Women doctors were not uncommon by the eighteenth century; they were, in fact, effecting some remarkable 'cures' among the people. For example, "Crazy Sally," a bone-setter, ". . . was so popular that the authorities of the town of Epsom offered her £100 a year to remain in that neighborhood. She used to come to town in her carriage, and receive patients at the Grecian Coffee House."[22] It is unfortunate that so little has been written about this woman, for she made medical history in a special way, in a dark period of social life. Here and there in old newspaper files are names of women who performed operations of various kinds in England. Where they were trained—and they must have had some experience—remains a mystery to this day. The work performed by these women surgeons is suggested, rather than explained.

A few decades later, the name of Ellen Haythornethwaite takes a conspicuous place in medical history. A letter written in 1788 states that this practitioner

Lives in the Forest of Bowland, [and] is supposed to be one of the best surgeons in the country. She has performed several amazing cures, given up for being incur-

[22] Hill, Georgiana. *Women in English Life*. Vol. II. Richard Bentley & Son. London. MDCCCXCVI. p. 282.

able by the Whitworth Doctors and others. . . . As for asthmas, coughs, fevers, and all internal disorders, she will not prescribe a great quantity of drugs, and yet effectually cure, if curable. But as for burns, scalds, fractured skulls, bruises, and all external wounds, she will, in a very little time make a perfect cure, . . . N.B.—She will take nothing in hand if she finds it incurable. Her charges are also very moderate; only 12d. a week if they come to her. She travels none abroad.[23]

The early part of the nineteenth century was a period of unrest and conquest. Exploitation was in the public mind—that is, volunteers would sail from some English port, hoping to return with quantities of coins, and precious jewels. It was an Elizabethan dream which brought uncertain results. Under such conditions, women in the lower classes had a bad time of it. Consider what a correspondent wrote for a monthly magazine in 1808: "I noticed that cases of the sale of wives at Smithfield with halters round their necks appears to be on the increase."[24] To become a household drudge was about the only work a woman could get. When hard times strike England, wealthy families employ very little help; they just close a part of their homes, and live in a few rooms—the only notice being an assortment of unwashed windows. The 'superior job' was still midwifery, something of a move towards the medical profession. Indeed, it was almost a step.

Elizabeth Blackwell (1821–1901), was the first English-born woman to receive a degree in medicine. This young woman spent the formative years of her life in the United States. Her family faced a desperate struggle for existence; and to add to the difficulty, Elizabeth's father died in 1838, leaving a widow and nine children with no means of support. The elder sisters opened a boarding-school for "young ladies" in Cincinnati, Ohio (U.S.A.). Apparently, the entire family entered into the business venture. Henry,[25] who was thirteen years

---

[23] Beale, Catherine Hutton. (Editor). *Reminiscences of a Gentlewoman of the Last Century.* Cornish Brothers. Birmingham. 1891. p. 69.

[24] Fremantle, A. F. *England in the Nineteenth Century.* The Macmillan Company. New York (U.S.A.). 1930. p. 415.

[25] Henry Blackwell married the gifted Lucy Stone, who founded the American Woman's Suffrage Association in 1869.

old, acted as cook—priding himself on the fact that he could make three different kinds of bread. In considering this period of her life, Elizabeth said in a letter that "The wider education of women was a subject then coming to the front; and we three sisters threw ourselves with ardour into the public conferences held in Cincinnati on this subject, . . ."[26]

Then, a chance happening changed the entire course of Elizabeth's life. She had a friend who was suffering from a painful disease, but refused to be attended by any of the home-town physicians. Elizabeth was deeply touched, and decided to study medicine, although she disliked everything connected with the profession. Applications were sent to all of the large medical colleges, and refusals came from each and every one. Almost in despair, she wrote to a small college in Geneva, New York (U.S.A.). The authorities, after some deliberation, found themselves unable to decide whether a young woman should or should not be admitted to the College. Thereupon, they asked the students how they felt about the matter. These young men held a meeting and adopted the now famous resolution:

RESOLVED—That one of the radical principles of a Republican Government is the universal education of both sexes; that to every branch of scientific education the door should be open equally to all; that the application of Elizabeth Blackwell to become a member of our class meets our entire approbation; and in extending our unanimous invitation we pledge ourselves that no conduct of ours shall cause her to regret her attendance at this institution.

2. RESOLVED—That a copy of these proceedings be signed by the chairman and transmitted to Elizabeth Blackwell.

T. J. STRATTON, *Chairman*.[27]

On the whole, Elizabeth had a very satisfactory course of study at Geneva University, for the men students did everything possible to smooth her way, not only in the classroom, but in the laboratory.

[26] Blackwell, Dr. Elizabeth. *Pioneer Work for Women.* J. M. Dent & Sons, Ltd. London. 1914. p. 9.
[27] *Ibid.* p. 53.

She received the degree, Doctor of Medicine, on January 23, 1849. The press, both in the United States and England, gave considerable space to the event. Even *Punch* waxed enthusiastic:

> Young ladies all, of every clime,
>   Especially of Britain,
>   Who wholly occupy your time
> In novels or in knitting,
>   Whose highest skill is but to play,
>   Sing, dance, or French to clack well,
> Reflect on the example, pray,
> Of excellent Miss Blackwell![28]

Dr. Blackwell understood full well that a degree in medicine was only the first step towards a medical career. Shortly after graduation, she left the United States with the twofold purpose of visiting relatives in England, and of studying medicine in France. A short time later, Elizabeth entered La Maternité, the State institution for training midwives. She worked in the hospital as an "experienced" *élève*, for the authorities refused to grant the slightest favor to a woman M.D. Day-to-day life in the institution was extremely trying, as sleep was lost every fifth night by schedule. It was while doing service in the infirmary that Elizabeth had a misadventure which caused her both pain and anguish: she contracted purulent opthalmia from a patient. The doctors did everything possible to save the sight of the infected eye. But the disease had done its worst.

This brave woman passed over her affliction as a "strange and sudden blow." The next few months were given over to rest, as professional work was out of the question. By the following spring, Elizabeth was making plans to continue her studies in London, She entered St. Bartholomew's Hospital as a student in the wards, and did special clinical work with well-known physicians. But the matter of earning a living became more and more urgent.

[28] *Punch.* Vol: Sixteen. London. 1849. p. 226.

Dr. Blackwell selected New York City (U.S.A.) as the place where a woman might carve out a career for herself. Even in the United States it was an uphill undertaking, for women physicians were frowned upon, not only by society, but by the medical profession as a whole. In reviewing the difficulties encountered in those early years of practice, Dr. Blackwell said:

> My first medical consultation was a curious experience. In a severe case of pneumonia in an elderly lady I called in consultation a kind-hearted physician of high standing who had been present in Cincinnati at the time of my father's fatal illness. This gentleman, after seeing the patient, went with me into the parlour. There he began to walk about the room in some agitation, exclaiming, 'A most extraordinary case! Such a one never happened to me before; I really do not know what to do!' I listened in surprise and much perplexity, as it was a clear case of pneumonia and of no unusual degree of danger, until at last I discovered that his perplexity related to *me*, not to the patient, and to the propriety of consulting with a lady physician! I was both amused and relieved. I at once assured my old acquaintance that it need not be considered in the light of an ordinary consultation, if he were uneasy about it, but as a friendly talk.[29]

All was not discouragement for the Society of Friends gave the woman-doctor hearty support—Elizabeth's "first baby" being born to Quaker parents. Later on, with the help of the Friends, Dr. Blackwell opened an infirmary where poor women could receive treatment three afternoons each week. From this small beginning arose the New York Infirmary and College for Women. It should be mentioned that up to this time no hospital had offered clinical training to women.

After ten years of active work, Dr. Blackwell sought a much-needed rest in England (1869). She had no sooner arrived in London than a request was made for a series of lectures on what women doctors were doing in the "New World." The first talk was given in

[29] Blackwell, Dr. Elizabeth. *Pioneer Work for Women.* J. M. Dent & Sons, Ltd. London. 1914. pp. 157–158.

Marylebone Hall to what proved to be an appreciative audience. As a result, a committee was formed to consider the whole subject of medicine as a profession for women. The following announcement was sent out:

> The Lectures recently delivered by Doctor Elizabeth Blackwell at the Marylebone Literary Institution have produced in the minds of the ladies who heard them a strong conviction of the necessity for a more general diffusion of hygenic knowledge among women; and have led to a proposition to found a hospital for a class of diseases, the ordinary treatment of which too frequently involves much avoidable moral suffering, to be placed under the direction of competent women physicians, in connection with a Board of consulting physicians and surgeons.[30]

Thus it was that an English woman paved the way for medical education in England by passing on to the Old World the knowledge that she had gained in a newer culture pattern. Elizabeth Blackwell was the *first woman* to have her name entered on the British Medical Register.

It was a lecture given by Dr. Blackwell that first turned Elizabeth Garrett's thoughts toward medicine as an absorbing interest. She was the daughter of Newson Garrett, a prosperous merchant of Aldeburgh, Suffolk. Miss Garrett (better known as Mrs. Elizabeth Garrett Anderson of London) was born June 9, 1836. It was a period notable for other reasons: a number of half-grown girls being ready to turn the world topsy-turvy—or as one writer has said, "butt like wild young heifers into the social life of England." The tiny Elizabeth was just another baby in another English home, and no one had the slightest idea that she would become a medical practitioner. Elizabeth, according to relatives,[31] was a normal child, responding in the usual way to home-life and home-lessons. In later years, she at-

[30] Blackwell, Dr. Elizabeth. *Pioneer Work for Women.* J. M. Dent & Sons, Ltd. London. 1914. p. 177.

[31] A letter to the writer from Louisa Garrett Anderson (daughter of Mrs. Elizabeth Garrett Anderson). June 28, 1938.

tended a school kept by the Misses Browning[32] of Blackheath, who had the reputation of educating young ladies in a most "sensible manner."

Elizabeth Garrett believed that every woman should have some engrossing interest in life. She was always making social contacts which would broaden her own horizon. Now comes the old, familiar story: place yourself where "things happen," and very soon "things will happen to you." Miss Garrett allied herself with an intellectual group in London, and before she realized what was happening, a friend mistook a kindly interest in the medical profession for a keen interest to become a woman-doctor. She was looked upon as a medical recruit before she had given the matter any serious thought.

A woman wishing to become a physician at this time set up a troublesome problem, not only for herself, but for members of her family.[33] This observation covers Miss Garrett's experiences in the early stages of her career. She made the rounds of English universities, and was refused matriculation in all of them. After this rebuff, Elizabeth appealed to the University of Edinburgh, but she was rejected by that institution as well. This young woman had made up her mind to study medicine regardless of opposition; accordingly, she entered Middlesex Hospital as a nurse. By not forcing the issue, a well-mannered nurse was allowed to attend classes; but she had no standing as a registered student in the medical college. The question of tuition was settled in this way: the Director accepted a sum of money which would correspond to institutional charges for all of the courses.

Just what a woman could study and still remain a "lady" gave college professors much concern. On April 1, 1862, the problem was summed up by a correspondent of *The English Woman's Journal:*

It would be impossible for a lady or a man to lecture to, or instruct, a number of young girls together on many of these subjects. Private lessons would be almost the only way in which instruction could be given, and the extreme repugnance,

---

[32] These ladies were aunts of the poet, Robert Browning.
[33] Miss Garrett was fortunate in that her father stood always as a stanch ally.

amounting to disgust, felt for this kind of knowledge, including physiology would frequently prove an obstacle, which could not be surmounted without the sacrifice of much which is very valuable in a young girl's mind.

Elizabeth had much to learn about medical schools. On March 23, 1861, after the first visit to a dissecting room, she wrote:

It was not nearly so shocking as I had been led to expect. The reports have been gross exaggerations. There were no bodies hanging over chairs or by their feet from the ceiling, nor any of the horrors that had been painted to me. . . .[34]

Despite the lack of training, Elizabeth proved an apt student; in fact, she came out first in the hospital examinations. It was not long before the authorities received a *protest* from the men students, who insisted that women be kept out of the classes. As a result, Elizabeth found herself barred from further study at the hospital.

Elizabeth Garrett was pitted against an impregnable force. Undaunted, she sought legal counsel, and made a hopeful discovery: the London Society of Apothecaries was pledged to confer its licentiate on all who passed the final examination. She started at once to seek further training from recognized medical practitioners. After a time, she passed the examination of the London Society of Apothecaries, and obtained a license to practice medicine.

The long fight was apparently won. But the Society of Apothecaries decided to put up strong bars against women-doctors; accordingly, they altered the constitution so that only graduates of medical schools could become candidates for the examinations. This change of policy looked like a serious handicap. Then came the thought of a foreign degree. Such study involved costs almost beyond the means of the average family. All efforts seemed to be leading up a blind-alleyway.

However, Miss Garrett did manage to go abroad; she studied at the University of Paris where she received a medical degree in 1870.

[34] Stephen, Barbara. *Emily Davies and Girton College*. Constable & Co., Ltd. London. 1927. p. 63.

The British Ambassador to France congratulated this young English girl who had made such great progress in entering the medical profession.

Returning to London, Elizabeth Garrett started on a somewhat strenuous career. She became a candidate for the London School Boards, and received the highest vote ever recorded in those elections. Not long after this, she married James George Skelton Anderson, thus taking upon herself the management of a home. But this woman-doctor remained true to her profession, giving constant attention to a dispensary for women and children in the Marylebone district. This was a private undertaking. Mrs. Garrett Anderson was, for many years, the *only woman* holding a membership in the British Medical Association to which she was elected in 1873. She followed the definite pattern set by the English-born Dr. Elizabeth Blackwell and went right ahead in spite of obstacles.

The Times of London, June 9, 1936, in speaking of Dr. Garrett Anderson, said:

> The second English women to become a doctor was born one hundred years ago today. Public opinion in the thirties and forties recognized women as a ministering angel, or a Sairey Gamp, but did not see her carrying out efficiently the many duties which custom has marked 'for men only.'

To complicate matters, Queen Victoria did not lift a hand to help women in any one of the professions. How Elizabeth Garrett Anderson managed to keep the respect of people in all classes of society, and at the same time to build up an extensive practice in a large city, stands as one of the most remarkable feats in the history of medicine. She was a lone figure in a changing world.

The next review is similar, and yet differs in many ways—the heroine being Sophia Jex-Blake (1840–1912). This young woman started out as an individualist, and entered Queen's College against the wishes of her father. Within a few weeks, she was asked to take a tutorship in mathematics, and was brought face to face with a well-established social prejudice. A letter from her father presents middle-class ideas on such matters. It began,

Dearest, I have only this moment heard that you contemplate being paid for the tutorship. It would be quite beneath you, darling, and I *cannot consent* to it. Take the post as one of honour and usefulness, and I shall be glad, and *you will be no loser*, be quite sure. But to be *paid* for the work would be to *alter* the thing *completely*, and would lower you sadly in the eyes of almost everybody. Do not think about it, dearest, . . .[35] [Later her father wrote:] . . . if you take money payment, you will make a sad mistake, debase your standing, and place yourself in a position that people in general, including many relations and friends, will never *as long as you live* understand otherwise than as greatly to your discredit.[36]

Against this point of view, Sophia used her brother's salary as an argument, to which her father replied: "Tom's being a *man* makes *all* the difference, he has just taken the *plain path of duty*."[37] As a result of this correspondence, Sophia waived fees for the first term of her tutorship.

After this experience, Sophia spent one year in Germany, and then set out to visit schools and colleges in the United States. It was in Boston, Massachusetts, that she first came in contact with women physicians. Apparently, these new friends turned her thoughts towards a medical career. She studied at the New York Infirmary and College for a short time, returning to England the following year. Sophia was convinced that if English women wanted to study medicine, they should strive to obtain medical degrees from British universities. With this idea in mind, she applied to the University of London, an institution that had always been more or less liberal in its views. She was informed by the Registrar that the existing Charter had been "purposely so worded" as to prohibit women from taking

[35] Todd, Margaret. *The Life of Sophia Jex-Blake*. Macmillan & Co., Limited. London. 1918. p. 67.
[36] *Ibid*. pp. 67–68.
[37] *Ibid*. p. 72.

medical examinations. Oxford and Cambridge were out of the question, as they did not have the facilities for giving a complete medical education.

The University of Edinburgh held out the only hope, for it stood quite free from ecclesiastical control, and offered medical degrees of a high standard. Sophia petitioned the authorities of that institution for enrollment in the medical course. Two bodies of professors agreed, but the University Court refused to open the doors to "one woman." As Professor Lorimer explained to her in a letter,

> The root of indelicacy is immodesty, and the root of immodesty is immorality, and the arrangement that would in my opinion be immodest, and might be immoral, would be that such subjects (*viz.*, anatomy) should be taught by *one* man to *one* woman.[38]

Miss Jex-Blake then advertised in the newspapers for young women who would like to take up the study of medicine. Within a few months, "four ladies" came forward, and Sophia wrote to the Dean of the Medical Faculty explaining the situation, and asking him to consider the matriculation of women in the University. She offered to pay whatever was required for conducting separate classes. The mention of payment was not lost on the authorities; they proceeded to look upon the new idea with considerable favor. A resolution to this effect was sanctioned by the Chancellor on November 12, 1869. The regulations were as follows:

> (1.) Women shall be admitted to the study of medicine in the University; (2.) The instruction of women for the profession of medicine shall be conducted in separate classes, confined entirely to women; (3.) The Professors of the Faculty of Medicine shall, for this purpose, be permitted to have separate classes for women; (4.) Women, not intending to study medicine professionally, may be admitted to such of these classes, or to such part of the course of instruction given in such classes, as the University Court may from time to time think fit and approve; (5.) The fee for the full course of instruction in such classes shall be four

[38] Todd, Margaret. *The Life of Sophia Jex-Blake*. Macmillan and Co., Limited. London. 1918. p. 250.

guineas; but in the event of the number of students proposing to attend any such class being too small to provide a reasonable remuneration at that rate, it shall be in the power of the Professor to make arrangements for a higher fee, subject to the usual sanction of the University Court; (6.) All women attending such classes shall be subject to all the regulations now or at any future time in force in the University as to the matriculation of students, their attendance on classes, Examinations, or otherwise; (7.) The above regulations shall take effect as from the commencement of session 1869–70.[39]

These privileges having been granted, the women students pursued their studies in the ordinary way, and received every courtesy from the men students.

In her book, *Medical Women*, Sophia Jex-Blake said,

I remember that on one occasion we crossed the quadrangle while some students were snowballing each other, and, simply by accident, a snowball struck one of our number. The howl of indignation and regret that burst from the students showed that their annoyance at the incident was infinitely greater than our own; — a straw shows which way the wind blows.[40]

The fact that women studied in classes apart from the men caused the first hostile demonstration against the women-students. The difficulty concerned the Hope Scholarship: one thousand pounds being offered to the four students who ranked highest in the first-year class. Mary Pechey, one of the five girl students, was third on the list; however, she was *denied* the scholarship on the ground of sex. Women were not members of the "regular class," the professor said, and could not be honored in this special way. This decision caused a furor throughout the British Isles. In London, *The Spectator*, April 23, 1870, said:

The female students almost deserve this rebuff, for making the concessions not made either in France, Austria, or the United States. The only safe ground for them to stand on is that science is of no sex, and cannot be made indelicate unless

---

[39] Jex-Blake, Sophia. *Medical Women*. Oliphant, Anderson, & Ferrier. Edinburgh. 1886. pp. 77–78.
[40] *Ibid*. p. 80.

made so of malice prepense, and that by the very conditions of the profession the modesty of ignorance must be replaced by the modesty of pure intent.

Miss Pechey was not awarded a Hope Scholarship. As a result, the Faculty of the University of Edinburgh was divided into factions. A few professors opened their classes to women, while others were so bitter that they actually aroused the men students to rebellion.

The actual trouble did not start until women—in the second year of study—were refused admittance to practice classes. Sophia at once petitioned the University authorities to be allowed to include infirmary work in the regular schedule. This so incensed the unfriendly professors that they denounced the women in even more threatening terms—going so far as to say that the men students deserved credit for not "pelting the ladies." This was a signal for trouble.

One afternoon, while approaching Surgeons' Hall, the girls found their way blocked by a mob of angry men-students. As Dr. Jex-Blake wrote later:

As soon as we came in sight of the gates, we found a dense mob filling up the roadway in front of them, comprising some dozen of the lowest class of our fellow-students . . . with many more of the same class from the University, a certain number of street rowdies, and some hundreds of gaping spectators, who took no particular part in the matter. Not a single policeman was visible, though the crowd was sufficient to stop all traffic for about an hour. We walked straight up to the gates, which remained open until we came within a yard of them, when they were slammed in our faces by a number of young men, who stood within, . . . they abused us in the foulest possible language, which I am thankful to say I have never heard equalled before or since. We waited quietly on the step to see if the rowdies were to have it all their own way, . . .[41]

Within a few minutes one of the students who had been watching the proceedings from a second-floor window rushed down to the gates, and wrenched them open. The girls entered the campus surrounded by a jeering crowd. It was a most unpleasant situation.

[41] Jex-Blake, Sophia. *Medical Women*. Oliphant, Anderson, & Ferrier. Edinburgh. 1886. pp. 92–93.

The riot at Surgeons' Hall was the incentive for Sophia to issue a public statement in which she suggested that the trouble-makers had been intoxicated. A libel suit was instigated against this remarkable young woman (1872). With prejudice so widespread, it was only to be expected that Sophia would lose out in court; she was fined one farthing, and ordered to pay the court costs, amounting to one thousand pounds. This sum was collected by voluntary contributions from all over the Kingdom.

The next step on the part of the opposition was to keep the women from taking their Professional Examinations. The girls resorted to legal opinion in order to get impartial judgment in the matter, and discovered that the Medical Faculty had no legal right to withhold examination papers from students who had completed a two-year course. Thereupon, several "ladies" took their Professional Examinations, and made a passing grade despite the worry and uncertainty to which they had been subjected.

The question now arose as to whether the women who had been studying medicine at the University of Edinburgh would be allowed to graduate. The University officials were determined that women should not become legally-qualified doctors, and offered them certificates of proficiency instead of college degrees. Certificates would be worth *exactly nothing*! The women took matters into their own hands and started court proceedings against the University. However, the University of Edinburgh won the suit on the ground that it could not legally accept women at any time. It was a discouraging outlook, for

The ladies lost their law-suit, and with it all the labour and all the pecuniary outlay of the past four years, and also had thrown upon them the superadded offence of having trusted implicitly to the good faith and legal knowledge of the University of Edinburgh.[42]

[42] Jex-Blake, Sophia. *Medical Women*. Oliphant, Anderson & Ferrier. Edinburgh. 1886. p. 146.

Five English women had given the best years of their lives to medical study. But they could not make use of this training without the necessary credentials. Therefore, in 1874, a number of men and women who were prominent in social and professional life came forward, and founded the London School of Medicine. As usual, Sophia Jex-Blake was the prime mover in the new undertaking. She found an old-fashioned house in Brunswick Square, which was well-suited to the needs of such an institution. The School was very successful, having twenty-three students the first year. But there were two obstacles: (1) There was no official recognition of the School from any of the nineteen Examination Boards. (2) There was no way to obtain the necessary qualifications—that is, actual hospital experience. Something had to be done, for graduates would need permits in order to practice medicine.

How to proceed was the question. Finally, Sophia Jex-Blake, Miss Mary Pechey, and Mrs. Thorne—one of the original five—applied to the Board of Examiners for Midwifery Certificates. It was a most unusual request. The Board accepted the credentials of the three women, but had no idea how to handle such a complicated matter. To solve the problem, every member of the Board resigned. After that decisive step, no examination was possible.

Meanwhile, Sophia had resorted to Parliament. She was well-known by that time, and had considerable influence with that august body. So it was that in 1874 friendly legislators tried to make it possible for institutions of higher learning to grant degrees to women. The matter was shelved for a time, because the University of Edinburgh requested the law-makers to postpone action until they could reconsider the subject. Two years later, the Russel-Gurney Enabling Act was passed; it permitted universities to grant degrees to women. In connection with this legislation, Sir James Stansfield said:

It is one of the lessons of the history of progress that when the time for a reform has come you cannot resist it, though, if you make the attempt, what you may do is to widen its character or precipitate its advent. Opponents, when the time has come, are not merely dragged at the chariot-wheels of progress—they help to turn them. The strongest force, whichever way it seems to work, does most to aid.[43]

Nevertheless, the University of Edinburgh still refused to grant any concessions to women, and the five pioneers in medicine were forced to seek help in Ireland. The request was granted, and Sophia Jex-Blake crossed to Dublin, where she passed a medical test entitling her to sign the register. In the same year, 1877, the Royal Free Hospital in London admitted women as interns. Not long after this time, the University of London offered all of its degrees to women. Edinburgh held aloof until 1894.

After years of bitter controversy over women studying medicine, it was only natural that Sophia Jex-Blake should feel some curiosity as to how the examination grades of women compared with those of men. In 1884 she consulted the Calendar of the University of London, and studied the examination grades in Arts and Medicine. The figures are given below:

For the Matriculation Examination during these five years, 7208 men went up and 3712 passed, *i.e.*, 51.5 per cent.; 619 women went up and 427 passed. *i.e.*, 69 per cent.

For the next examination, the 'Intermediate in Arts,' 1635 men went up and 938 passed, or 57.3 per cent.; 139 women went up and 107 passed, or 77 per cent.

For the final B.A. Examination, 833 men went up and 408 passed, *i.e.*, not quite 49 per cent.; 68 women went up and 50 passed, or rather more than 73 per cent.

Now as regards degrees in Medicine. For the first professional or 'Preliminary Scientific' Examination, 1027 men went up and 538 passed, or 52.3 per cent.; 20 women went up and 12 passed, or 60 per cent.

For the second or 'Intermediate Examination in Medicine,' 431 men went up and 240 passed, or 55.6 per cent.; 7 women went up and 6 passed, or 85.7 per cent.

For the final M.B. Examination, 116 men went up and 91 passed, or 78.4 per cent.; for this only 3 women had gone up (to the end of 1883) and *all* have passed, *i.e.*, 100 per cent.[44]

[43] *The Woman's World*. Edited by Oscar Wilde. London. 1888.
[44] Jex-Blake, Sophia. *Medical Women*. Oliphant, Anderson, & Ferrier. Edinburgh. 1886. pp. 221–222.

The University of London did not ask the sex of the candidates seeking an examination; it was the only university in the three kingdoms self-sufficient enough to mark papers on content alone. Thus, the right of women to take their place in a difficult profession was unquestioned.

The first decade of the twentieth century might be called a period of frustration for English women. Then it was that many parents sought to educate their daughters for a useful, rather than a useless way-of-life. But these efforts were to no avail, as prejudice against girls who worked for pay still gripped a large portion of society. Selfishness played a part, men trying to protect their jobs in a labor market that had long been feeble, really insecure. On the other hand, women had no idea of giving up the skills in which they had become proficient, and in which they could be of service to mankind.

At this time, Mrs. Emmeline Pankhurst and her followers came into the picture; they began a strenuous campaign to free all women from what amounted to a tightly regulated employer-association. Just when the movement got well under way, the Germans, with their lust for power, started all the turmoil involved in World War I. Suffrage activities stopped at once—undivided attention being given to the needs of the nation. Small wonder that a statue of Mrs. Pankhurst now stands in Westminster Park, London.

A selfless approach to war was a one-sided affair. For men in both business and professional circles kept on with their strangle-like technique. It is an amazing fact that in this critical period, the War Office refused to accept women doctors. The "ladies were told to *go home* and *keep quiet*." Many women were well prepared for this national emergency; they had been gaining experience all through the long struggle for enfranchisement. The few who had medical degrees held meetings, and discussed the question of military service.[45]

It was known that France needed physicians and hospitals; ac-

---

[45] Unfortunately, the names of these brave women have been passed over as inconsequential.

cordingly, two women doctors called at the French Embassy in London, and offered to raise and equip a surgical unit for the French Government. Within one week, the French authorities sent a formal acceptance; they asked that the Corps be organized as soon as possible. These courageous women faced obstacles quite formidable in character; they needed money for equipment, and they needed a suitable staff. The unexpected happened; in less than a fortnight the women's medical unit was ready for duties abroad. The baggage, which was extremely bulky, attracted considerable attention as it passed through London to the railroad station. The supplies included,

> More than a hundred packages—many large Red Cross cases with padlocks, all labelled and painted with 'Croix Rouge Francaise' and 'Women's Hospital Corps,' with lists of their contents noted on them and the address. Piled on top of them were enormous bales of wool and blankets, pillows, and clothing.[46]

It was generally understood that the Suffrage Cause would be advanced one hundred years if this small body of women doctors succeeded in their unique undertaking.

The story of how this small band of women left their native land to do medical work in France will bear retelling. A large group of friends carrying fruit and other tokens of affection gathered at Victoria Station to wish the Corps Godspeed. In the Women's Hospital Corps were,

> Surgeons and anaesthetists, a physician, a pathologist, and dressers, together with a staff of trained nurses and men orderlies, and, because one of the 'English' lady doctors was a Scotch woman, every member of the Corps wore a sprig of white heather.[47]

It was a happy send-off for a not-so-happy piece of business. The ladies arrived in Paris late at night, too late for dinner or even

[46] Murray, Flora. *Women as Army Surgeons*. Hodder and Stoughton, Limited. London. c. 1920. p. 10.

[47] Bennett, A. H. *English Medical Women*. Sir Isaac Pitman & Sons, Ltd. London. 1915. pp. 116–117.

a *chocolat*. Rooms in the Hôtel Claridge had been set aside as a hospital; unfortunately, they had been arranged so that no sunlight ever entered them. But the women doctors went ahead with their preparations. Before the actual cleaning had been finished, a doctor from the American Hospital[48] called to see whether the women's hospital could care for an overflow of patients. "We can take twenty-four this afternoon and another twenty-six tonight," replied Dr. Murray, well knowing that the baggage was still at the station, and conscious of the expression on the faces of those who heard her.

'Good! Will you take officers?' he said.
'Yes. We have a ward for officers.' she answered, remembering for the first time that officers got wounded as well as men, . . .
'Well, I shall bring officers,' he said: 'British ladies are the right people to look after British officers.'[49]

By the end of the first week, the women's hospital was a smooth-running concern filled with patients who were more than content with their surroundings. This institution soon made a place for itself in the hearts of the French people; the stretcher-bearers sometimes pausing for a moment to praise the "wonderful" English doctors. Stories such as these reached England in due time, and the War Office in London sent a representative to France in order to learn what was being done in the hospitals. This move was, to some extent, a face-saving operation.

The "mi-lord" who inspected the work of the Women's Hospital Corps was an impressive-looking individual. He wore khaki, a shining brass-hat, and an order of some kind hanging from his neck. This particular official attracted so much attention that the simple French peasants stepped aside as he entered the women's hospital—the

[48] This hospital had been established by the American Colony in Paris; it provided the only efficient ambulance service near Paris during the early days of the war; the French had a few small ambulances, the British none.

[49] Murray, Flora. *Women as Army Surgeons.* Hodder and Stoughton, Limited. London. c. 1920. pp. 26–27.

first to be inspected. The visitor strode through the corridor, his spurs clicking all the while; then he proceeded to interrogate the senior medical officer:

'Who is in charge of this place?'
'What are you doing here?'
'What have you got behind there?' pointing at the glass partition rendered opaque by white paper.
'A French hospital! How can it be a French hospital? You're British.'
'All women! No proper surgeons?'
'Have you British soldiers here? Any officers?'
'What are you doing with them?'
'Where do they go when they leave you?'
'Versailles! Who told you to send them to Versailles?'
'Colonel Smith! How do you know about Colonel Smith?'[50]

The women doctors smiled and went about the business of nursing. They had seen too much distress and suffering to be impressed with a bluffing-game, even a bluffing-game sanctioned by high officials in Whitehall. The doctors and nurses treated the officious one kindly, and allowed him to wander at will through the hospital.

The visitor had arrived during the rest hour; he saw men reading and smoking in most attractive wards: pretty colored blankets on the beds, and fresh flowers on the tables. All of the patients, including the officers, expressed their gratitude for a "good home." Despite this assurance, the official from the War Office managed to interview a French woman. He said, ". . . is it possible that the soldiers tolerate such an arrangement?" Madam was much mystified by the question. Later she asked the doctors, *"Qu'est-ce qu'il avait? Il me semblait mécontent."* So it was that a British official made his way in war-torn France.

By the spring of 1915, hundreds of medical cases were being sent to England; some of the hospitals were taking on the character of

[50] Murray, Flora. *Women as Army Surgeons*. Hodder and Stoughton, Limited. London. c. 1920. p. 49.

clearing-houses for men of different nationalities. The Director General of the Army was forced to seek accommodations for large groups of disabled soldiers. He got in touch with the Women's Hospital Corps in Paris, and asked whether he could get help from the women doctors stationed there. The weather was very cold, and the nursing duties in the French hospitals were lighter than they had been for many weeks. The need for medical work at that time undoubtedly lay in England, and the two senior physicians from the Corps left Paris for London; they must have felt a thrill of satisfaction at the sudden turn of affairs.

The now famous interview with Surgeon-General Sir Alfred Keogh was held at the War Office. The two ladies were questioned in this way:

'Who is running you?' . . . 'Nobody. We run ourselves.'
'Yes! But who is behind you? What lady?' 'There is no lady.'
'Who gets your money?' 'We get it ourselves.'[51]
'Well, but who is your committee?' 'We are the committee.'
'Ah then,' he said—with a twinkling eye—'then we can talk.'[52]

As a result of this conversation, the Women's Hospital Corps was moved to England.

The women doctors were stationed in the old workhouse of St. Giles,* Bloomsbury. It was necessary to make extensive alterations in the buildings—lifts for the stretchers, and labor-saving devices for the kitchens. At first, there was a shortage of equipment such as knives and forks for the service-trays. The hospital was planned to accommodate five hundred cases. After 1916, additional beds were put up and never taken down. The Army had a help-yourself way of opening new hospitals; it would transfer troublesome patients from old wards to newer quarters. The Women's Hospital in Endell

[51] This reply shows the strength of the women's movement at this time—plenty of money being available.

[52] Murray, Flora. *Women as Army Surgeons*. Hodder and Stoughton, Limited. London. c. 1920. pp. 114–115.

* St. Giles is said to be the workhouse where Oliver Twist interviewed the Guardians.

Street was opened in May, 1915 — one hundred convalescent patients being sent from other London hospitals within a week. All of the beds were soon filled, for fighting in France had begun in earnest.

To the surprise of officials in both France and England, women-doctors had almost no difficulty in keeping order in the hospitals. The work was conducted under difficulties, the British government refusing to give women-doctors the titles which befitted their training. The women were in an embarrassing position; for a medical group to carry on such duties without a single badge of honor was an absurd arrangement. It meant that the women had to make the best of it as far as discipline was concerned. The women-doctors just ignored the petty jealousies of men in the War Office. As for the soldiers, they were ofttimes speechless with surprise when two young girls appeared before them with a stretcher. Women gained the reputation of being "gentle stretcher-bearers." The Chief Surgeon (a woman of course) made it a rule never to hurry a man into the operating theatre. In the quiet hours of evening, she would visit the more severe cases, and explain the surgical situation from all angles. This was a great comfort to the men, many of whom had no idea whether they were ever going to get well again.

Disciplinary measures were necessary at times, especially when a patient thought he was quite well, and the nurse in charge knew that he was far from ready to leave the hospital. It was a problem that came up again and again. For instance, a patient would enter the Commander's office and say:

'I wish to mak' a complaint. There's a lot of men in the ward gone to the theatre and the Sister kep' me back.'

Under discussion, it transpired that he was not so well, and being kept in bed, he had risen and dressed to come down and make his complaint.

'It's true the doctor said I was not to leave my bed, me being with a temperature again.'

When asked whether he would have wished the other men to stay in, since he could not go out, he replied with dignity that he was not 'an onreasonable man';

and on being advised to return to his bed and take care of himself, he said: 'Would ye say a word to the Sister?' Then with a 'thank ye kindly, lady,' he retired to bed all smiles.[53]

The time came when some of the problems were not so easily handled. Peace Day was a general holiday; it brought extended privileges to convalescent men. The question which presented itself was this: how to get the patients back to the hospital before midnight, or even before the following morning. At the Endell Street Hospital the challenge was met in this way: the nurses let it be known that a large tea would be held in the afternoon, and a substantial meal would be served at 10 P.M. *Not one man was absent*. It was a triumph for woman-made methods of enforcing discipline— that is, treating disabled soldiers, not as irresponsible boys, but as *brothers* ready to enjoy the little amenities of social life.

Physicians, like men and women in other professions, differ greatly. Some treat their ability to cure as a duty, others as a lucrative business undertaking. It is a delicate relationship, with the economic angle ever-present, yet seldom the topic of an extended conversation. There is a joke in the inner circle that a bill paid unexpectedly means an urgent call from the patient some time soon. Dr. L. Martindale, in her book, *A Woman Surgeon*, says,

> When I look back on my own life as a consultant, I realize that one-third of my work was not paid for. I spent at least two days every week in my hospital rounds and operations, which of course were unpaid—it never occured to me to complain, for life was much too interesting. I do not know of any other profession in which its members have given of their time and skill so generously and willingly.[54]

Undoubtedly, this record has been duplicated many times, the average physician being too busy to rebel against overwork or service without pay.

When warfare was again forced upon England in 1939, the medical

[53] Murray, Flora. *Women as Army Surgeons*. Hodder and Stoughton. Limited. London. c. 1920. pp. 149–150.
[54] Martindale, Dr. L. *A Woman Surgeon*. Victor Gollancz, Ltd. London. 1951. p. 244.

Women's Federation got in touch with the War Office in an effort to learn just where their organization stood in Government arrangements. It was found that they stood just exactly where they were standing *twenty years earlier*, not the slightest thought having been given to women physicians.

After "Mr. Chamberlain and his umbrella" had crossed the Channel for the last time, officials in the precincts of Whitehall took notice of the fact that their country was not prepared to fight a war, and an order for gas-mask instruction went out to all medical schools. It is safe to assume that every student co-operated. But the job was too big for an unorganized group to handle. The one thought-provoking note was this: children enjoyed being conditioned to war; they took to gas-masks with the greatest enthusiasm, even holding contests to find out who could wear the beastly contrivances the longest.

All dilly-dally proceedings came to an end in Whitehall with the fall of France. Every fit person was asked to put personal interests aside and help the country in the emergency. After this appeal, 800,000 women enlisted, this group representing all classes of society, and all districts of the country. Medical problems arose almost at once, for earlier experiences—that is, dealing with a small number of women in an earlier war—was of no help at all.

The need for doctors became more and more apparent, and the War Office appointed Dr. Letitia Fairfield adviser to the Director General of the Army Medical Service. From this time on, there was great activity, the medical services for women being fitted into the various branches of the Army. The chief in command had the final word, the duties of women being advisory rather than regulatory. As war conditions grew worse, women-doctors ". . . were appointed to every recruiting base, women specialists to every hospital to which women were admitted, and a medical woman was appointed to the headquarters staff of every command in Great Britain."[55]

[55] Bell, E. Moberly. *Storming the Citadel*. Constable & Co., Ltd. London. W.C. 2. 1953. p. 186.

World War II dragged on to a finish. Little mention was ever made of the splendid work done by women in the medical profession; but these English doctors were kept busy from the first to the last day of hostilities. Unfortunately, their work was not fully appreciated—people huddled in places of safety could not possibly understand the dangers of street travel at night. Think of the fogs, the blackouts, the half-shaded street lights!

Then too, there were the unskilled groups who took turns at nursing. Many of these women were high-strung, hardly responsible for any swing from normal behavior. Hospital attendants tell of young volunteers who would rush for air-raid shelters the minute a siren sounded. Apparently, these workers gave little thought to the fact that men and women who were bedridden might call for help. The preservation of life is an urge not easily overcome, but this was no excuse for losing all sense of propriety. As for the patients, there was nothing for them to do but say a few prayers—thus making the best of a bad situation. Women physicians did many odd jobs around the hospitals in those hectic days. This was war, the struggle a peace-loving people had tried to stave off by appeasement, the soothing remedy which so often leads to disaster.

Peace brought new problems: a large number of women began to miss outside work. This longing took a strong hold on the leisure class. It was among the members of this group that part-time employment made its initial bow. These activities were made possible through the invention of labor-saving devices which revolutionized household duties.

Girl students who make plans for a fifty-fifty working arrangement may become medical technologists. They will have little competition, and in some cases may name not only their hours, but their salaries. There are more openings than graduates available. Consider the following occupations: (1) Investigating research problems; (2) Running tests for diagnosis by pathologists; (3) Evaluating drugs in the treatment of disease. As specialists, students should select all subjects carefully; they should give about one-third of their time to the study of anatomy, chemistry, physiology, and bacteriology.

Medical technologists retain a certain prestige—that is, they enjoy professional status whether the employment is in a hospital, a university, or a private research enterprise. This may be one of the reasons why so many parents favor a medical career for their daughters. The Census of 1951 listed 6,487 women as fully qualified physicians.

In recent years, the people in England have had to face reform measures of a disturbing nature. It is difficult at this time to place a value on changes of this kind, as people become evasive in discussing such matters. But let these good people get abroad—the United States, for instance—and much of this reserve takes leave. Sir Francis Walshe, a British physician, managed to express a few of his worries on a recent visit from the homeland. On one occasion he said, "We have sold our birthright for a pretty poor mess of pottage."[56] These few words express his opinion of England's health-plan. The plan was evolved because many people in the low-income brackets could not afford adequate medical protection. This distinguished visitor specializes in diseases of the nervous system, and is the author of a textbook used in some medical schools.

From the doctor's point of view, the inflexibility of the legal restrictions imposed on them through socialized medicine is a matter of great concern. Compensation for professional services performed does not allow the doctor much money to spend on the little niceties of life. The prospect of receiving a high fee has been taken away by legislation of a really harsh nature.

To some extent, doctors now are like cogs-in-a-wheel; they must move along day after day in a set pattern. The incentive for dedicated service has been weakened. Consider prestige: in times past,

[56] *The Cincinnati Enquirer*. Cincinnati, Ohio (U.S.A.). April 19, 1959.

physicians who possessed exceptional ability were consulted by patients from many different cities, even from far-away countries. All of these services meant additional income, to say nothing of additional satisfaction. In discussing the reaction of persons who have free access to professional care, physicians as a group, feel that a patient who receives free medical advice is not as grateful as the one who pays a fee.

But there are two sides to every question. Consider another appraisal of socialized medicine: Dr. Robert Steiner, a professor of radiology in England, said on February 8, 1963, (*Post & Times Star*, Cincinnati, Ohio, U.S.A.), that the new medical program is not really socialism, but rather a "humanitarian approach" to necessary care. The good doctor expressed his views further by saying that "everyone in England is entitled to free hospital care, physician's services[57] and low-cost drugs." To cover the cost, the employer in England pays roughly two-thirds and the employee one-third of the cost—and the national Government also contributes a share.

The physician receives one pound ($2.80) per patient per year, regardless of the many patients he has on his books. A large number of people who were against "sickness meddling" in the nineteen-forties, are all for the plan in the nineteen-sixties—eager for its continuance.

A lack of clinical experience has long been a formidable barrier standing in the way of women in the medical profession. For this reason, they have been stopped before they could get started. To become skilled in any art without full instruction and practical experience is an uphill road. This barrier to medical training for women was not overcome until 1944, when the Government was forced to change its policy.

What amounted to a revolution in methods came by way of the *Goodenough Report*; it covered about every abuse that had to do with

---

[57] The writer found the service very unsatisfactory under the Labor Government—three months being required for a certificate of vaccination.

the higher education of women-doctors. This document declared that "There must be no sense of superiority or of privilege."[58] Men and women students were to be classed from now on as one group. This opinion was followed by a timely statement concerning preparation; women must have adequate training, otherwise they ". . . cannot qualify themselves properly for general practice, much less can they train for advanced medical work or specialist practice."[59]

The subject of student-patient relationship was also dealt with, emphasis being placed on the fact that both are equally important in the general curriculum of medical instruction. It was also recommended that there be a teaching-centre which would include a university medical school and adequate clinical facilities for the student body. There were many other valuable recommendations in the report, a document far too involved for full discussion in this chapter. It was clear that England was going ahead with an important medical program.

The *Goodenough Report* was very explicit. It recommended that co-education become the established policy of every medical school in the United Kingdom, and that the payment to any medical school of Exchequer Grants-in-aid of medicine ". . . should be conditional upon the school being co-educational and admitting a reasonable proportion of women students."[60] It all sounded too good to be true, but there were still other traditions to be broken. For it was recommended that,

The number of women students in any school should be a reasonable proportion of the whole, say about one-fifth; otherwise the women will not form a sufficiently numerous body to ensure proper status and position. The grudging admission of a few women is unsatisfactory. The group must be large enough to feel itself to be an important but integral section of the whole, whose members are trained on a

[58] *Report of the Inter-Departmental Committee on Medical Schools (Goodenough Report).* London. His Majesty's Stationery Office. 1944. p. 99.
[59] *Ibid.* p. 100.
[60] *Ibid.* p. 99.

basis of complete equality with their male colleagues and given access to all the usual facilities, including staff appointments. There must be no sense of inferiority or of privilege. . . .[61]

The last recommendation will fall, no doubt, into routine lines of action, for there are questions here of sex, prestige, and personality, all of which play a part in hospital assignments. The prospect of motherhood will militate against a woman, even though she is not yet married. The time will come when a woman will be allowed *maternity* leave of absence, just as a man now gets leave for *surgery*. For when a people no longer adhere to a custom, the custom no longer exists as a social force.

English physicians really had a bad start, forced as they were to abide by a set of rules laid down by the "Medieval Guilds." Strangely enough, this semi-foreign program worked fairly well until far along in the nineteenth century. Then, this body of learned men encountered a social problem that was almost beyond their comprehension: should women be allowed to heal the sick and injured on equal terms with men? By making an honest study, this troublesome problem could have been settled within a short time. But nothing was done about the situation. It took World War II with its tragic implications to *force* men doctors to work with women doctors. Indeed, a depressing story has been brought to light—that is, how English women made their way into the medical profession.

[61] *Report of the Inter-Departmental Committee on Medical Schools (Goodenough Report)*. London. His Majesty's Stationery Office. 1944. p. 99.

V. Civil Service

To trace the Civil Service is like trying to see through an Asian mystery. But this much is known: from earliest times, reigning monarchs surrounded themselves with clergymen who gave their labor in exchange for food, fuel, and lodging. It required learned men to use the Latin system of calculation, and answer countless letters in one or more of the foreign languages. In the fourteenth century, English rulers began to employ laymen—their staffs being recruited as a rule from aristocratic, land-owning families.

Then a strange thing happened: just as flowering plants take root in unexpected places, intellectual seedlings began to thrive in the halls of government. Chaucer (1340?–1400), who had only a half-mile to walk from the Customs House to his living-quarters over the tower of Algate—the streets may be followed still—had the urge to report what was probably an average day:

> Wherfor, as I seyde, y-wis,
> Iupiter considereth this,
> And also, beau sir, other thinges;
> That is, that thou hast no tydinges
> Of Loves folk, if they be glade, . . .
> Thou herest neither that ne this;
> For whan thy labour doon al is,
> And hast y-maad thy rekeninges,
> In stede of reste and newe thinges,
> Thou gost hoom to thy hous anoon;
> And, aslo domb as any stoon,
> Thou sittest at another boke,
> Til fully daswed is thy loke,
> And livest thus as an hermyte,
> Although thyn abstinence is lyte.[1]

[1] Skeat, The Rev. Walter W. *The Complete Works of Geoffrey Chaucer*. Vol. III. At The Clarendon Press. Oxford. MDCCCXCIV. p. 20.

Government work as Chaucer knew it continued for more than one hundred years. Henry VIII, with his strong will and keen intellect, introduced many changes in affairs of state. For one thing, he established a postal service for the exclusive use of the Crown, letters being carried by couriers who traveled at great speed on horseback. In time, London merchants who were doing considerable business on the Continent, took up the idea and started a mail service of their own. The first post offices were placed some distance apart and were restricted in service. In fact,

The particulars are not correctly afcertained; except that fome old ftatutes exift on the fubject, and that the poft was reduced to a pyftem and made more an object of revenue during the commonwealth, than it had been previous to that time.

On the Reftoration, however, in 1660, the Poft was placed wholly in the hands of Government, and one General Poft Office eftablished . . . by Act of Parliament.[2]

In the year 1710, the postal system was "new-modelled" and extended over Great Britain and "all other countries beyond the Seas."

Apparently, the morale of the Civil Service had long been questioned. It was said that government workers were not only lazy but incompetent. Towards the end of the eighteenth century, an investigation was begun to find out

The real ftate of things, whether it be good or bad, whether the abufes be many or few, or nine at all. Without fuch knowledge, dark furmifes fill the place of truth, and improvement is at a ftand, even in thofe cafes where it is moft practicable; nor have we any anfwer to give to clamours for Reform, in thofe cafes where alteration could be conductive to no good purpofe: but information, founded on unqueftionable evidence like this, may give rife to meafures of judicious and temperate regulation, without leading the mind too far, or occafioning any premature or inconfiderate change in eftablifhments of high antiquity and great public importance; for there is no fentiment to which the Editor more readily fubfcribes, than to that of the Commiffioners of Public Accounts in their

[2] *The Former and Present State of the Principal Public Offices in this Kingdom.* Printed for F. and C. Rivington. London. 1794. p. 17.

fixth Report—'That Eftablifhments of fuch a defcription are entitled to the utmoft refpect, and that alterations in them fhould be well weighed, and propofed with caution and diffidence.'[3]

Fifty years passed before the Service again came under the fire of public criticism. It was usually government workers in low-paid posts who voiced their grievances. One of them pointed out that employees

> Could obtain leave of absence, or remain away without it, for any time, from an hour to six months. A feeling of giddiness on reaching business in the morning was sufficient reason for a trip to Gravesend, 'a cold in the head' for several weeks absence, a medical certificate, 'of no use to any one but the owner,' for half-a-year. Cessation, or diminution of salary under such circumstances was, of course, a thing unheard of.[4]

At that time, comparatively young men were allowed to retire to what was known as an "Englishman's Paradise": a house in the country, a garden hedged in by a wall, and a regular pay-check from the Government. But far-reaching reforms were bound to come, for the forces operating for correction were much stronger than the forces operating for corruption.

It was the brazen approach to office-seeking which finally led to the downfall of a patronage system in England. In a few words, the Service was no longer worthy of respect. Competitive examinations offered a way out; they could at least be given a trial. Even Queen Victoria had "considerable misgivings" over the new arrangement; she felt that the ability to pass an examination did not indicate general competence. But Mr. Gladstone in his patient way assured Her Majesty that only "qualified persons" would be allowed to take up Government work.[5]

[3] *The Former and Present State of the Principal Public Offices in this Kingdom.* Printed for F. and C. Rivington. London. 1794. p. VII.

[4] *Political Tracts, 1865–1896.* "Heads and Tales in the Civil Service." By a Civil Servant. British Museum. London. c. 1896.

[5] The theory was that an industrious student would make an industrious clerk.

The old system of making appointments gave way slowly. There was competition, but often the tests were deceptive in character. It was possible to select men for the examination in much the same way that hostesses arrange bridge guests—that is, place a favored friend with poor players. Herbert Preston-Thomas in his book, *The Work and Play of a Government Inspector*, says:

> It was towards the end of the year 1859 that, fresh from Marlborough, I distinguished myself by gaining first place in a competition held by the Civil Service Commission for a Clerkship in the Privy Council Office. Frankness compels me to add that the two other nominees (required by the regulations to make up the prescribed number of three) may have been the special couple known as the "Treasury Idiots" who could not pass anything and were sent to give a walk-over to any minister's protegé able to reach the minimum of qualifications. At any rate, they could hardly read and write, and so I found myself entitled to a desk at Downing Street.[6]

The idea got abroad, in due time, that the Government was no longer offering easy employment. The various departments had taken on added responsibilities, and officials in the service had long been gathering facts on countless subjects—"all information being strictly impartial, based on the collective experience of every aspect of administration."[7]

Needless to say, the different departments run into snags when trying to adjust social problems. Consider the question of raising funds: the Exchequer is very cautious about making suggestions, for there is always a chance that requests will be tossed back as "political dynamite." For instance, it would be unwise to ask members of a trade union to pay fees for the privilege of marching to Hyde Park on May Day. It is said that ministers develop an instinct for what they can do—in the jargon of the street, "what the public will swallow."

Only men had been employed in government offices up to this

[6] Moses, Robert, *The Civil Service of Great Britain*. Longmans, Green & Co. New York, 1914. pp. 99–100.
[7] Campbell, G. A. *The Civil Service in Britain*. The Whitefriars Press, Ltd. London. 1955. p. 10.

time. Public officials expressed doubt as to the efficiency of women. The general belief was this: a few women are clever, but the majority are stupid. Then a man highly placed in the postal service rose to the defense of wives and daughters. Strangely enough, this reformer—for such he was—is known today only as "Mr. Scuddamore"—nothing more. This champion of women workers noted in the first place that they . . .

Have to an eminent degree the quickness of eye and ear, and the delicacy of touch, which are essential qualifications of a good operator.[8]

In the second place, they take more kindly than men or boys do to sedentary employment, and are more patient during long confinement to one place.

In the third place, the wages, which will draw male operators from but an inferior class of the community, will draw female operators from a superior class.

Female operators thus drawn from a superior class, will, as a rule, write better than the male clerks, and spell more correctly; and, where the staff is mixed, the female clerks will raise the tone of the whole staff.

They are also less disposed than men to combine for the purpose of extorting higher wages, and this is by no means an unimportant matter.

On one other ground it is especially desirable that we should extend the employment of women. Permanently established civil servants invariably expect their remuneration to increase with their years of service, and they look for this remuneration even in the cases, necessarily very numerous, in which from the very nature of their employment they can be of no more use or value in the twentieth than in the fifth year of their service. . . . Women, however, will solve these difficulties for the department by retiring for the purpose of getting married as soon as they get the chance . . . and those only will return whose married life is less fortunate and prosperous than they had hoped.

On the whole, it may be stated without fear of contradiction that, if we place an equal number of females and males on the same ascending scale of pay, the aggregate pay to females will always be less than the aggregate pay to the males; that, within a certain range of duty, the work will be better done by the females than the males, because the females will be drawn from a somewhat superior class; and further, that there will always be fewer females than males on the pension list.[9]

[8] This "delicacy of touch" is an important requirement in the manufacture of electrical equipment—hence a preference now for women in this field.

[9] Martindale, Hilda. *Women Servants of the State, 1870–1938*. George Allen & Unwin, Ltd. London. 1938. pp. 17–18.

No one realized at the time what a momentous decision was in the hands of authorities. In spite of opposition, Mr. Scuddamore won the day; moreover, he lived to see thousands of women employed in the post offices throughout the country. Within a few years the question of employing more women came before the Government. In this connection, Mr. G. R. Smith, the Controller, appeared before the Civil Service Enquiry Commission (known as the Playfair Commission). His testimony follows:

What general result have you found from the employment of female clerks there; has it been successful or otherwise?

So far as it has gone I consider that it has been a perfect success. . . .

Do you find that they are both quick and accurate in the performance of the work?

Very much so. They have completely surpassed my expectation in that matter; they are very accurate, and do a very fair quantity of work; and, in fact, more so than many of the males who have been employed on the same duty. . .

Do you find the female clerks are as easily kept in discipline as the male clerks?

Quite so. I have never had the slightest occasion to reprove any one of them. . . .

Is there any condition as to their being married?

It appears not, because I have recently had a young woman sent to me who is married. What the consequence of that will be I do not know. I am getting rather alarmed.

I suppose that she might have leave of absence under certain circumstances?

That would be a question when the time comes. I do not know that there is an immediate probability of it. . . .

In fact, you are judiciously and cautiously extending their work?

Just so. We think that we shall ultimately succeed in getting them to do more of the work, but we must be cautious in the matter, because the questions arising in connection with it are so numerous. . . .

Is there much jealousy as to the employment of female clerks in your department?

There is some jealousy. I have not heard it so much expressed on the part of the clerks themselves who are doing actual clerical duties as on the part of the men who are doing a kind of intermediate duty, and who are a class termed 'assistants.' They do not like the females coming in at all.

They think that the females are placing their labor at a disadvantage? Certainly.[10]

Many men in the post offices did not take kindly to the idea of working with women. Some "gentlemen" in the various departments went so far as to call "indignation meetings," and what they said about the "young ladies" was enough to bring blushes to pale Victorian cheeks.

Every attempt was made to prevent women extending their field of work, and we have a clerk making a solemn declaration before the Playfair Commission that, although women might do the lighter part of office work, there would be a difficulty in their writing cross-entry acknowledgements, because they have to be written 'with heavy pressure by means of very hard pens and carbonic paper.' A hard pen was apparently more difficult to wield than a scrubbing brush.[11]

In an effort to bar women from certain types of government work, The Royal Commission offered the well-known excuse that "structural difficulties," (meaning the lack of rest rooms for women) prevented their employment. The idea spread that it was not quite proper for women to work in the same room with men, although for centuries they had eaten their meals in the same room with men, and had even knelt and said their prayers in the same room with men. How little any one realized that countless obstacles would be overcome. The way lay straight ahead for thousands of women in the business world.[12]

An outsider can best judge the Civil Service by way of the postal system. Up until World War II, the delivery of mail in England was in all respects remarkable. In Chelsea, for instance, the postman would deliver letters in a matter of hours. Like so many experiences on this little island, there was tradition as well as sentiment tucked

[10] Martindale, Hilda. *Women Servants of the State, 1870–1938.* George Allen & Unwin, Ltd. London. 1938. pp. 21–22.

[11] *Ibid.* pp. 25–26.

[12] It is not generally known that an additional number of women were employed in the post offices during both world wars.

away in those envelops; it might be a midsummer notice that the
rent is due, or a midwinter notice that Michaelmas is here—and
your agent sends holiday greetings. There were letters from friends
and relatives to cheer the day. It was a tranquil way-of-life cherished
in memory. Now the English postal service is more like the service
in other countries—not quite so prompt.

An important part of the postal service is the sale of stamps, and
the payment of pensions and allowances. Certificates and defence
bonds are sold along with gun, dog, radio, and television licenses.
The authorities also act as distributors for Government leaflets. For
the general public, the postal branches really represent the Civil
Service—the work of other departments being less intimate in
character. Unlike most countries, the postage stamps of England do
not carry a name, just a picture of the reigning Sovereign. The low-
value stamps are now colored, as in other countries.

The face of society was changing. Now and then, the transformation caused some comment. Most certainly, a woman of good family
could not take a paid position without losing friends, especially those
with newly-acquired social position. It is clear that the wife or
daughter who ran counter to public opinion possessed more than ordinary courage. Marie Constance Smith, member of a scholarly
family, belongs in this category; she braved all censure and entered
the postal service as a clerk in 1875. At the end of the first year, Miss
Smith was placed in charge of a large number of recruits. The youthful supervisor—she was twenty-four years old—insisted from the
first that every girl, every woman, should obey governmental rules
to the letter. Then officials in other departments began to look with
interest on such an innovation in government work. In due time, the
Board of Education, the Registrar General's Office, and the National
Health Insurance Commission appealed to the post offices for women
clerks. Miss Smith with great foresight sent her most efficient workers; she was moving silently but effectively to advance the cause of
women.

It is clear that the employment of women in the postal service was an opening wedge into other professions. In the eighties, the Local Government Board appointed Marianne Harriet Mason to inspect homes where pauper children were "boarded out." It was necessary to have some responsible person determine just how regulations were being enforced. The new inspector made her rounds regularly; she brought back first-hand information on conditions in the various homes. Her reports give a vivid picture of how pauper children fared in the last quarter of the nineteenth century. Miss Mason's duty was

> To go about the country and to turn up beds and inspect blankets and generally satisfy herself that the children in cottage homes were washed and well cared for. . . . I very clearly remember her [Miss Mason] coming to Lady Margaret Hall and telling us all about her work. Village ideas of cleanliness and sanitation were still elementary. When she mentioned baths in one cottage, the foster-mother called up her charges to show the lady that they were washed every day 'down to the high-water mark,' a line around their necks about at the top of their pinafores.[13]

The Guardians watched the experiment with interest; but they played safe, and kept Miss Mason as a "temporary" worker for seven years.

Very little has been said in this book about workshop conditions in England. Yet in the long ago, factories were often located in tumbledown buildings, and crowded with machines that had no protective devices. There were many accidents. Then a far-reaching event took place: the Factory Acts were passed in 1833. From that time forward, factory regulations were enforced by well-paid employees of the Government. As the number of industries increased, the number of duties increased—many offices being swamped with unfinished business. Then university women were asked to join the staff of factory inspectors, and these new workers gave great satisfaction. It is amusing to note that women inspectors were first known as

[13] Courtney, Janet. *The Women of My Time.* Lovat Dickson, Limited. London. 1934. pp. 122–123.

female inspectors, then as *lady inspectors*, and finally as *women inspectors*. These terms reveal to a great extent how the position of women was changing.

A pioneer who fits particularly well into this picture is Adelaide Mary Anderson, D.B.E., and she became known as an outstanding social worker. Adelaide was born in 1863 in Melbourne, Australia. She was the daughter of Alexander Gavin Anderson, a ship-owner, and a man of considerable wealth. Her grandfather, Dr. Alexander Anderson, was long Principal of the Gymnasium of Old Aberdeen. The Anderson family moved to England while Adelaide was still a small child, and they lived in a large house in the newly-built Fitz-John section of London. As for schooling, Adelaide—who was named for Beethoven's famous song—was educated first at home, and then in France and Germany. At the age of twenty, she entered Girton College to read Moral Sciences. There is no one left to give a first-hand account of those days. But Miss K. Jex-Blake did write an article saying this:

> I found her there [Girton College], when I joined the staff in 1885, and until shortly before her Tripos, I hardly knew her personally, though I remember her very well, quiet, reserved, rather aloof from any but the best minds among her generation of students. Her perfect simplicity carried with it a touch of dignity which made her seem more grown up than the average student, and although liked and respected for her friendly and unselfish spirit, she was not a vital force in the college.[14]

From these few lines it would appear that Miss Anderson was self-reliant in a quiet sort of way.

But girls will be girls! And Adelaide Anderson was called "The Widow" all through her stay at college. This image stood her well in the years to follow, for she could go to the most "impossible

[14] *A Pamphlet*. "Dame Adelaide Anderson, D.B.E." From the *Girton Review*. Cambridge. February, 1937. p. 1.

places," on the most "impossible errands" without any special credentials. She looked for all the world like a meek, little "missionary
lady."

Student days ended and this young woman devoted herself to
writing an essay on Joannes Scotus, which was called *Erigena*. She
was awarded the Gamble Prize in 1893 for this work. Miss Anderson
had been giving lectures from time to time to groups of working girls
on philosophy and economics under the auspices of the Women's
Co-operative Guild. There came a definite break of interest as a consequence—Adelaide was concerning herself with social problems in
the homeland. Enquiries into the "sweated system" had revealed
miserable wages, bad sanitation, long hours of work, and unfair
penalties in the workrooms. At least one English woman was up in
arms! She would not accept this way-of-life for women, however
low they might be in the social scale.

It is not surprising to hear that Miss Anderson was, in due time,
made Principal Lady Inspector of Factories, taking charge of the
women inspectorate in the Home Office—work which lasted from
1897 to 1921. She was later named Dame of the British Empire.[15] She
had great powers of endurance, and never faltered in her long years
of painstaking service. There was at this time considerable agitation
over the number of women who were being injured while doing
laundry work—steam laundries had taken the place of hand laundries. The prosecution of offenders served as a warning to guilty factory owners, and scientists were called in to produce safety devices.
A pathetic side of the picture was this:

Little girls were usually set to feed or to clean such machines, often without
any training or supervision. Their thin hands would be nipped in the rapidly re-
volving rollers and arms would be drawn in by the relentless machine before its
motion could be arrested. Not infrequently the poor little victim was held tight in

---

[15] This was a mark of public appreciation for a service both unique and splendid.

the grip of the heated rollers while expert assistance was procured and screws and nuts loosened before the pressure was relieved. Terrible injuries by crushing and burning resulted, and the girls after prolonged suffering, were maimed for life.[16]

This was a sorry period of industrial life.

An amusing story is told about Miss Anderson by a junior inspector:

'I was honored,' she says, to receive an invitation to visit laundries with the chief inspector. But . . . after a long morning of most energetic inspection of laundries in one of the least salubrious of suburbs, and when the inner man called for refreshment as one o'clock came, Miss Anderson said brightly, 'Now we can take the opportunity to pay some mealtime visits.' It was not until three o'clock that she said: 'I think a cup of tea somewhere would be pleasant before we go on to the next place.'[17]

Miss Anderson was rewarded for her hard work—for really dangerous laundries became safe places in which to work. This is but a sample of the pioneer work carried on in the last years of the nineteenth century by a very remarkable English woman.

In later life, Miss Anderson was invited to study labor conditions in China;[18] she was able to offer many helpful suggestions to officials in that country.

It was not only China which she whole-heartedly served in 1930 but she set out alone to Egypt to make enquiries into the conditions of child labour in that country, and her report on the subject which has been described as a most moving human document had far-reaching consequences. This journey called in a marked degree for the display of the courage, tenacity and persistence in face of difficulties which never failed her.[19]

[16] Square, Rose E. *Thirty Years in the Public Service.* Nisbet & Co., Ltd. London. 1927. p. 150.

[17] Martindale, Hilda. *Some Victorian Portraits.* George Allen & Unwin, Ltd. London. 1948. pp. 48–49.

[18] Dame Adelaide Anderson liked to visit the Chinese Embassy in London because she was given such a warm welcome there.

[19] Martindale, Hilda. *Some Victorian Portraits.* George Allen & Unwin, Ltd. London. 1948. p. 50.

At the age of 72, Dame Anderson returned to her cottage at Kew. She died on August 28, 1936.

This was a period of change, not sudden, but cumulative in character. Charles Robert Darwin (1809–1882) was working on his theory of evolution, and Alexander Graham Bell (1847–1922) was trying to perfect a hearing device. But there was an awkward question: would a new flow of thought produce a good, really practical culture-pattern? Wives and daughters did not have long to wait, for they were handed the Sex Disqualification (Removal) Act of 1916. This law had given women very definite rights. However, there was this innocent looking proviso which all but nullified the document: ". . . notwithstanding anything in this section, His Majesty may by Order in Council authorize regulations to be made providing for and prescribing the mode of admission of women in the Civil Service of His Majesty."[20] This clause made it possible for officials to ignore the place of women after World War I, and to employ hundreds of ex-service men in the various departments. The Government had formulated rules for just such an emergency, and English women were the victims.

Men in high places would consider social problems in a half-hearted way, knowing full-well that they intended to vote against any measure which would give members of the opposite sex a better advantage in life. Small wonder that so little was accomplished over so long a period of time. Consider a meeting held in the late nineteen-twenties: Lord Tomplin's Committee was trying to find a way to improve conditions for women. After many hours of debate, the members found themselves so confused that they *did not even vote* on the clear-cut question of equal pay. There was, however, a large amount of first-hand evidence gathered during the investigation. For one thing, the prejudice which had long existed against women work-

[20] *General Information Regarding Examinations Held Under the Direction of the Civil Service Commissioners*. His Majesty's Stationery Office. London. 1937. pp. 1–2.

ers was discussed quite freely. The consensus was this: prejudice can only be overcome by giving women a chance to show what they can do. The individual views of committee members were summarized, and passed on to the authorities, this procedure being a *cul-de-sac* in political matters.

It stood as an encouraging sign that the employment of women in the Civil Service was at least being discussed. Sir Russell Scott gave the opinion of Treasury personnel as follows:

> It is necessary to have regard to two facts, which I think do tend to differentiate the value of women's work as compared with men's work; the fact is that women retire on marriage and do not make the Public Service their lifetime career; the second reason is that we are not yet past the age of prejudice about women in employment and that is still the fact, and a fact that cannot be ignored when you are judging the value of the work as measured by its results, that there still is, to some extent, a prejudice on the part of men in the matter of doing business with a woman. I am not stating that as defending it, I am merely stating it as a fact; I think as a fact it does still exist. I am quite clear it is a fact of diminishing importance, but there can be no question that the fact does exist at the present time and ought not to be ignored when people compare the value of men's and women's work as measured by results.[21]

At least, women in the Civil Service knew where they stood.

There was a great deal of ill-will among women over the way they were being treated, and most human beings have what is known as a 'breaking point.' Ray Strachey had this to say:

> The main facts of the situation are all too plain. Parliament decided . . . that women were to be admitted to, and employed in the Civil Service upon the same terms as men, save for the three important points of pay, eligibility for service over-seas, and dismissal on marriage. . . .
>
> But the authorities of the Civil Service (conveniently called *the Treasury*) believed that this was an impulsive and absurd position. . . .
>
> Anyone who has watched Civil Service matters closely for the past ten years will have ample evidence of how this Treasury attitude has worked in practice.[22]

[21] Evans, Dorothy. *Women and the Civil Service*. Sir Isaac Pitman & Sons, Ltd. London. 1934. pp. 51–52.

[22] *The Woman Leader*. London. August 7, 1931.

Mr. Strachey went on to say that all matters relating to this subject (fair practice for women) were left much as they were found—in "a very bad state."

This period became known as "the doldrums." No English woman had come forward to match the record of Mrs. Pankhurst, who had worked so tirelessly for women's rights. But this dull period was to pass—for soon an American-born woman, Nancy Langhorne Astor, became a predominate figure in the social and political life of England. She was a member of Parliament from Plymouth.[23] The consensus around Crosby Hall—where almost everyone was a University graduate—was that this gay, hard-working politician "got what she went after." This idea of self-assertion was reaching down to the lowest ranks of office clerks.

Over a long period of years working conditions for civil servants had been bad, crowding and under-heating being the rule rather than the exception. In one government office a room originally planned to hold fourteen was occupied by twenty-six girls. Stenographers complained that they spent their days alternating between the warm comfortable rooms where they took dictation, and the cold, damp quarters where notes were transcribed and typed for mailing. Bronchial trouble was quite general, sometimes causing the absence of a quarter of the staff in the cold months of winter. Women discussed their troubles amongst themselves, but they lacked leaders to force the issue in a determined manner.

In 1931, the women office workers did make demands on the Government for heating,[24] hot water, window cleaning, and wool foot-mats. The request was ignored—the workers received exactly nothing. Such a complaint upset many highly-placed officials, for they did not take kindly to the notion of notoriety in such matters.

[23] As a member of the American Woman's Club in London, the writer often heard Lady Astor speak. Her favorite theme was: we shall never have a well-ordered society until the English-speaking people stand together on what they think is right.

[24] Foreigners cannot possibly understand how uncomfortable it can be in England because of insufficient heating. The writer used to sit first on one foot, then on the other, when reading in the British Museum.

Sir Malcolm Ramsey, Comptroller and Auditor General of the Treasury, possibly expressed the attitude of most colleagues when he said, "Civil Servants used to regard the heads of departments rather as Gods on Olympus obscured by the clouds from the people in the valley below."[25]

An increase in Civil Service duties had led to change in official routine—the executive class doing work that had formerly been in the hands of administrative groups. This trend was especially noticeable after World War II. Women began to wonder about their own status—that is, would favoritism help ex-service men as it had done twenty years and more earlier? No one was in a position to answer this question. Soon several highly-placed officials were asked to consider recruitment; they lost no time in declaring themselves opposed to any plan that might adversely affect public business. Going even further, the committee went on to say that services must not be hampered "a second time" by untrained workers. It all sounded very good. The Government seldom puts up a fight against really strong social pressure. English women were delighted at the turn of events—a new era was dawning.

The Civil Service attracts university women from among the upper classes. They prefer, as a rule, posts in one of the several grades of the Administrative Class. In this branch of the Service training of a high order is required. The salary schedule established in 1935 set a precedent as to what educated women should be paid for their services. Even so, a study of the accompanying scale shows that higher pay was established for men than for women. The argument that men have family expenses to shoulder and should therefore receive higher salaries is a distortion of fact. What about the bachelors who are financially responsible only for themselves? On the other hand,

[25] *Daily Herald.* (Organ of the Trades Union Congress & Labor Party). London. December 16, 1930.

many women—widows with young children, or daughters with elderly parents—have financial burdens quite as heavy as married men with families.

	MALE SCALE		FEMALE SCALE	
	Basic	*Inclusive*	*Basic*	*Inclusive*
Assistant Principal	£200 by annual increment of £20 to £240 by annual increments of £25 to £500	£274–£629	£200 by annual increments of £20 to £400	£274–£511
Principal	£700–£25–£900	£840–£1051	£600–£25–£750	£732–£898
Assistant Secretary	£1000–£50–£1200	£1154–£1354	£850–£50–£1000	£1004–£1154[26]

An adequate salary scale is only one phase of the problem, for the paths leading to the higher grades of the Civil Service are strewn with obstacles. The examinations are so difficult that it takes a year or more to prepare for them. Twenty-seven women entered the competition in 1925, and of this number three came through successfully. For a time, the lack of coaching, or possibly the lack of ability, brought candidate after candidate down to defeat. T. J. Curtin, writing in *The Daily Telegraph* (London) of October 24, 1932, made this statement:

This year's examination for the Administrative appointments in Whitehall was a landmark in the history of women's efforts to succeed at this examination.

Not only did they fail to win a place, but—a more ominous feature still—they only put six candidates in the field. This is the smallest number of women attending the examination since they first became eligible in 1925. . . .

The only conclusion to be drawn is that women are finding the competition for Class I, from which all the highest posts in Whitehall are recruited, including the permanent heads of departments, too formidable a hurdle to surmount, and that in

[26] Day, A. J. T. *Civil Service Guide.* Sir Isaac Pitman & Sons, Ltd. London. 1935. p. 40.

the higher reaches of University education they are unable to hold their own against men. . . .

It looked very much as though the best government posts would remain in the hands of men.

But this was not the case. The graduates of women's colleges undertook a publicity campaign; they made addresses and secured funds for the special training of women students. What happened is what always happens when women make a determined effort; women came through with flying colors in the examinations. On January 21, 1938, *The Times* of London, had this to say:

The completed results of the recent examination for the Civil Service Administrative Class are now available, and a feature is the remarkable success of the women candidates, who have won a record number of places. At first six women were declared successful, but in the final shuffle, after the several preferences have been taken up eight have received appointments.

When women were first allowed to compete in the higher examinations there was considerable doubt as to the wisdom of such a move. In the past, only honours men from Oxford and Cambridge had been able to hold their own in these difficult tests. Women did not know what they could do, for they had never been offered any worthwhile opportunities. But the bad years were forgotten, as women continued to make top grades in the higher examinations. These ups and downs were helpful in an indirect way, for college girls began to show a preference for subjects hitherto regarded as only for men. There is no better test of an educational trend than the data afforded by examinations. Political organization, was a subject chosen by one woman—she scored 75 per cent. Another, "plumped for economics," industry and trade, public finance, economic history, and English literature—her grades going all the way from 69 to 90 per cent. Several competitors chose metaphysics (three papers), logic and psychology. Women have proved that logic is no longer a male specialty, for in this subject they were awarded 88 per cent. Of the 400 who took the examination, no man reached this level of excellence.[27]

Everyone places a high value on security. As one Civil Servant remarked:

When unemployment is unfortunately so rife that merely to have a job is to be the envy of quite a considerable proportion of the community, parents are more than ever attracted by the permanency of State employment. It is true that Civil servants hold office at the pleasure of the Crown, and that theoretically they have not the contractual rights of other employees, but in practice they enjoy virtual security of tenure. When, to this major advantage, are added the attractions of an assured income, increasing up to the maximum of the scale by modest but regular annual increments, the possibility of promotion to a post with a substantial salary, and the certainty of a pension when working days are over, the Civil Service presents itself in a very favorable light.[28]

This is not a one-sided affair, as the high standard of recruitment makes for considerable efficiency in the Service.

A permanent post is not everything. Women are eager to get into the Foreign Service, and certain obstacles have long blocked the way of this dream. For one thing, women do not take kindly to compulsion; they understand full well that such a practice makes for high-handed proceedings in human relationships. In this connection, George Nasmyth wrote that in England,

Women are allowed to vote in municipal affairs and county affairs, but are debarred from participation in national and imperial policies because, as the imperialists claim, women cannot understand imperial affairs. In reality this means that the imperialists fear that the social institutions of women would revolt at the application of the philosophy of force to imperial ambition, and this fear is probably justified.[29]

---

[27] It is not possible to pass these examinations by way of a memory system. Here is a question included under the heading, "Moral Philosophy": Give an historical and critical account of the part played by the notion of self-preservation in modern ethical systems.

[28] Day, A. J. T. *Civil Service Guide*. Sir Isaac Pitman & Sons, Ltd. London. 1935. p. 1.

[29] Nasmyth, George. *Social Progress and the Darwinian Theory*. G. P. Putman's Sons. New York and London. 1916. pp. 263–264.

If the mailed fist is so important in affairs of state, then women must wait a while before gaining full rights to Her Majesty's Service.

Women are watching developments in fields where their suitability is unquestioned. They feel especially well-qualified to judge the value of articles passing through the Customs, for it is the wives and daughters who purchase the largest part of all goods sold in the retail shops. How many travelers have been amused at the ignorance shown by custom officials—all men in the writer's experience.[30] The traveler who has had her silks and laces pulled about by rough, none-too-clean hands, would welcome women into this branch of the Service.

The knowledge and ability of candidates seeking superior positions is judged by written examinations and personality tests. This system gives fairly good results, although far from perfect. The Board of Interviewers tries to place recruits into the niches for which they are best fitted by training, background, and natural endowment. A study of the following table for 1935 shows the number of women brought into the Service through competition or nomination at that time, as compared with the number of men. The individual items as well as the totals reflect the gains that had been made by women in about three quarters of a century—the years since they were first employed by the Government:

	Males	Females
1. Number recruited by written competition under regulations made by the Civil Service Commissioners —		
Post Office.	352	1,472
Other Departments	1,168	2,834
2. Number recruited by written competition limited to candidates accepted by a Department —		
Post Office.	730	472
Other Departments	48	..
3. Number recruited by interview competition under regulations made by the Civil Service Commissioners —		
Post Office.	17	..
Other Departments	164	10

[30] In Russia, custom officials wasted time going over a pack of my canceled checks. The writer's diary. August, 1932.

	Males	*Females*
4. Number recruited by interview competition limited to candidates accepted by a Department —		
Post Office.	..	..
Other Departments	94	9
5. Number recruited by composite competition under regulations made by the Civil Service Commissioners —		
Post Office.	41	1
Other Departments	469	11
6. Number recruited by composite competition limited to candidates accepted by a Department —		
Post Office.	91	..
Other Departments		..
7. Number recruited by nomination of persons already in the established Civil Service —		
Post Office.	100	74
Other Departments	142	13
8. Number recruited by nomination of persons not already in the established Civil Service —		
Post Office.	4,808	1,772
Other Departments	1,563	185
9. Number recruited by nomination of persons who came within the scope of the reports of the Temporary Staffs Committee .	4,604	1,682
Totals	14,491	8,535[31]

In the same report, the varied character of appointments is shown. The Department of Agriculture listed a woman as Assistant Botanist. And for some time, a woman had been employed as organist at the Chelsea Royal Hospital. In the British Museum, two women had been given posts: one as Guide Lecturer; one as Assistant Keeper of Books. Women were working in the Board of Control as Commissioners and Occupation Officers. Two women had been assigned to executive positions in the Customs and Excise Office, and others had received appointments in the Ministry of Health, the Ministry of Labour, the Post Office, the Board of Trade, and the Home Office — seven had been made inspectors of factories. The Ministry of Health had named five women as assistant workers in the insurance department. However, there was only one medical officer. The Board of Education had recruited the greatest number with fourteen as assist-

[31] *Report of His Majesty's Civil Service Commissioners in the year 1935*. His Majesty's Stationery Office. London. 1936. pp. 25–26.

ant inspectors, and one in the junior grade of the administrative class. These appointments showed that the field of employment for women had been widening year by year.

A study of the Civil Service would not be complete without some mention of its divisions. The officials who care for State affairs are quite outside the ranks of those who handle the daily round of office duties. The ministers of different departments are almost always lay-men who have been selected for general, rather than special ability. The Exchequer might be headed by a barrister, the War Office by a journalist, the Admiralty by a merchant—these temporary officials have the last word in statecraft. The most influential positions in Great Britain are those of Prime Minister, Governor of the Bank of England, and Secretary of the Treasury (head of the Civil Service).[32] Just how much influence a given official exerts at a given moment depends upon the character of the individual. It is *taken for granted* that these ministers will not promote the interests of any special class.

There have been overtones of discontent among employees in the Service at times. Such a situation developed in the nineteen-twenties, and the Government lost no time in posting some stiff rules on the bulletin boards:

> No established organization of which the primary object is to influence or affect the remuneration and conditions of employment of its members, unless the organization has been approved by the Treasury. The Treasury certifies approval if (a) the association is confined to persons employed by the Crown, (b) it is in all respects independent of, and not affiliated to, other such associations or federations including them, not confined to Civil Servants, (c) it is not associated with political objects, (d) it is not associated with any political party or organization directly or indirectly.[33]

[32] There is a demand in some quarters for a new type of Governor for the Bank of England, an economic expert, perhaps, who could cope with unemployment problems and trade cycles.

[33] Finer, Herman. *Civil Service (Approved Associations) Regulations, 1927, No. 800* (made by the Treasury).

All associations within the Service must meet the approval of high officials. The Head Registrar of Friendly Societies handles all advisory and reporting work for the Treasury. The State now assumes the role of manager in the various departments of the Civil Service.

Complaints reach the Government occasionally on the question of promotions. The heads of departments have great difficulty in handling experienced workers whose education is below accepted standards. The three Tithe Commissioners came under censure in the late nineteen-thirties because they sought outsiders for vacant posts. The employees protested at what they called "an unwarranted insult to their efficiency": moreover, they threatened to take up work in departments less strict in matters of promotion.[34] To anyone outside this circle, pressure of any kind stands as an example of poor taste.

The Government offers to every man and woman on its regular staff a certain amount of security, and in return for this show of confidence expects the employees to be loyal, and to do all in their power to improve the quality of public service. A danger that threatens England, a danger that has long threatened France, is the possible union of Government workers for the sole purpose of gaining higher wages and an easier way to promotion.

Anything which makes for efficiency-of-service is encouraged by the British Government. As a consequence, *The Civilian*, a journal established for Civil Service clerks, has prospered for more than eighty years. The paper gives last-minute news of various departments, and it presents special articles that have a great deal of literary merit. *The Civilian* is the nucleus for all social reforms within the Service.

Superannuation rights for both men and women are based on earning power. This means that women receive smaller pensions than men, because they receive smaller salaries. The marriage gratuity is

[34] *The Star*. Sheffield, England. August 23, 1936.

based on the idea that most women will, in time, be tied down with home-making responsibilities—this attitude prevailing at a time when families are growing smaller, and household duties lighter. A few notes of interest will be given at this point: (1) civil servants usually retire at the age of sixty, and are required to retire at the age of sixty-five; (2) pensions are reckoned at one eightieth of salary at the date of retirement, multiplied by the number of years spent in government work. Here is an example: retirement salary, £560 divided by 80 equals 7; and 7 times 40, (the number of years of service) equals 280, which would be the number of pounds received annually. There is an additional allowance provided—one-thirtieth of the retiring salary, multiplied by the number of years of service. The plan has one disadvantage: it makes no allowance for the fact that women live longer than men—old age often entailing heavy expenditures for personal care.[35]

The Civil Service is so far removed from the market-place that the public knows almost nothing of what goes on in the many offices. The Government seldom makes headlines in the press, although its ancient halls are forever buzzing with activity. By a "gentleman's agreement" between officials of State and newspaper reporters, an aura of secrecy is maintained in all departments. This freemasonry makes for a smooth-running organization, important matters being side-tracked before they reach the Cabinet. The Government has other methods of control that are quite effective. It can, for instance, straighten out the worst kind of official muddle by calling for investigations—a few desks being moved from one office to another. "Keeping face" is very important in British affairs.

A study of the following table will show the number of scholarly individuals who had penetrated the various levels of Civil Service up to, and including, the year 1955:

---

[35] Further, there is a very high rate of accidents after the age of eighty.

CIVIL SERVICE STATISTICS

1st July, 1955

ADMINISTRATIVE CLASS

	Men	Women	Total
Permanent Secretary to the Treasury	1	. .	1
Permanent Secretary	31	. .	31
Deputy Secretary	61	1	62
Under Secretary.	209	5	214
Assistant Secretary	644	29	673
Principal	1,143	116	1,259
Assistant Principal	245	42	287
Total	2,334	193	2,527

EXECUTIVE CLASS

	Men	Women	Total
Heads of major establishments	21	. .	21
Principal executive officer	110	. .	110
Senior Chief executive officer	251	3	254
Chief Executive officer	688	23	711
Senior executive officer	2,525	166	2,691
Higher executive officer	7,279	1,349	8,628
Executive officer.	17,313	5,675	22,988
Total	28,187	7,216	35,403

CLERICAL OFFICER GRADE

Men	Women	Total
49,799	25,639	75,418

CLERICAL ASSISTANT CLASS

Men	Women	Total
15,917	19,307	35,224[36]

The Civil Service faces a problem that is seldom mentioned; it concerns the staff. These groups are recruited at an early age, and some few workers prove to be inapt at almost everything. There is a period of probation, but this fact does not prevent dozens of shiftless

[36] Extract from the *Report of the Royal Commission on the Civil Service*. 1953–1955. Cmd. 9613.

individuals from slipping into the various departments—becoming little more than slackers. One misfit can disorganize an entire office. Officials are in an awkward position, for it is much easier to make a charge, than to prove its accuracy. Co-workers are tight-lipped when questioned about routine duties in any branch of the Service. Unless an employee is willfully causing trouble, he or she stands on firm ground as far as employment is concerned. A list of figures of dismissals for inefficiency is given below:

	NEW ENTRANTS	DISMISSALS
1950	.63,072	127
1951	.61,893	103
1952	.48,198	117
1953	.36,209	94[37]

In the case of higher officials, the failures numbered only one out of 900.

Prestige plays a large part in upper-class business circles. When recruitment by open competition was first suggested for the Home Office, any number of people came forward to plead for "no such nonsense" in civic work. But that was long ago; now, members of the most important bodies qualify by stiff examinations. The requirements are as follows: a high grade of intelligence, and what may be called a "pleasing personality." These posts are greatly prized as the daily grind is said to be less severe than in other branches of the Service. The Home Office has always been close to Buckingham Palace—sometimes called the link between the Throne and the people. Next to the Prime Minister, the Home Secretary has the most important duties to perform, receiving all petitions, and sending them to the Queen with a list of recommendations. Small wonder that parents covet these assignments for their sons and daughters.

It is clear that there is nothing haphazard about the Civil Service. Consider the age-old institution of wedlock: for many years women

[37] Campbell, G. A. *The Civil Service in Britain.* The Whitefriars Press, Ltd. London. 1955. P. 359.

had a "marriage bar" held against them; they had to choose between the loss of a job, or the loss of a life companion. The rule was never in harmony with common sense thinking. If a couple fell in love, it usually caused trouble for some supervisor. Now and then women in the higher grades were retained. But the procedure was very often questioned, as few people are indispensable in any department. But times change. There is now a deep-set feeling in the Service that women should be allowed complete equality with men. After all, ". . . getting rid of a social obstacle is fundamentally a matter of civil liberties to be envisaged from the point of view of the citizen and not merely that of a public service. Thus, the general idea is that all individuals should conduct their lives as seems best to them."[38] The authorities of the Civil Service were lacking in foresight when they imposed restrictions against marriage, for such an order was doomed to failure.[39]

It is surprising how many lives are shaped by the State. Consider the figures for April 1, 1954:

> There was a non-industrial staff of 645,758, with expenses running over £350,000,000 a year in salaries.[40] Unfortunately, many of these people are employed on an unestablished basis—a force representing 45 per cent in 1949. But, by the spring of 1954, the unestablished employees had been reduced to 164,120, or about one in four of the total non-industrial complement.[41]

Small wonder that music-hall comedians—exaggerating a little—tell jokes about the week-to-week worker who holds a place in the Civil Service from youth to old age. Workers take pension rights for granted these days—and few benefits are more highly prized. It is said that one out of every twenty-two of the insured population of England works for the Government.

[38] *Civil Service Opinion*. Published by the Society of Civil Servants. Palace Chambers, Bridge Street, London, S.W. 1. November 15, 1929.

[39] The "marriage bar" was removed in 1946—an exception being the Foreign Service.

[40] Campbell, G. A. *The Civil Service in Britain*. (Figures for April 1, 1954). The Whitefriars Press, Ltd. London. 1955. p. 9.

[41] *Ibid*. p. 283.

New rulings very often introduce unforeseen problems. For example: an eight-hour day was established throughout the Service during World War II, and this change of schedule led to questions concerning hours of work, and vacation periods. In 1954, the Treasury put forward a plan ". . . designed to provide for a 10½ day fortnight in return for longer hours and shorter holidays, a less favourable arrangement than that rejected by the staff five years earlier."[42] Workers never hesitate to say that the prestige of being a Government worker outweighs all other benefits; but men and women are hard to please. Recruits are not now coming forward as they did in former years. Young people, especially girls, like to be near home, and most of the jobs in this field are in large industrial centres. The authorities are trying to meet the problem by employing workers who have been out of secondary school for a year or two; only the top third of a particular class are considered.

With faults or no faults, the Civil Service enjoys the confidence and respect of the majority of citizens. This attitude of trust and veneration is fostered alike by the Church of England, the House of Commons, and geographical factors which lead to a common way-of-life. Traditional ideas which are accepted without question, lead quite naturally to an abiding faith in highly placed officials, especially those drawn from old, aristocratic families, and the Government carries its burdens with ease and a firm approach to matters at hand. There have been drastic changes of policy to test the strength of State machinery, but the general belief is that the Government will hold fast under all circumstances.

The question arises as to what women have accomplished in the Civil Service. They have been moving ahead in all departments. It is a common sight in England to see one man and two women busily engaged together in some form of government work. As for salaries, women receive about 20 per cent less than men. They will eventually have the same weekly income, the principle of equal pay having been

[42] Campbell, G. A. *The Civil Service in Britain.* The Whitefriars Press, Ltd. London. 1955. p. 291.

accepted in an odd sort of way. A plan was devised whereby wages were to be increased in seven-yearly-stages, beginning with the year 1955. More and more positions are being opened to women, as indicated by the following list: engineers, surveyors, architects, psychologists, clerical assistants, and assistant information officers. The Government has adopted a helpful service by publishing reports of its activities at regular intervals—usually every two years. These reports offer valuable information to the public at small cost.

During the last ten years or so, the pioneer women administrators, who entered the Home Civil Service when the administrative grade was first opened to women forty years ago, have reached the culmination of their careers, as the following four biographies indicate:

DAME EVELYN SHARP claims the accolade of being the *first* woman to become head of a Department. This was in 1955 when she was appointed Permanent Secretary at the Ministry of Housing and Local Government, a Department with which she had been associated for a number of years since the War. Possibly her contemporary at Oxford University, Alix Kilroy, who took the examination successfully the previous year, may have influenced her in turning from teacher training to compete for the Civil Service. She is the daughter of a London clergyman, who believed in educating his daughters, being educated first at St. Paul's Girls School and then Somerville College, Oxford. When her first big promotion came in 1946 with her appointment as Deputy Secretary at the Ministry of Town and Country Planning, she was at that time the highest paid woman in the Civil Service at the age of 42. Personally attractive and elegant, she is said to be a voracious reader, to have a great fondness for foreign travel, to be a great walker and lover of the countryside.

DAME MARY SMIETON was the *second* woman to achieve the highest rank in the Civil Service. She was made Permanent Secretary at the Ministry of Education in 1959. The earlier part of her career was spent in the Ministry of Labour, dealing with health and welfare problems—she rose to Deputy Secretary here in 1955. These were subjects very probably of particular interest to Dame Mary, whose grandfather, James Smieton, had been a pioneer in industrial welfare in Scotland 100 years ago. Just before World War II Dame Mary was given the job of organising the Women's Voluntary Services. In 1946 she was the first Director of Personnel at the United Nations. Educated at the Perse School, Cambridge, Wimbledon High School, London, and Lady Margaret Hall, Oxford, Dame

Mary is perhaps more domesticated than some of her fellow women administrators — to the extent that the long hours of work will allow. Dame Mary is to retire soon, and will then be taking up work with UNESCO.

DAME ENID RUSSELL SMITH, whose career began the same year, 1925, has spent most of it in the Ministry of Health, where she reached the position of Deputy Secretary in 1956. After 38 years as a civil servant, Dame Enid is soon to retire, but from next October she has been appointed Principal at St. Aidan's College, Durham University.

Dame Enid has an unusual hobby. She is an expert in Judo, in fact the senior woman expert in Europe. She is one of the few female holders of the Black Belt of the third Dan, a highly prized mark in Judo circles.

DAME ALIX KILROY is in private life Lady Meynell, the wife of Sir Francis Meynell, poet and publisher. After a brilliant early career in which her work at the Board of Trade included the administration of clothes rationing and the utility furniture schemes during the War period, she became in 1949 the Secretary of the Monopolies and Restrictive Practices Commission. After 30 years in the Service, Dame Alix retired in 1955 to 'combine part-time appointments with more leisure.' She and her husband run a farm in Suffolk, which takes up much of her time. Dame Alix has had a fair share of the public eye. Elegant, charming and brilliant, it was her fate as a civil servant to oppose the Dior 'new look' — because of difficulties at the time in the supply of clothing materials.[43]

The following table shows the number of men and women of the permanent staff of the Civil Service in post as of April 1, 1962:

	Men	Women	Total
ADMINISTRATIVE CLASS (Grades from Permanent Secretary to Assistant Principal)	2,238	191	2,429
GENERAL EXECUTIVE CLASS (Principal Executive Officer to Executive Officer)	30,816	7,992	38,808
DEPARTMENTAL EXECUTIVE CLASSES	27,540	3,523	31,063
GENERAL CLERICAL CLASSES	45,562	33,018	78,580
OTHER CLERICAL (Departmental Grades)	21,576	15,251	36,827
CLERICAL ASSISTANT CLASS	14,408	21,656	36,064
	142,140	81,631	223,771[44]

[43] *The Fawcett Library* (Research Department). London. April 23, 1963. pp. 1–3.
[44] *Ibid.* p. 4.

Some mention of the Diplomatic Service might be in order here. It is a system of practice by which political negotiations are conducted between two or more countries.

It involves intercourse on each side through accredited representatives, according to customs prescribed by international law; these agents, in order of rank, are embassador, envoy extraordinary and minister plenipotentiary, minister resident, charge d'affaires, secretary of legation, and attaché. The greatest nations send to each other envoys of the highest rank; smaller countries appoint those lower in dignity, and receive representatives of like rank.[45]

What a diplomatic official does is not backed by tradition, for indulgent behavior was not a part of either Greek or Roman culture. As relations between political parties grew more complex, there developed a need for closer co-operation between the different countries. A diplomatic officer must concern himself with the welfare of his own government, and the rights of fellow citizens living or traveling in his district. At all times, business proceeds according to polite ceremonials and studied cordiality. Workers in the diplomatic departments enjoy great privileges, for they are direct representatives of sovereign powers.

The consular system of a country is not part of the diplomatic service. A consul differs from a diplomatic representative in that the former attends to commercial affairs, while the latter is interested primarily with political relations. There are three ranks in the trade-service: consuls, general consuls, and commercial agents, the first named having charge of all operations in a particular zone. It is a complicated arrangement devised for groups with widely-scattered interests. A pleasing personality can be a great asset for a consul, for in the absence of an embassador—far from large cities—a consul can act as a social link between the ruler of a country, and any special guest who visits his territory—that is, he can arrange conferences or make introductions. It is exacting work—nothing can be taken for granted.

[45] *The World Book Encyclopedia* (Limited Edition 905) for the library of Nellie Alden Franz. Volume 1. W. F. Quarrie & Company. Chicago, Ill. 1928. p. 1955.

This chapter on the British Civil Service has attempted to relate how this great institution serves the public. Within one hundred years, the British Civil Service has grown from an inert political body, to a highly respected division of the Government. Prudence is the watchword, for the representatives of Whitehall must be, in all respects, above reproach.

VI. Architecture

In the long ago, a German scholar described architecture as "frozen music." This was a pertinent comment from an individual who no doubt understood the value of stones and marble—that is, as they stirred the æsthetic emotions.

Architectural designs do not necessarily follow any set rules, buildings given over to worship of the Almighty differing in many respects from the less-complex structures erected for educational purposes. Further, nations display their diversities of character by the prominence which they give to certain moral standards. For example, when domestic life becomes vigorous, utilitarian principles take precedence over any hard set ideas concerning beauty or symmetry. It is safe to assume that the higher the state of cultural growth, the more marked will be the features of architecture in a given society.

It is surprising to find that artists, rather than architects, sent out the first call for more gracious building designs. In this connection, the influence of John Ruskin—art critic and social reformer—can hardly be over-estimated. He wrote voluminously on art as an expression of a people's soul, feeling that good designs were especially necessary in the building industry. For is not

The art of Building—the strongest - proudest - most orderly - most enduring of the arts of man; that of which the produce is in the surest manner accumulative, and need not perish, or be replaced; but if once well done, still stand, more strongly than the unbalanced rocks—more prevalently than the crumbling hills. The Art is associated with all civic pride and sacred principles; with which men record their power—satisfy their enthusiasm—make sure their defense—define and make dear their habitation.[1]

[1] Ruskin, John. *Sesame and Lillies*. The Macmillan Company. New York. 1919. p. 116.

Until recent years, the mention of art in a school program was enough to bring on a family discussion of some length, and often of some bitterness. This was an unfortunate situation, as children take quite naturally to creative work, composing their own songs, writing their own plays, and sketching any thing from the cat, to the cook, to the head of the household. However, during the past fifty years, the long-neglected arts have been receiving more than passing attention; music came first, then dramatic training, finally a slow approach to any number of crafts. It is usually an interest in drawing which often leads to a career in architecture. A great obstacle has been the daily time-schedule, almost all schools stressing the importance of a grammar-type education. This approach to school work has more or less blocked the way for pupils whose interests lay in a particular form of self-expression. It is a complicated situation, for with all this attention to sound scholarship, many people—including a few in professional groups—cannot write or speak English with any degree of competence.

For centuries, students had received about the same type of preparation in architecture, acquiring knowledge of the masterpieces that had been produced in former years; they were never expected to do more than work with the frame-work of their time, just making improvements here and there. In England, the training offered in architectural schools was always somewhat below the standard set for the other learned professions.

A builder must work as a rule with the materials at hand. Ichmus, for instance, used Parian marble for roof covering in 500 B.C. And this procedure was well suited to that period, the old world having plenty of unskilled labor, and a wealth of natural resources. But in recent years, a new movement has dominated structural work— changes growing out of calls for aerodromes, factories, and office buildings. Thus, the "international style" has been introduced into towns and cities all over England. This is a severe break with the past. Think of a skyscraper rising almost a quarter of a mile from the ground (the Empire State building in New York City being an example). Changes keep coming by way of new inventions, and the steady evolution of techniques handed down from father to son.

How architecture started in England is something of guess work. It is known that William of Normandy[2] made a mark on the building industry in the eleventh century. This reckless invader is remembered as the man who disregarded the distinction between *meum* and *teum*, giving huge tracts of land to his followers, in some cases to his personal servants. The newcomer finally established his position, and became known as William the Conqueror. He proved to be a man of wisdom and understanding. Indeed, it was he who built a large number of churches and monasteries, along with smaller structures like the Tower Chapel in the East end of London. As workmen, the Normans were not only proficient, but exceedingly clever in that they were able to work with new materials, and adjust themselves to a new way of life. The time-worn buildings of England have a charm, a delicate air that is usually lacking in modern real estate developments.

Today, except for places of worship, the average building contract is a business proposition from start to finish. Church properties have always been important factors in community life; they have been used century after century as schools, libraries, even play-rooms. Many of these structures have stained-glass windows which present stories of kings, commoners, and saintly characters—features possessing educational value. Many churches built in the long ago are still being used in England; they are found for the most part in isolated country districts and are a great delight to tourists who come upon them unexpectedly. Static land values have had a hand in this.

[2] The Normans were at this time the most cultivated people in France.

But it is a different story in the large cities, where many well-preserved buildings have been torn down to make way for huge blocks of iron and concrete.

In speaking of earlier days in the building industry, a truly remarkable book (undated) should be mentioned—for it offered very good suggestions on how to select a building site, and how to proceed with the structural work. Consider the following lines which have to do with "goods":

> There goeth to buyldnge, many a nayle, many pynnes, many lathes, and many tyles, or slates, or strawes, besyde other great charges, as tymber, bordes, lyme, sand, stones, or brycke, besyde the workmanshyp and the implementes. But a man the whiche haue puruyd, or hath in store, to accomplysshe his purpose, and hath chosen a good soyle and place to cytuat hys howse or mansyon, and that the prospecte be good, and that the ayre be pure, fryske, and clene, Then he that wyll buylde, let hym make his fundacyon vpon a graualy grownde myxt with clay, or els let hym buylde vpon a roche of stone, or els vpon an hyll or a hylles syde, And ardre and edyfy the howse so that the pryncypall and chefe prospectes may be Eest and weest, specyally North-eest, Sowth-eest, and Sowth-weest, . . . whan all this is fynysshed, and the mansyon replenysshed with Impl:men*tes*, There must be a fyre kept *con*tynually for a space to drye vp the contagyous moyster, of the walles, & the sauour of the lyme and sande.[3]

All through the experimental stage—the years prior to the sixteenth century—England had no standard architecture in the technical sense of the term. As a result, what is known as the "provincial style" was developed by village carpenters. Judging from old prints in the British Museum, the average home was put up with very limited accommodations. Many of these structures had but one small sleeping-room, and one barn-like living room.

The manor houses were erected with some thought of elegance, many of them having private chapels, large reception rooms, and countless guest suites. The decorations were elaborate—cupids in every direction—the work being done more often than not by crafts-

---

[3] *The Fyrst Boke of the Introduction of Knowledge* made by Andrew Borde. F. J. Furnivall (Editor). Published—by Trubner & Co. London. MDCCCLXX. pp. 237–239.

men from the Continent. Frequently the kitchen, always a fire hazard, was built some distance from the main residence. In the fourteenth and fifteenth centuries buildings could be put up under very favorable conditions, expert workers receiving but three pence a day with food and lodging. This wage scale—if such it may be called— would cost the owner of a large estate very little.

At least some thought was being given to the art of building. This change was especially noticeable during the reign of Henry VIII. It was then that German and Flemish architects entered the field; they began to build houses[4] of plaster and timber—structures that outlasted any number of limestone productions under similar time exposure. By the year 1590, several wealthy families had erected really inviting homes, instead of the fortress-like quarters that had long been the choice of upper-class families. The greatest innovation was the chimney and the cheering fire-place. The tea kettle did not appear on the hearth until some time later. It was not until September 25, 1666, that Samuel Pepys wrote about a "China Drink" that was very pleasing. During this shift in living conditions, practically all small houses were built with thatched roofs that often sprouted into flower gardens high up in the tree tops.[5]

All buildings were designed in a more or less haphazard way until a few trained architects set themselves up in proper business style. In most cases, these men had obtained a good background abroad— Greece, France, Italy. For Inigo Jones (1572–1652), the work of Andrea Palladio was especially inspiring, for the two builders were not far apart, their life-spans overlapping. This Italian architect had very unusual ideas:

[He] . . . floated leisurely up and down the Brenta Canal—there were many villas going up at the time—on a splendid guilded barge, equipped with a studio for his ten to twelve apprentices, shaded by a yellow-and-black linen awning.[6]

[4] A map drawn near the end of the sixteenth century shows London closely built up around the Tower, with houses dotted here and there along the river bank.

[5] Anne Hathaway's cottage at Stratford-on-Avon is an example of art fused with nature.

[6] *Time*. (Magazine). Rockefeller Center. New York 20, N. Y. (U.S.A.). January 13, 1958.

The Latin people have a special way of encouraging artistic develop-ment, be the work taking shape on the corner of a busy street, or on the deck of a quiet canal boat—the proceedings are treated with complete indifference.

Needless to say, no British architect ever called attention to his profession by sailing up and down the Thames. English students did absorb worthwhile ideas on grand tours which they put together in their own way, in their own country. A few builders ignored the make-shift styles then in vogue, and submitted original designs which closely resembled the pure Classic. Christopher Wren (1632–1723), gained recognition through daring and somewhat different adapta-tions of the classic forms. A few decades later, Sir John Van Brugh (1666–1726), gained great fame as a builder; he erected many of Queen Anne's churches, and was known for his emphasis on loca-tion—that is, the lay of the land. This particular architect obtained a completeness of style hitherto unknown on the island. Nicholas Hawksmoor (1661–1736), also worked with Wren. Because they used local materials in new ways, Wren, Van Brugh, and Hawks-moor, are known as the "original" architects. Decorative features became an integral part of architectural design through the work of Robert Adam (1728–1792). This architect—with the help of his brothers—erected a number of dwellings which gave great satisfac-tion, not only to English patrons, but to a clientele extending to the Colonies.

Up to the eighteenth century, no special attention had been given to the problem of designing really elegant small homes, contracts of this kind being handed over to a local carpenter. These unskilled workers often placed kitchens below the street level, and arranged sleeping rooms without hall exits. Unfortunately, London has plenty of houses of this type. It is clear that the voice of woman was seldom heard in the discussions between patron and builder. Home-talent in the field of architecture was non-existent for at least a hundred years.

Plans reflected the Greek or Roman or Gothic (the pointed-arch style) according to the taste of prospective clients. The orderly development of English architecture was lost in a "battle of the styles."

The Institute of British Architects came into being in 1834; it was founded not only to stimulate interest in architecture, but to set standards for the profession as a whole. The Institute was organized to stop what had long been known as a "haphazard building program." The objects of the Institute were originally set forth as follows: (a) The desire to cultivate friendly relations between architects; (b) The desire to offer technical information to all citizens; (c) The desire to encourage civic reforms in crowded areas.

The founders of the new organization realized that Royal Sanction would add a certain prestige to the Institute. To this end, the following charter was drafted in 1837:

VICTORIA, by the Grace of God of the United Kingdom of Great Britain and Ireland Queen Defender of the Faith. To all to whom *These Presents Shall Come Greetings*. ¶ Whereas Thomas Philip Earl de Grey did by a Petition to His Majesty King William the Fourth humbly represent among other things that he and divers others had associated together for the purpose of forming an Institution for the general advancement of Civil Architecture and for promoting and facilitating the acquirement of the knowledge of the various arts and sciences connected therewith it being an art esteemed and encouraged in all enlightened nations as tending greatly to promote the domestic convenience of citizens and the public improvement and embellishment of towns and cities . . . ¶ And whereas His said Majesty did thereby grant especial license and authority unto all and every person and persons Bodies Politic and Corporate (otherwise competent) to grant sell and convey in Mortmain unto and to the use of the said Society and its successors any messuages lands tenements or hereditements not exceeding such annual value as aforesaid. ¶ And whereas the Original Charter contained further provisions for the constitution and management of the said Institute. ¶ And whereas on the eighth day of August One thousand eight hundred and thirty seven in the first year of Our Reign We graciously consented to become the Patron of the said Institute and did afterwards grant and do annually grant and confer at the recommendation of the said Institute a Royal Gold Medal for the promotion of Architecture. And whereas on the eighteenth day of May One thousand eight hundred and sixty six We were graciously pleased to command that the said Institute should thenceforth be styled the Royal Institute of British Architects (hereafter called the Royal Institute).[7]

The Royal Institute of British Architects has three classes of membership: Fellows, Associates and Licentiates.

Fellows (F.R.I.B.A.) are elected from the Associate and Licentiate classes; they must be at least 30 years of age and generally have been in practice as principals for at least seven years. Associates who are not principals may, however, be admitted to Fellowship if they are or have been in positions involving responsibility for the design of architectural work or if they are otherwise considered eligible by reason of their professional attainments.

Licentiates who wish to become Fellows are required to pass a special qualifying examination unless they are over 60 years of age.

To become an Associate a candidate must have passed the R.I.B.A. final or special final examination or the final examination at a recognised School of Architecture. Subsequently 12 months practical experience must be gained before taking the examination in Professional Practice and Practical Experience. A candidate must then apply to have his name put on the register of the Architects Registration Council of the United Kingdom (which enables him to practice under the title of architect) after which he can apply to become an Associate of the Royal Institute (A.R.I.B.A.).[8]

It might be well to consider the fee system, which dates back to 1813. At first, 5% was set as the recognized commission for all types of building work. In 1872, 1919, and 1957 it became necessary to revise the remuneration for building projects, as extra requirements had greatly increased the architect's expense, both in office and field operations. The charges are based upon a percentage of the total cost of the structure, as shown by the following: (1) In any contract or order which exceeds £2,000 the percentage is 6 per cent; (2) In any contract or order which does not exceed £2,000 the percentage is 10

---

[7] *The Charter, Supplemental Charters, and By-Laws of the Royal Institute of British Architects.* London. 1937. pp. 6–8.

[8] *Letter* in the writer's file. (R.I.B.A.). London. September 8, 1959.

per cent. There is a lower charge (about 5 per cent) in any estimate which involves a repetition of units. In general, these percentages apply to the bulk of work done by an average firm, and provide a basis for computing fees that are fair to both client and architect.

In due time (c. 1875), young men began to work in the offices of well-known architects, and in this way prepare themselves for examinations which were given at stated intervals by the authorities. However, this somewhat informal system was satisfactory only as long as architects followed established traditions; it proved quite inadequate when technical requirements began to play an important role in the building industry. As a consequence, students were forced to take regular training in schools of architecture. This was a move in the right direction. To support a plan of this kind, the Royal Institute of British Architects went so far ". . . as to accept evidence of satisfactory training in approved schools as equivalent to passing its own examinations to students attending such schools."[9] The controlling body was concerned with but one question: Have the candidates received a thorough grounding in architecture? Rules have had to be changed. At present, all architectural schools are open to women. Before World War II, some institutions were known to have limited the number of women students. This practice was finally dropped, "If, however, there were a substantial increase in the number of women applying for places, individual schools might well decide to impose a limit."[10] If such a policy were adopted, women would consider establishing their own schools of architecture.

Murmurs of unrest at different times have caused the Royal Institute of British Architects to assume the role of guardian. However, this organization remains in the background most of the time; if trouble arises, action can be swift and uncompromising. When the subject of student-training came under criticism, a special board was

[9] *Architectural Students' Handbook*. By F. R. Yerbury. Technical Journals, Ltd. London. c. 1912. p. 12.

[10] *The Status of Women* (submitted by the R.I.B.A.). London. June 12, 1958.

created to provide a set of regulations for just about all forms of professional conduct. Many building firms took stock of their personnel, faced as they were with serious problems. For there still remained

> A number of persons practising as architects who were not members of the R.I.B.A., who had not passed its examination, and who were not bound by its Code of Conduct. Only an Act of Parliament could prevent such people from entering the profession . . . it was resolved to work for the necessary legislation. In 1927, following unremitting hard work and many discouragements, the Royal Institute succeeded in having the Architect's Registration Bill introduced to the House of Commons. The two Architect's Registration Acts subsequently became law in 1931 and 1938.[11]

This legislation proved of great value, not only to the trained architect, but to the public at large.

Turning to the business aspects of architecture, clients are unpredictable. The difficulty, one of them at least, lies in the fact that many people wait until they are in trouble before sending out a call for help. Proper guidance should be all things to all men from the moment building ideas take shape in the mind; will the structure be well-proportioned, is the style going to be suited to the purpose—a church must not look like a school house nor a residence like a shelter house. Large building must please the eye, and fit into the landscape, not as an addition, but as a part of the whole scheme. Trained architects understand these fine points, and they should be given a free hand in matters pertaining to over-all appearance. In constructing public buildings, the main consideration is apt to be the greatest amount of over-head for the least amount of money. This policy tends to deaden creative instinct. Some reputable architects refuse to have anything to do with commitments of this kind, the struggle hardly being worth the effort in time and energy.

There was another problem in the practice of architecture:

> A man may have been in an office, say, for eighteen months or two years as a 'temporary', and have probably received no increase during that time. He finds

[11] The R.I.B.A. *Kalendar*. 1957–1958. 66 Portland Place, London, W. 1. p. 4.

that other men are being taken on, owing to comparative scarcity, at much higher salaries, and he himself makes application for an increase, which is refused. He then attempts to obtain a job as 'temporary' in another large office at a higher salary, . . . [there are] cases where on a first application a man has been informed of a vacancy at £7 a week, subsequently to be told, however, presumably after communications have passed between the offices concerned regarding the previous salary, that the post is available only at £6.6 S.[12]

These firms could hold workers to one post, and still be acting within the law. The practice constituted what might be called a "union of employers." Keen competition was a rule of the day all through the nineteen-thirties.

As for appointments, Her Majesty's Office of Works employs a number of architects, and office assistants. If a Post Office is to be put up, or even altered, the Office of Works will supervise all details of construction. The architects selected for this service must be fully qualified. The Ministry of Health employs a small staff of trained workers to assist local authorities with housing schemes and town planning. Architectural departments are maintained by the various County Councils; these bodies are responsible for the erection of hospitals, fire stations, housing estates and school buildings. Applicants for posts in the different branches must satisfy the authorities that they have passed one or more of the examinations held by recognized institutions. All regular employees are covered by insurance. A few critics say that the spirit of adventure is being stifled in architecture. Some youthful graduates are making every effort to secure steady employment by way of "official channels," and this could lead to an unhealthy state of affairs. However, there will always be individuals who place a higher value on security, than on any form of personal achievement.

This was the state of affairs when women first invaded the profession of architecture. It was a matter of concern to friends and relatives that any woman would want to take up such an occupation

---

[12] *The Architect and Building News.* Iliffe Technical Publications, Ltd. Dorset House. Stanford Street, London, S.E. 1. October 29, 1937.

—so unlike the mother-job of teaching children. Then too, there was this question: Could architecture as a profession be considered altogether lady-like? It was not considered proper for wives and daughters in upper-class society to do hard work in the home—to sweep the front steps would have been unpardonable. Everyone seemed to be concerned with what the neighbors would say!

As the story goes, it was not long before Ethel Mary Charles (listed as an Associate of the R.I.B.A.–1898), and Bessie Ada Charles started out on a great adventure—the study of architecture. Through the kindness of Miss Ethel, the writer is able to set down a few facts concerning this period. These young women belonged to a family of some stability, the father, Thomas Edmonston Charles, having held the post of "Honorary Physician to Queen Victoria." Their schooling was carried on at home. The two sisters were no doubt ambitious, for they went on to Somerville College, Oxford University (c. 1889), at a time when sewing, calling and afternoon tea just about covered the daily schedule of young women in upper-class society. This varied program, as it turned out, was really a preparatory step to the study of architecture. But ". . . *pour rire*, the architectural schools stood aloof; they would have nothing to say."[13] As a result of this non-commital attitude, the girls picked up what they could—rather a poor start in any profession. Fortunately, the Misses Charles had been given the advantages of travel. From childhood, they had visited relatives across the Channel; but apparently, architectural study was the main interest. Then of all things, the Essay Medal which is offered with some regularity by the Royal Institute of British Architects, was won by Ethel Mary Charles in 1906. The winning paper had to do with "The Development of Structural Art as Influenced by Structural Requirements,"—a controversial issue even today.

This summary covers only part of an early struggle for recogni-

[13] *Letter* in the writer's file. November 12, 1959.

tion. The women who took up professional work in those early days had to be brave—ridicule facing them on all sides. Considerable credit must go to Dr. Charles, for as Miss Ethel says, "It was he who had a go-ahead disposition and looking around and seeing no women engaged in architecture, said, 'Let there be women architects.'"[14] However, clients were anything but responsive; they dared not violate well-established rules of conduct. So it was that "the poor father was much disappointed" with what his daughters could accomplish in the building industry.

Another pioneer in architecture was Mrs. Edith Gillian Harrison, who was born and bred in London. Her father was a patent lawyer who saw to it that his daughter should be given a good education. Edith attended day-school until she was fourteen, and then went on to The Rodeau School, where she studied for the usual four-year period. About this time, a story got about that the Architectural Association School—in its new home in Bedford Square—would welcome both men and women students. There was no time to waste. Edith wrote,

> I had always intended to be an architect, so I seized this opportunity to go and interview the headmaster. . . . I was accepted as the *first* woman student and entered the school in 1917. There were few men at this time as most of them were at war. I was shortly joined by three other women students and we became known as the 'Big Four.'[15]

According to reports, these girls had the advantage of an excellent teaching staff. The groups were small, quite different from the crowded classrooms of today. Then came a success story: Edith won three traveling scholarships—one being a trip to Italy. Later, she was presented with a medal by the Ecole des Beaux Arts as the best student of the fifth year in a French School of Architecture. Edith Gilliam married an architect. However, she has managed to practice

[14] *Letter* in the writer's file. November 12, 1959.
[15] *Letter* in the writer's file. November 17, 1959.

quite independently. This is a good arrangement for the woman who must combine office work with the daily routine of housekeeping. Mrs. Harrison, in speaking of student days, says, "I was received in this school [of architecture] with cordiality and treated with consideration by all, and there was no feeling of resentment by the male students, as was encountered when women first entered the medical profession."[16] This statement, short and to the point, suggests that emotion and reasoning had been brought under control in the undergraduate ranks of at least one professional school.

Another architect, Mrs. Winifred R. Maddock, is the daughter of Dr. Reginald J. Kyle, who carried on an extensive practice in Brighton for many years. She received her early education in the local schools, taking the elementary grades in stride, and then going on to the Brighton and Hove High School for girls. Soon thereafter, Winifred began training at the Brighton Municipal School of Art. She says of this period, "I took the full three year course for book illustration and poster design. I won a scholarship to the Regent Street Polytechnique School of Art in London, but had hardly started work there when we heard that the Architectural Association School had just opened its doors to women."[17] This announcement brought a change of plans, for there had been several members of Winifred's family who had gained fame by way of building projects. It was only natural therefore for this young woman to want to take up the study of architecture. Later, she married an architect, and eventually, their son became an architect. Mrs. Maddock practiced her profession alone for some years, and then went into partnership with her husband. Of this venture, she wrote,

After the end of the last war, a sudden rush of War damage repair and rebuilding work enabled us to start properly in practice together. Our work has been mainly domestic-private houses and one small housing scheme locally (in Sutton

[16] *Letter* in the writer's file. November 17, 1959.
[17] *Letter* in the writer's file. November 22, 1957.

Surrey). We have built a new Quaker Meeting House, our first attempt at 'contemporary, all glass, frosted style.'[18]

Taking everything together, this is a review of some significance; it goes to show what the "weaker sex" can do in a changing society.

The career of Gertrude W. M. Leverkus was similar to that of the Misses Charles in that this young woman also felt the influence of a strong-minded father. It was he who put the idea of architecture "into his daughter's head" while she was still a school-girl. However, there was good reason for such advice as Gertrude had long shown marked ability in drawing. In later years, she said,

I was always making models and apparently saw objects 'in the round.' My mother put no difficulties in my way and I had taken my B.A. degree in Architecture at the University of London by the time I was 20.[19]

After graduation, Miss Leverkus, like many architects, shifted from one line of interest to another, starting out with a small practice, and then spending five years—after the outbreak of World War II—in a local government office.

This is truly a success story, for Miss Leverkus is now working independently with a company doing business in all parts of the world. Her speciality is housing development and she works not only inside the office, but outside on the building sites. In summing up her long experience, Miss Leverkus wrote,

I think on the whole we enjoy our work with its great variety of interests. Architecture is an art but also a science . . . we meet people of all kinds, we have to be theoretical but also practical, we must have common sense and some experience in business and law, but also possess a sense of beauty and appropriateness. So there is no time to be dull.[20]

In observing the large group of men and women who work along with her, Miss Leverkus concludes that there are no "official diffi-

[18] *Letter* in the writer's file. November 22, 1959.
[19] *Letter* in the writer's file. October 3, 1959.
[20] *Ibid.*

culties" in the way of any capable architect. She goes on to say that a large number of women have married "fellow architects, but that it is too soon to know whether their children are bound to become architects."

In all of the professions, beginners understand full well that the first few years of practice will be spread with difficulties. For there are always worries that have to do with income, working conditions, to say nothing of personal obligations. In architecture, the "open contest" provides a unique way of displaying exceptional skill. The man or woman who takes up such a challenge must have unbounded courage and a considerable amount of energy; for it is not easy to do without regular hours of sleep, just to work on a plan which may be turned down by a few judges. For with all awards, personal opinions are bound to affect the outcome. And unfortunately, the line between good judgement and bold obstinacy is very thin. All an applicant can do is stand aside, and say a prayer.

Before long, the general public grasped the fact that women were doing especially well in competitions. Chance operations have always been popular in England. Various competitions for design of projects have been held

Under the auspices of the Institute of British Architects, including 113 town halls, law courts, fire stations or art galleries, 80 schools and other buildings of an educational character, 52 housing and town planning schemes, 43 hospitals, between 30 and 40 war memorials, 14 churches or Sunday schools, and over 130 for buildings of a miscellaneous character. Of these totals, . . . 30 educational buildings, 22 housing and town planning schemes, 13 hospitals, 4 churches and 36 miscellaneous buildings have been competitions promoted since the spring of 1933.[21]

The inequitable awards which flourished through the Victorian period are no longer possible.

Another woman to achieve prominence in the field of architecture is Elizabeth Whitfield Scott. By way of introduction, Miss Scott

21 The R.I.B.A. *Kalendar*. 1939–1948. London. 1950. p. 708.

comes from a family of distinguished architects—being related to Gilbert Scott, R.A., and George Bodley, R.A. And prestige goes even further, Sir Giles Scott, a second cousin, gained fame by winning an open competition for the design of Liverpool Cathedral. With a background so rich in color, Elizabeth entered the Redmoor School, Canford Cliffs, Bournemouth. According to teachers, she displayed considerable aptitude for drawing and arithmetic. It was her natural disposition, as well as her family background, that pointed the way to architecture as a profession. In due time, Elizabeth entered the Architectural Association School in Bedford Square, London, receiving her diploma in 1924. As for experience, Miss Scott moved right along—that is, she worked for several different firms: first with Louis Soissons, F.R.I.B.A., at Welwyn, Garden City; then with Maurice Chesterton, F.R.I.B.A., at Hampstead; and Oliver Hill, F.R.I.B.A., in London. This experience was to show up clearly in the events which followed.

The old Shakespearian theatre at Stratford-on-Avon had been destroyed by fire, and scholars everywhere recognized the need to replace it with a modern playhouse that would provide a suitable background for the works of Shakespeare. In January, 1927, an open competition was announced and British and American architects were invited to submit designs for this unique project. The architects who took up this challenge were faced with long hours of research. Consider such a project: the structure, the scenery, the acting, all have to be treated as a unit. Further, drama has deep roots in religious ceremonies. This point can easily be overlooked by inexperienced architects—comparatively few are familiar with the formal ritual of church life. Such a complex problem was enough to deter all but the brave in spirit. However, seventy-two men and one woman entered the contest and submitted their designs for the theatre. It was a singular contest, the judges being faced with designs for a very special theatre, in a very special place.

Everything concerning the contest was conducted in the British way—very carefully thought out—the designs submitted had no marks of identification.[22] Finally, the great day of decision arrived. Architects everywhere were amazed when it was announced that Elizabeth Scott, a young English woman still under thirty years of age, had won the coveted award.

The *Manchester Guardian* of January 6, 1928, commented on Miss Scott's design as follows: "Her design was unanimously selected by the assessors, and Mr. Bernard Shaw, when seconding the adoption of their report, said it was the only possible design, a very good one, and the only one that showed any theatre sense." On the same day, the London *Daily Express* in speaking of this architect's achievement, said ". . . those who know her say that, having regard to her age, her flair for arresting and original design is almost akin to genius."

The first reaction to this renown award was more or less favorable. But on second thought, the critics took up their cudgels, and struck out in every direction. This was England still under the spell of Victorian prejudice. Miss Scott's winning design was called "un-English," as though architecture could be confined within restricted national lines. Indeed, the appreciation of Shakespeare's work has gone far beyond the limits of any particular group.

In starting research on a Shakespearian theatre, Miss Scott faced architectural problems quite out of the ordinary. She had to submit plans for an up-to-date theatre

For an island site in a small and low-built fifteenth century town, a large modern playhouse which would harmonize with its surroundings. Fake Tudor was an evasion of the difficulty which she properly disdained. As to the problems hinted at in the foregoing lines, . . . [there was] the added problems of foreseeing any and every fashion in which Shakespeare may be worthily performed by succeeding generations, ...[23]

[22] The Committee of Judges had no way of knowing whether the plan under inspection was the work of a man or a woman.

[23] Jellicoe, G. A. *The Shakespeare Memorial Theatre, Stratford-upon-Avon.* (Foreword by W. Bridges-Adams). Publisher, Ernest Benn, Ltd. London. 1933. p. VIII.

While the theatre was going up, English newspapers withheld praise, a few going so far as to print satirical comments from men and women in the street. But when the great structure was finished, approval came from unexpected sources. *The Times* of London, on April 22, 1932, reported that everything in the way of decoration

> Is addressed to creating in the audience the mood of well-being that is favourable to the appreciation of what is taking place on the stage. Just as the stage machinery conduces to ease of production, so the decorations conduce to ease of appreciation. There are no distractions, and everything is strictly relevant to the architectural character of the building.

The *Manchester Guardian* of April 25, 1932, was even more eloquent when it said:

> Of course all those who think that good architecture is something with 'knobs on' will resent the absolute rejection of 'ye olde' and the plain functional solidity of the new theatre. . . . The result is that Stratford has now the finest working theatre in England. For it has been planned as no other in this country, with ample resources to meet the workaday requirements of the producer and the actor as well as the comfort of the audience.

The foundation stone was laid on July 2, 1929, and the theatre was formally opened on April 23, 1932, by H.R.H., the Prince of Wales. Unpleasant comments concerning the practical, very up-to-date theatre at Stratford-on-Avon, will probably be heard for many years to come. As heretofore suggested, a good theatre conforms to no ordinary conditions; even its outline seldom conforms to geometrical terminology. It is a place of make-believe.

Young people of today cannot possibly understand the great thrill that came to English women (the writer was in London at the time), when a woman-architect was presented to the world as an outstanding genius. Miss Scott still wears a halo, for the people of England do not forget great achievements. But she has taken success as a part of every-day happenings, now being connected with the firm of A. J. Seal & Partners, in Bournemouth. This architect was kind enough to express her views on professional life for the writer (December 7, 1957). She said: "I would not like to speak for women architects generally, but I do not think many have maintained themselves in private practice. On the other hand, there have been rather good opportunities for salaried architects since the war, both in England and over-seas, and I think there is very little prejudice now against the employment of women." To continue, Miss Scott thinks that women, as a group, like professional work that can be combined with home life. The foregoing comment from an able architect covers the situation quite well.

Of course, there is the problem of wages, women receiving less pay than men in all departments of architectural service. But the word has gone out that this abuse is to be corrected. The proposal is this: to give women a gradual equalization of pay, with the promise of full equality in the nineteen-sixties. There are overtones of uncertainty here, but it is a move in the right direction. For conditions must be improved. In looking back, the question is, how women have kept going in a society that was not only selfish, but completely deaf to reason. For the price of food, lodging, and bus fare is the same for everyone, sex playing no part. The answer lies perhaps in the thinking of so many Latin poets: strength comes with struggle.

Another woman, Mary L. J. Wall, also became a well-known architect. She received her preparatory education in good private schools, and then entered the Architectural Association School in London. In a letter (November 29, 1959) to the writer, Miss Wall said, "I became an Associate of the R.I.B.A. in 1930, and practised independently from 1932 to 1934—chiefly reconditioning Hobbing Hill slums, and from 1934 to 1939 there was a good patch in Robert Atkinson's office where I did a lot of interesting work (flats, film studios, etc.) at high speed." Then came a break: driving an ambulance, and holding a Top Secret job with the Government. This was a difficult time for everyone. However, the late nineteen-forties brought a certain normalcy in both social and business life. It was then that Miss Wall began teaching in a school of arts and crafts. She covered such subjects as building construction, and the history of architecture, carrying on in this way for three years full-time, and for eight years part-time. This architect says of her profession: "Architectural practise is a thermometer of international conditions."

Kathleen A. Veitch, a very successful architect, was born in 1907, just when women were being freed from what amounted to a helpless existence. As a young girl in school, Kathleen showed a marked aptitude for drawing and arithmetic, and for this reason was advised by her teachers to enter the Architectural Association School in Bedford Square, London. She proved to be a good pupil, winning the Owen Travelling Scholarship for Colour Decoration. Her travels amounted to a course in graduate work, for the time was spent in the study of Spanish tiles, a subject used later in a required composition. During the war years (1939–1943), this architect worked on miscellaneous projects in the building line: army canteens, ambulance rooms, air-raid shelters, and bomb-shaken cottages. These assignments proved to be a rich source of experience, and later on, Miss Veitch was able to establish her own office. She was fortunate in that World War II had provided a boon to architects. Enemy operations had produced a shelter-pinch of large proportions.

A question often asked is this: What part of career work has been the most rewarding? As for architecture, this sincere answer came to me from Miss Veitch:

A satisfied client, of whom I am happy to say I have a considerable number, gives me the greatest satisfaction and when some one says, 'we are pleased with our house' it repays me for all the trials and anxieties of the process of nursing a building through the different stages, permits and construction. You may be interested in this small incident. I can remember thinking on one Christmas Day, 'three families are gathered round a Christmas tree in their *own* home this year who would still have been living uncomfortably in makeshift accommodations without my efforts in the past months.'[24]

[24] *Letter* in the writer's file. January 5, 1960.

In discussing a woman who has varied interests, it is safe to assume that she does not follow the crowd. These few words suggest the career of Jessica M. Albery, an architect who has many ties in London. Miss Albery comes from a family of intellectuals, two members having been successful dramatists. Her father was a member of Parliament for more than twenty years, and was knighted by King George V for service beyond the line of duty. Jessica led the life of many upper-class English girls; she studied at home under a governess, and when eighteen years of age, took what was known as a "finishing course" on the Continent. Her studies so far, did not satisfy her aspirations as to a life career and when most of her friends were starting out on a social career, or making plans for marriage, Jessica began serious work at the Architectural Association School in London. In 1931, just when she was ready to practice, the business depression had disrupted the economy and it was almost impossible to find employment. However, through the kindness of friends, a temporary job was obtained.

The following year brought openings of another kind: Miss Albery entered the Civil Service, first with the Ministry of Town Planning, and later with the Kent County Council. As is so often the case, architects become very unhappy with the subtle politics in civil administration and leave the service for employment which offers more freedom of expression in their chosen profession. So it was that Jessica Albery made another change, this time becoming a full-time teacher at the Brighton School of Building. She described her activities thus: "I teach building construction, specification, and town planning principles and history to architects and surveyers, and I also carry on a small private practice."[25] In 1949 this teacher-architect adopted two small boys, one a baby four months old. This short review[26] reflects a time-tested truth: life offers a wealth of opportu-

---

[25] *Letter* in the writer's file. November 15, 1959.

[26] Concerning women-architects of today, Miss Albery says, ". . . of the 12 known to me personally, six are married, and six are single."

nity. But the initiative rests with the individual to recognize the demands of the time and occasion and blaze his or her own path to
achievement and happiness.

Another success story features Jocelyn Frere Adburgham. She
was born May 24, 1900. Her parents' home was located far down a
valley in the County of Surrey. There was a scenic quality about the
surroundings: "heather carpeting the hills, gypsies camping in the
pine forests down the road."

From her father, no doubt, Jocelyn inherited a love of creative
work, coupled with a spirit of uncommon strength. For Edmund W.
Adburgham became editor of the Hull *Daily Mail* when he was only
twenty-three years of age. One year later, he went to London where
he founded the *Architectural Review* (a quarterly) and the *Architects
Journal*, both attaining great success in the years that followed, and
still today, leading architectural publications.

Very little education was available in the local schools, and at the
age of five, Jocelyn was sent to a boarding school in Guildford—a
market place to the West. Along with her studies in reading, writing, and arithmetic, she acquired some knowledge in the art of
gardening—that is, she was allowed time off from classes to help the
gardener with the flower beds. Years later, Miss Adburgham wrote:

> I like to think, and believe it to be true, that the peaceful convent garden, . . .
> encouraged the conscious interest in gardening and landscape that resulted in my
> becoming a Fellow of the Institute of Landscape Architects.[27]

Before Mr. Adburgham realized what was happening, his two
small daughters—having spent so much time with the nuns—began
to converse in French instead of English. Another school was selected; it was located in Putney, a suburb of London. Any number of
courses were offered, but the time-table stressed natural history,
with field trips and tadpole-catching in the weedy ditches around
Barnes and Wimbledon Commons.

[27] *Letter* in the writer's file. May 23, 1960.

Two years later the Adburgham family moved to Hampton-on-Thames, and three of the children were registered in the local schools. It was a fortunate change, for Jocelyn began to work in a painting class. She wrote that

It is to these classes and the comprehension of colour and form exhibited by the Art Mistress that I think it is possible to trace my interest in decoration in relation to building.[28]

Continuing her studies, she entered the Notting Hill High School in London. This school belonged to the Girls Public Day School Trust. Instruction was given in the usual subjects including literature with emphasis on poetry, and botany and chemistry—both favourite subjects.

Various aspects of city life in London affected Jocelyn acutely. She never forgot the sight of "hunger marchers," a long line of drab, forlorn-looking men making their way up Holland Park Avenue. Miss Adburgham wrote,

Perhaps it was due to the deep impression this cavalcade made, that years after I became a founder of the Housing Centre whose *raison d'etre* is fundamentally, the eradification of slums, and the improvement of the emenities of the living quarters of people at large.[29]

Jocelyn entered Bedford College in the autumn of 1917. It was a special concession as she was the youngest student enrolled. This college is a branch of the University of London. It was during this interval as a student in the college that this keen-minded English girl learned to appreciate architecture of the Regency Period, the view from her window being over the lake to the famous terraces of park in the Regency idiom. This fondness still persists. Later, she studied at the London School of Arts and Crafts, giving special attention to the various types of pen and brush work, and measured drawing for architectural use. By now it was evident that this young woman was preparing herself for work in a special field.

[28] *Letter* in the writer's file. May 23, 1960.
[29] *Ibid.*

It was not long before Jocelyn found employment with a well-known firm of architects in London, specializing in marine architecture—and particularly, the interior arrangement of ships. Among the assignments were ships of the "Empress class," owned by the Canadian Pacific Railways and Shipping Lines. Often the work of refurbishing had to be done between sailings, under pressure of time and with attendant labor problems. Jocelyn was faced with trying tasks—but it was a good beginning.

Time passed, leaving a wealth of experience in its trail. As for likes and dislikes, Miss Adburgham is an architect who denies preferences of any kind. She considers herself fortunate in having been commissioned to do many different types of work: schools, factories, private and local authority houses, restoration of period towns and construction of a number of farm buildings—the latter projects often turning out to be rehabilitation or repair jobs—and restoration of period houses to preserve them from demolition.

Miss Adburgham was the *first woman* to be elected to membership in the Town Planning Institute—as an associate member in 1928, and as a full member in 1948. In 1932, she became a partner in the firm of W. R. Davidge & Partners, Planning Consultants, in London. Recalling the events of the past few decades, Miss Adburgham wrote:

> It seems unreal now to think that since then I have been a member of the Town Planning Institute Council, have served on the Education Practice, Library and Membership Committees, and as one of the Examiners of the Candidates who submit testimony of study for their qualifications; represent the Institute on the Council which directs the Town Planning Summer School . . . and toward the end of the last war served on the Royal Academy Planning Committee.[30]

A coveted goal was reached that same year (1932) when she became a Licentiate of the Royal Institute of British Architects. In 1956, she was elected a Fellow of the Institute of Landscape Architects.

[30] *Letter* in the writer's file. May 23, 1960.

After World War II, the British Government recognized the need for a well-regulated building program to cope with the problem of rehabilitating towns and cities badly damaged by enemy air raids. To meet this emergency, the Dudley Committee was established whose terms of reference were, among others, to make a thorough study, and report on all aspects of the housing situation in relation to the design and equipment of dwellings. Miss Adburgham was asked to assist on the Committee. Evidence was gathered from all parts of England in order to determine the needs of a people sorely-pressed for living accommodations.

Not long ago, Miss Adburgham accepted an unusual assignment; she undertook the rebuilding and re-location of an old windmill from Partridge Green at Gatwick Manor, now a famous inn on the Brighton Road. The mill was built in the last half of the eighteenth century, and is described as "a smock mill (one in which the cap and sails only revolve, as opposed to a post mill, in which the whole structure revolves about a central post)."[31]

The framework was still in good condition. It had a beautifully shaped cap, and stood nearly fifty feet high; the diameter of the sweeps being seventy feet. Gear wheels, including the nine-foot diameter brake wheel, were made of hornbeam timber. Here was an odd assortment of woodwork which had to be moved to a new location, and it had to be handled with great care. Parts of the main frame were sawed from side to side, and each of the octagonal pieces broken down completely—this being the most practical solution of the cartage problem. Thus, a rejuvenated windmill was to be set in motion again by the fitful winds after careful re-assembly by a long established family of mill-wrights.

Miss Adburgham is still active in her profession. Her duties are manifold, many having to do with calls for advice on various building regulations; as an expert witness in Town Planning appeals, and as a designer of layouts and landscape concepts.

[31] *The Woman Engineer.* Vol. VIII. No. 14. London. Autumn, 1959.

In discussing English women in any profession during the first half of the twentieth century, it is well to remember that they have faced uncommon difficulties. Consider the case of Enid Mary Wilmot. She was born in Solihull, Warwickshire, the daughter of W. H. Wilmot, a manufacturing silversmith. As for education, this followed a familiar pattern: she had a governess from the age of three to five, a preparatory school from five to eleven, a secondary school from eleven to eighteen—the last mentioned being the Edgbaston Church of England College for girls in Birmingham. After deciding upon a career, Enid undertook a somewhat unusual schedule—that is, she interrupted her period of formal training at the Brighton School of Architecture for one year of steady employment in an architect's office.[32] It was a good approach to more serious work.

In 1933, Enid became a member of the Royal Institute of British Architects, and was ready to practice independently; but she was faced with a serious business depression. She wrote:

> At the time I qualified, the architectural profession was at a very low ebb and it was extremely difficult to find work. My name was one of many on a register kept by the Birmingham Architectural Society and eventually my turn came. The inquiry was from an office where no woman had been employed before—not even as a secretary. But they agreed for the sake of fairness, to give me a fortnight's trial at a very small salary. I am able to say that during that fortnight I was able to break down the prejudice, and at the end was offered a substantial rise in salary, although now it would not be accepted by even an unqualified architect.[33]

This goes to show how men, in at least one office, had to change their ideas concerning women-workers—their prejudice giving way to the calls of modern life. Continuing, she said:

> The war made a bad break in my experience. All private work ceased completely and my time was mostly spent on surveying courtyards and cellars in the slums of Birmingham with a view to their stability to provide air-raid shelters, and subsequently designing the necessary reinforcement for cellars or the design of

[32] This is the pattern of almost all co-operative programs of education.

[33] *Letter* in the writer's file. February 5, 1960. (There is another angle: English money had very good purchasing power in the nineteen-thirties.)

over-ground shelters; also inspection after air-raid damage. It meant miles of walking as no petrol was available.[34]

This upset in every-day life—the petrol shortage affecting everyone—came as a result of enemy action. In retrospect, some incidents had all the emotional overtones of the stage. But they were real, far too real for comfort. So it was that Enid Wilmot moved ahead, overcoming obstacles year by year.

A number of architectural firms have been established by families—usually a husband and wife partnership. A plan such as this requires considerable adjustment. Otherwise, one of the team will almost surely fall back as a helper, rather than a mainstay in the organization. Jane B. Drew (Mrs. Maxwell Frey) and her husband have been very successful in such a venture. This couple, in association with the French architect, Le Corbusier, designed the plans for the new capitol of East Punjab, India. It was a large undertaking with many complications, as officials of the Indian Government wanted designs that were modern in function, yet intricate in pattern. This demand reflected a devotion to the native arts. This new development started with practically nothing—just a plot of ground.

The project includes Government buildings, an industrial area, a hospital of 500 beds, five health centres, 15 nursery schools, 11 junior schools, 3 colleges, one of them residential, and six community centres, not to speak of 3,208 houses. The latter are designed to accommodate 15 different income groups, and the cheapest of these houses, consisting of two rooms (for the sweeper class), costs only £154 to build.[35]

To the many who have known only shanty-life, this building program has been a great blessing.

Designing houses for the English people presented a very different problem for Miss Drew. A question often asked is this: Should people of refined taste eat in the kitchen? This practice does save time.

[34] *Letter* in the writer's file. February 5, 1960.
[35] *The Woman's Service Library.* 27 Wilfred Street, London, S.W. 1. April 24, 1957.

For those families who have no objection to this practice, she has designed modern cook-rooms that are large and afford plenty of room to move about and have real prettiness, as well as a liveable quality. Fancy shelves are built along one or two sides of the room so that the housewife can display her fine china—a reminder perhaps of childhood elegance. This idea is proving to be of practical value as well. In one house she had installed a larkspur-blue glass hood over the kitchen range—while decorative, it also deals effectively with unpleasant fumes. This architect does not like the wholesale similarity of modern American kitchen units. However, standardization does offer convenience at low cost to many people.

Mary D. Wales may also be classed with the women pioneers in the field of architecture. She is the daughter of a medical practitioner who lived in Shipley, a village not far from Skipton. Mary was carefully educated by indulgent parents. She went to "a day school until 13, then to a boarding school, Brentwood, Southport (60 miles away on the coast)."[36] She completed a five-year course in a school of architecture, followed by three years of apprenticeship in an architect's office—this last fruitful period being spent in the city of Leeds. To an outsider, the career of Mrs. Wales, who became a Fellow of the Royal Institute of British Architects in 1956, appears ideal in every respect. She has a private practice among old acquaintances ". . . in a Country Market Town in the 'Dales' part of Yorkshire, and the work is scattered, which entails spending quite a lot of time travelling [seeing to] houses, village halls, alterations or extension to schools, shops, public houses, office premises, small factories, garages and farms."[37] In addition, Mrs. Wales has the added responsibility of inspecting churches,[38] and looking after repairs and alterations to halls, schools and homes. She does all this with a small

[36] *Letter* in the writer's file. November 16, 1959.

[37] *Ibid.*

[38] Mary D. Wales is the only woman employed at this time as a Diocesan Surveyor—that is, by the Church of England.

working force—two male assistants and one female secretary. It is always interesting to know how different people provide different backgrounds for their work-a-day lives. This particular firm has offices in the gate-house of Skipton Castle, a beautiful pile of masonry dating from the year 1100.

Elizabeth M. Thomas comes from a long line of professional people. Like many English girls and boys, she had to live in a boarding school during the years when her father, a civil servant, was occupied with duties abroad. After finishing secondary school work, and a secretarial course, Elizabeth entered the Architectural Association School in Bedford Square, London. She passed the R.I.B.A. External Final Examination in 1938. Her story is typical of a number of women architects: a period of employment, followed by marriage and ten years in the role of wife and mother—four sons taking up much of her time. But an education is seldom wasted. Since 1953, Mrs. Thomas has been kept busy on what she calls "a free and easy basis." Her practice is concerned mainly with garden and landscape design. She explains, "I work eight to nine months in a year, and this is . . . just enough to make both ends meet and employ a woman to keep the house clean."[39] This is a brief report of an English woman who has managed to merge wifely duties with the demands of a career.

The big question fifty years ago was whether young girls should enter the business world, or give serious thought to marriage in the not too distant future. College students have been interviewed often in order to get their first-hand opinions on the subject. The problem has gradually resolved itself. Women have graduated from college, married, raised a family of children, and then picked up the threads of earlier days as a matter of course. This is a severe test in adjustment, but women have responded courageously to changed conditions. This ability to set things right surprises some male observers—army life being an example. Some professions lend themselves to change much better than others—architecture belongs in this category.

[39] *Letter* in the writer's file. November 22, 1959.

The previous commentary, in one instance at least, suggests the career of Margaret MacDonald (Lady Casson), the daughter of a physician in South Africa. This young girl spent very little time in her native land as she was sent to a boarding school in England at the age of eleven. This was the time when young girls were beginning to feel the urge for more freedom.[40] After completing work in a secondary school, Margaret went to London for training in architecture, finishing the required course of study in 1936. What promised to be an agreeable occupation was interrupted by her marriage in 1938. Thereafter family obligations—the care of three children—occupied most of her day-to-day activities. It was not until 1947 that this architect could turn again to the practice of her profession. She has been ". . . mainly interested in interior work of all kinds—domestic, offices, exhibitions, display showrooms [and] a certain amount of designing in china and glass ware."[41] Lady Casson has been a tutor in the School of Interior Design at the Royal College of Art since 1952.

The following sketch will introduce Elaine C. Denby, who belongs to a later group of professional women. A half-century has passed since the "ladies Charles," most certainly the pioneers, took up the study of architecture. Elaine is the daughter of Robert Coventry Denby, a well-known solicitor (lawyer) in Bradford, Yorkshire. As a young girl she was sent to the Casterton School, near Kirkby, in Westmoreland. (Charlotte Brontë attended this school— later injecting many intimate details of student life into the story of *Jane Eyre*.) Possibly, the appreciation of art came from the maternal side of Elaine's family, several members having had the zeal to carry on creative work in a "mild way." In this household architecture stood out as a worthwhile profession. Elaine spent five years in the Leeds School of Architecture, qualifying for practice in 1947. The following years she worked in both private and public situations,

[40] The movement to educate girls was gaining in popularity, not only in England, but elsewhere in the world.

[41] *Letter* in the writer's file. October 11, 1959.

being employed at one time by a local authority—the City of West-minster—in London. But apparently these activities were only stepping-stones to independent practice, and in due time, Miss Denby was able to set up her own office. This was no doubt a wise move—the satisfaction of individual effort outweighing the trying problems faced by persons engaged in the building industry. For the majority of women architects, their job contracts do tend to be domestic in character. Friends say that at times, Miss Denby longs for a broader field—perhaps designing an up-to-date theatre, a playhouse of dreams. Elizabeth Denby is one of the few architects who has turned to writing. She has contributed articles for the popular magazine, *Ideal Home*, and book reviews for various other publications. Also, she has produced a colorful book for a paint firm. This short review portrays a checkered career.

It is a joke among members of the Royal Institute of British Architects, that lady architects "lose no time" in getting married. Of the women in practice, about 40 per cent or, two out of five, were married according to an informal survey made by the R.I.B.A. in the nineteen-fifties. It takes courage for an educated woman to take on the role of wife, mother, housewife and wage-earner. For often the scales are weighted—the woman, not the man, cooking and washing the dishes[42] after the day's work in office or factory is finished. But social workers in England say that men in the upper-middle-class are gradually assuming a greater share of responsibility in the home. This may be the solution to a serious domestic problem.

In conclusion, there should be some words of commendation for the Royal Institute of British Architects. Briefly, this organization stands ever ready to give special honors for special achievements. The Institute may admit as

Honorary Associates any person not professionally engaged in practice as architects who by reason of their position or of their eminence in art, science,

---

[42] Yet it is an old custom for a man to wash a dish: ". . . as a man wipeth a dish, wiping it, and turning it upside down." *Holy Bible: Old Testament.* II Kings 21:13.

literature or any other matter or of their interest in matters relating to architecture, the Council may consider eligible for that honor.[43]

There have been eighty-five British subjects singled out for this tribute-of-praise in recent years. The names of four women were included in the list: Mrs. Marjorie Queennell (1938), Miss Elizabeth M. Denby (1942), Miss M. S. Macdonald-Taylor (1946), and Miss Joan Evans (1950). The Institute also gives proper consideration to other architects—not British subjects—who have made worthwhile contributions to the building industry.

Another regulation, somewhat gracious in character, is this: any Fellow, Associate, or Licentiate who has reached the age of fifty-five, and has retired, subject to the approval of the Council, may be transferred without election to what is known as a "special class." As far as women are concerned, the list of retired personnel follows: Fellows -o-; Associates -1- (Miss Anne Farewell Jones, elected in 1927); Licentiates -3- (Miss Florence Fulton Hobson, elected in 1911, Miss Winifred Barbara Ackworth, elected in 1934, and Mrs. Ella Briggs, elected in 1948).[44] The architects who give up practice are still a part of the main organization, having the privilege of reading in the library, and attending all business meetings, but they are not allowed to vote on any matter pertaining to architectural policy.

According to an informal Census of the nineteen-fifties, there were 658 women belonging to the Royal Institute of British Architects—a commendable record. These newcomers do especially well with projects demanding ingenuity, imagination, and that priceless virtue called patience. Women entered this exacting profession when mechanical inventions were reshaping the industrial pattern— splendor giving way to utility. The devastation of towns and cities caused by World War II, and its aftermath, offered unparalleled opportunity to women architects to practice in their chosen field. Much was lost, but much has been gained.

[43] The R.I.B.A. *Kalendar.* 1957–1958. 66 Portland Place, London. W.1.
[44] *Ibid.*

VII. Engineering

ENGINEERING, as a profession, requires a brief survey of past events—that is, how human beings have solved their problems from the dawn of history to the present time. Men have always had an inner craving for mechanical devices. They began by making chisels, planes, saws, even a pulley that could hoist bodies of great bulk and weight.

> Man, [said the professor in *Sartor Resartus*] is a tool-using animal . . . Feeblest of bipeds! Three quintals are a crushing load for him; . . . Nevertheless he can use tools, can devise tools: with these the granite mountain melts into dust before him; he kneads glowing iron, as if it were soft paste; seas are his smooth highways, winds and fire his unwearying steeds. Nowhere do you find him without Tools; without Tools he is nothing, with Tools he is all.[1]

The engineer of today might have profited from the great projects of long ago, but unfortunately, little is known of technical work as carried on by man in the earlier stages of civilization. Writers rely upon guess-work to some extent for facts concerning the Pyramids — how heavy hauling was done, how tools were shaped. No doubt a saw and tubular drill played some part in these imposing structures. Archæologists more or less agree that the blades of the saws were made of bronze—green stains having been found on the saw-cuts, and also on the refuse scattered about the pits. As for the common chisels used by all masons, these are not to be found in any of the tombs. It is quite possible that tools would be classed with national wealth, and passed on from one government worker to another.

From the beginning of time, machines have had one function in common: they are mechanisms put together to help men in the performance of their work. Therefore, the stout stick, the grooved wheel, and the twisted rope were implements in transportation in

[1] Carlyle, Thomas. *Sartor Resartus*. The Macmillan Company. New York. MCMXXVII. p. 32.

ancient times, as the modern locomotive, with its massive body and power-driven engine, is in modern civilization.

Engineering projects carried out centuries before the Christian era by methods unknown today are referred to as "archæological wonders," *i.e.*, the huge boulders brought to England from a foreign land and erected in a semi-circular group at Stonehenge. Self-exaltation was the motivation sometimes which brought about these archæological wonders—many rulers having monuments erected to perpetuate the family name.

It is clear that in England engineering lagged behind other professions. Of course, there were occasions when repairs had to be made on roads, bridges, and harbors; but little was done in the way of reclamation until the seventeenth century. Most likely, the elders of towns and cities held meetings from time to time, and then adjourned without making any plans for really worthwhile improvements. It was the old story: fear of criticism by a tax-conscious community.

Finally, the Thames embankment started to crumble in no uncertain way. This unexpected catastrophe became a source of great embarrassment to the Crown, and Charles I (1625) employed Vermuyden, a Dutch engineer, to make the repairs. The restoration was such a gigantic operation that it dragged on year after year, and was not finished until the early part of the nineteenth century. The people on this island have had anything but an easy time with their engineering projects because so much of the land is low, flat, and water-soaked by sluggish streams making their way to the sea. It has been more or less a question of where the sea starts and the land ends.

Considerable praise for construction work must go to the Benedictine monks, for they were not only ambitious, but extremely capable. These churchmen could always get a closely-knit group of workers together, and a building started was almost always finished. Little is heard of labor shortages until the Tudor period, when really skilled artisans were required for the growing export trade. This upset in business life necessitated changes in manual training. As a consequence, hundreds of half-grown boys were given instruction in the different trades. They were called apprentices, and treated like undisciplined children.

The guilds kept a watchful eye over everything; how the products were being made; how the workers were conducting themselves. Instead of an examination, as required in schools and colleges today, the student was asked to "submit a proof-piece." For example,

[The Needleworkers expected] . . . a display of 500 needles of different sizes, and the Shoemakers required four pairs of shoes, while other guilds gave the applicant freedom of choice. In some cases test work was required, and an apprentice applying for admission to the Clothworkers Company had to work for three days in the Common Hall of the Guild under the supervision of the Master Wardens.[2]

Without doubt, customs were being scrutinized—the Baconian method. Examine the following table (people being asked to use the human hand as an expression of length):

The Digit, ...equals 1 part
Palm or hand reach, ...equals 4 parts
Span, ...equals 12 parts
Foot, ...equals 16 parts
Cubit, ...equals 24 parts
Step or single pace, ...equals 40 parts
Double pace, ...equals 80 parts
Fathom, ...equals 96 parts[3]

Even today, it is a common sight to see a woman-shopper measure a remnant of cloth from finger-tip to shoulder—the correct length being easily reckoned in this way. After a time, standard yards were adopted by Parliament. This legislation was covered in two Acts: the first in 1824, the second in 1878. The principle of fine measure-

[2] The Woman Engineer. London. Winter. 1953.

[3] Hallock, William and Wade, Herbert T. Outlines of the Evolution of Weights and Measures and the Metric System. The Macmillan Company. New York. 1906. p. 6.

ment is the basis of all engineering work, for errors involving the fraction of an inch can upset the most painstaking calculations.

The first English engineers undertook work which was quite beyond their understanding. Therefore, it was thought wise to form some kind of an organization for the exchange of ideas. So it was that in 1818 the Institution of Civil Engineers was started, and it proved to be a wise step in the new, ever-changing profession. The first Charter, dated June 3, 1828, describes an engineer's work as,

The art of directing the Great Sources of Power in Nature for the use and convenience of man, as the means of production and of traffic in states both for external and internal trade, as applied in the construction of roads, bridges, aqueducts, canals, river navigation and docks, for internal intercourse and exchange, and in the construction of ports, harbours, moles, breakwaters and lighthouses, and in the art of navigation by artificial power for the purposes of commerce, and in the construction and adaptation of machinery, and in the drainage of cities and towns. . . .[4]

This short comprehensive document was framed in the reign of George the Fourth.

The various ways of applying mechanical devices are visible on all sides: the transport of goods by sea, rail, air; the transmission of messages by telegraph, telephone, and later by radio. It was the adoption of steam as a tractive power which lifted England out of the doldrums, economically speaking. A serious unemployment problem had long plagued Government officials. This condition was especially noticeable after 1815 — a post-war period. For then it was that a large number of sailors and soldiers were thrown back on a soil that could not support them.

The demand for better transportation relieved the situation, and before long men were being transported from isolated districts to build the first railway. Indeed, more than ". . . fifteen thousand persons found employment on the line which was laid down between

---

[4] *The Institution of Civil Engineers. Charter. Supplemental Charters, By-Laws and Regulations.* Published by the Institution. London. 1935. p. 5.

London and Liverpool.''[5] Strangely enough, many influential citizens held out to the last for horse-power, as opposed to steam power. These events, far reaching in importance, took place a few years before Queen Victoria came to the Throne.

It must not be forgotten that improved ways of handling iron and steel have played a large part in the development of machinery. At first, the method of producing iron was extremely crude—the local smith building a fire, and then heating and stirring a mass of refuse-laden ore until it was almost free of impurities. Further kneading produced a usable product—known to the trade as "wrought iron." This metal was so scarce that manufacturers kept it under guard at all times. To ease the situation, English machinists copied a German furnace which was fired by coal instead of wood. This was a boon to the home industry, as the supply of timber was decreasing rapidly, while the supply of coal was quite enough to satisfy all requirements. As a result, important smelting works were moved from the wooded areas to the coal fields.

If there is any romance in cutlery, it began at Sheffield when the townspeople heard of a clockworker who could make steel that was both soft and workable, far superior to anything produced on the Continent. The process was finally uncovered by stealth. It was on a winter night that the artisan was approached:

> An old beggar appeared at the door of the works and begged to be allowed to enter, and as he soon fell asleep, the work continued apparently unobserved. The 'beggar' was a neighboring iron founder, who, whilst feigning sleep, observed all the details of the process. Other works in Sheffield began immediately to make steel by this method . . . practised with little alteration at the present day.[6]

All of these trial and error operations signalled the opening of an inventive period.

Engineering, as a profession, continued to make progress, and in

[5] Fleming, A. P. M. and Brocklehurst, H. J. *A History of Engineering.* A. & C. Black, Ltd London. 1925. pp. 164–165.
[6] *Ibid.* p. 178.

another fifty years a new kind of fuel was attracting attention. Indeed, the advantage of gas was all but shouted from the housetops; it was said that arrangements could be made "to have every apartment lighted and heated from the kitchen or from the wash-house, whichever proves the most convenient."[7] But people were skeptical; they refused to invest money in such an undertaking—oil, wax, and tallow being both plentiful and satisfactory. In spite of opposition, a Parliamentary Committee was set up to investigate the idea of lighting the streets of London by gas.

'Do you mean to tell us,' asked a legislator, 'that it will be possible to have a light without a wick?'

'Yes, I do, indeed,' answered the witness.

'Oh, my friend, . . . You are trying to prove too much.'[8]

Time does not stand still, and by 1850, even small villages were lighted by gas. One individual reported that on a dark night the face of his watch "stood out clear as anything near a public lamp."

Some time elapsed before gas was used for power. On the whole, England "muddled through" the gas age fairly well; but she was very reluctant when it came to the use of petrol. It cannot be doubted that the motor industry was held back several decades by short-sighted legislators. Consider the following:

It was not until 1896 that the Act was repealed which limited the speed of motor vehicles traveling British roads to 4 miles an hour. This Act required that each vehicle should be in charge of three persons, one walking in front carrying a red flag (hence known as the Red Flag Act), . . . The ruling for travel in towns was even more drastic; 2 miles per hour being the limit of speed allowed.[9]

The idea was sound, as pedestrians did need some protection from the "power-buggies" which were soon to dot the highways. It is well

[7] Fleming, A. P. M. and Brocklehurst, H. J. *A History of Engineering*. A. & C. Black, Ltd London. 1925. p. 212.

[8] *Ibid.* p. 219.

[9] *Ibid.* p. 219.

to remember that the law-makers had no thought of self-gain, only a fervent desire to protect the public.

Then came social disturbances of other kinds. The English housewife had just settled down to the use of gas equipment, when along came electrical appliances. A strange force had been thrust upon the world—doing away to a great extent with back-breaking drudgery. Mechanical servants were about to revolutionize industry; they stood for good, efficient service in a day when labor groups were becoming difficult to manage. But an invention is not just a gadget; it must have value as a social tool. Often it is a device so simple that people remark, "how strange that no one ever thought of it before." Electricity is more expensive than gas, but the extra cost is offset by greater cleanliness.

The rise of the motor-car industry paved the way for aeroplane development, the cumulative process working as usual—one invention indicating the method for another. Men had thought about flying through the air for centuries—stories of these attempts being both legendary and historical. At first, scientists used balloons,[10] but these contrivances were always dangerous, their great size making them susceptible to fog, hail, and high winds. Aeroplanes could not be made to stay aloft because the propelling equipment was too heavy for the machine's lifting capacity.

In the development of original ideas, there exists a clear-cut ratio between free and slave civilizations. For it is no secret that during the past one hundred years, practically all of the important inventions and new ways of doing things have come from people born to a free way of life in the North Atlantic area—France, Britain, and the United States. These countries have produced seventy per cent of the world's inventions and yet in 1950 they totalled only ten per cent of the world's population.[11] This has long been a delicate subject with

[10] In the nineteen-thirties, the writer sat on the roof of Johnson Hall, Columbia University, until long after midnight in order to see the Graf Zeppelin pass over New York City.

[11] *Freedom and Union*. Vol. 2, No. 11. December, 1956. Washington, D. C., U.S.A.

nations employing slave labor. It is one reason why the Russians make so many false claims.

Too little has been said about the way nature creeps into laboratory experiments[12]—oysters for the hinge, lobsters for the pincer, mosquitoes for the hypodermic-needle, humming-birds for the gyroscope. It all sounds simple, but the way is anything but smooth. A scientist may work for years on end, only to be defeated by a missing-link—that is, the means by which a device or project can serve a useful purpose.

It sometimes happens that truths which have barely been indicated will strike several people at once. Sleepless nights may follow for a few research workers. Consider an actual situation: Elisha Gray (1835–1901), and Alexander Graham Bell (1847–1922) discovered the telephone simultaneously—the two applications reaching the United States Patent Office only a few hours apart. An event of this kind presents a problem for all concerned. There is nothing to do but consult notebooks on day-to-day operations—really "case histories." A heart-break for some one is quite in order.

A thing assumed in default of knowledge is usually greeted with distrust. Wilbur Wright (1862–1912), and Orville Wright (1871–1948) had to face downright ridicule during their years of research in Dayton, Ohio—the neighbors having plenty to say about "those fly-minded mechanics who keep their lights burning all night." But scorn was no deterrent. The two brothers never lost sight of a coveted goal: to build a flying machine. At last, they brought out a tiny craft that could stay in the air for several minutes.[13] Shortly thereafter, the Wrights made a few exhibition flights.[14]

In spite of these achievements, the inventors received little recognition in their own country. Then in 1900, Wilbur left for France,

[12] *The Digest of World Reading.* "Nature Got There First." Published by the *Australian Digest.* Melbourne. April, 1956.

[13] The petrol engine finally gave aeroplanes a light and reliable source of power.

[14] There are people still living in Cincinnati, Ohio (U.S.A.) who witnessed one of these flights. Wilbur Wright took off from a small baseball field on lower Reading Road.

hoping to prove that travel by air was practical. This dream-plan worked out very well, for the young aviator made a spectacular trip over Paris—thousands of people watching the experiment. Without further ado, the American aviator was decorated with the French Legion of Honor. Officials in the United States suddenly awoke to the value of the new invention, buying several Wright machines for use in the Army. It is said that every important principle of modern aviation was introduced in those "first air ships." These small-town boys did not "grow-up" like Topsy; they were carefully nurtured by a scholarly father—a Bishop of the United Brethren Church.

One fact is clear from this discussion: men and women who delve into the unknown must have not only original ideas, but a hard shell of confidence. Fortunately, industry is making an effort to provide a suitable climate for "inventive people"—many large engineering firms maintaining costly research departments. A scientist is told what to invent, and proceeds to carry out the order to the best of his or her ability. At times, an invention is not practical from the standpoint of expense, but often a problem of this kind is corrected as new ways of production come into use.

It cannot be denied that inventions are producing chaos in society. Therefore, an important question arises: How shall children be educated? It is said that grammar schools stress the study of English, and pass over science as a non-essential for all but the gifted pupils. But facts must be faced. Today, England is greatly mechanized. All boys and girls should be taught how to investigate simple problems —this being an operation which ties in closely with pure science. As for girls, even the very young, take to systematized knowledge with enthusiasm. Teachers are often surprised at the "natural behaviour" of girls who are studying in technical schools—many of them reaching out for tools as though they were picking pins from a lace-covered cushion. Life in the twentieth century is unlike anything that has gone before. The idea now is to get out of old ruts and fit into new patterns, be it a way of thinking or a way of acting.

The House of Commons made a move in the right direction early in 1957 by taking notice of the need for scientific and technical education at all levels, matching to some extent the national program for automatic power. The plan is to increase the number of scientists and technologists now being produced in England each year, about 10,000, so that in 10 to 15 years it would be 20,000.[15] Additional signs appear along the way: "the number of boys and girls obtaining passes at advanced level in mathematics and physics had increased nearly 50 per cent between 1952 and 1956."[16] The following statement concerning *talented girls* became a part of legal record in 1957:

> There was a pretty big reserve of talent among girls untapped, and the matter presented a big social problem. There were a considerable number of occupations where girls could contribute to scientific and technical man-power. There was no closed door in such occupations, and it was reported that girls . . . found little difficulty in getting jobs.[17]

From time to time, there have been other considerations for the engineer. Great changes were wrought by the increased use of concrete. It is certain that buildings made of concrete demand considerable knowledge of mechanical principles—line and color taking second place. A great deal of work handled by the architect may eventually be turned over to the engineer. As one writer has said:

> The modern building, with the exception of the small house, has become an engineering structure. . . . The design of industrial buildings, theatres, public halls, large blocks of flats, garages, railway stations and bridges has become essentially the work of the structural engineer, the services of the architect being only required in regard to facial and internal decoration where these are needed.[18]

Possibly this view is too pessimistic, yet the rows of "skyscrapers" going up all over England do suggest a definite change in methods of construction. To the layman, many modern buildings

---

[15] *The Times Educational Supplement.* London. March, 1957.

[16] *Ibid.*

[17] *Ibid.*

[18] *The Architect and Building News.* Iliffe Technical Publications, Ltd. Dorset House. Stanford Street, London, S.E. 1. November, 1957.

suggest little more than the block-houses of nursery days. This effect is due, in part, to the installation of air-conditioning, which has revolutionized the technique of bringing fresh air into homes and offices.

Since concrete is now taking an important place in construction work, many young people look upon imitation stone as something new. But it was widely used by the Romans—their volcanic ash being ideal for this purpose. The value of Italian cement lies in the fact that it hardens under water—the ash being taken from pits in the Campagna.[19] The discovery of concrete was a god-send to untrained builders, as they could cover up mistakes with large amounts of material. To some extent, engineers of today favor concrete—with its suggestion of solidity—for they prize low costs, coupled with massive effects. Early workers turned in due time to experimentation, building arches with longer spans, and fewer supports.

English builders as a group have been accused of timidity. In truth, it takes a bold person to face investment companies who are looking for more and more revenue from less and less space. Then too, men and women engaged in this line of work must contend with the ever-increasing cost of labor, and building codes which are constantly being changed. From sheer necessity, a company in London has erected a nineteen story apartment block with concrete bearing walls spaced at fourteen feet centers. These walls are only seven inches thick throughout their nearly two hundred feet height. To add to the wonder—and for the layman, fear—"only every other wall is reinforced."[20] To return to building codes, the approach of the Government has been anything but satisfactory. Far too often questions of change have come before voluntary groups who were unfamiliar with existing practices—to say nothing of the complex factors involved in the new technology.

[19] Lighthouses in many parts of the world rest on foundations of lava-concrete.
[20] *Sydney Morning Herald*. Sydney, Australia. March 6, 1956.

Some mention should be made of the various technical bodies in England, for in a way, they are the backbone of all engineering projects. The Institution of Civil Engineers, established in 1818, stands as the senior regulating body, and the qualifications obtained by passing its examinations have been generally recognized as having pride of place. Within recent years the increasing applications of science to all processes of engineering have made specialization inevitable, and have led to the formation of other bodies closely associated with scientific development. Following are a few examples:

Mechanical Engineers (1847), originating from events during the beginning of the era of steam locomotion; the Institution of Naval Architects (1860), associated with the first applications of steel construction to shipbuilding; and the Institution of Electrical Engineers (1871), associated with the early applications of electricity to telegraphy and telephony.[21]

The qualifications for the prospective engineer may be summed up as follows: (1) the passing of examinations; (2) the serving of a period of practical training as an engineer—in most cases not less than three years; (3) the attainment of a post of responsibility in engineering work. Individual circumstances vary the method of approach, but as a rule the ambitious girl or boy manages to hurdle the obstacles.

In creative work women have played a minor role through the centuries. It seems that they do best when working on home projects, especially kitchen equipment. But a career of this kind is anything but smooth sailing. Consider the neighbors in a section like Soho: they would not understand the girl who cluttered up her room and the family kitchen with odd parts of a gadget still unnamed—the usual procedure with boys. It is a question how far Madam Curie could have gone with the discovery of radium without the moral support of her husband. For make no mistake, this scientist worked at a

[21] *Engineering—Choice of Career Series*, No. 16. Printed and Published by His Majesty's Stationery Office. Adastral House, Kingsway, London. W.C. 2. 1936.

time—during the years prior to 1898—when women were not recognized as ingenious individuals.

The writer visited an exhibit of inventions in London some years ago, and found that many articles contrived by the wife had been invented by the husband. In the case of a knitting device, it was the woman whose eyes brightened while the invention was being demonstrated; it was the man who stood aside as a casual, somewhat indifferent observer. All in all, there is every reason why women should hold their own in the inventive field.

The unknown inventor may have some difficulty, for patents are not only hard to get, but hard to protect. An individual may struggle along in a make-shift laboratory—finally perfecting a really useful device—and then meet defeat—the invention being rejected. A semi-tragic event of this kind occurs when a contrivance does not satisfy the requirements of officials in a patent office, or the Courts where patent cases are appealed. An outstanding example of such a case occurred in the United States when ". . . the Supreme Court knocked out a patent on a device in wide use in supermarkets—an extended counter and a movable frame that enables the cashier to pull the customer's groceries alongside the cash register."[22] The finding on this contrivance sounds more like the cautious British, than the not-so-cautious Americans, as witness the following statement by Associate Justice William C. Douglas: "a patent must serve the ends of science, push back the frontiers."[23] This declaration must have been disheartening for any number of research students, especially those who had long been digging away on some pet project. As for controls, the inventor has few—a new idea often being exploited in a big way. Sometimes the filing of an application amounts to little more than a formality.

The writer recalls a college professor saying of her home city (population 700,000): "All this place needs is about twenty deaths."

[22] *United States News and World Report.* Dayton, Ohio, U.S.A. November 23, 1956.
[23] *Ibid.*

This somewhat airy remark was meant to infer that many prominent men were helpless in the face of social dislocations. To be more specific, the adjustments which have grown out of inventions are not easily understood. The thesis is, that different parts of culture do not change at the same rate, some going full tilt ahead, others remaining more or less static. Mr. William Fielding Ogburn has presented the idea in this way:

> Industry and education are correlated, hence a change in industry makes adjustments necessary through changes in the educational system. Industry and education are two variables, and if the change in industry occurs first and the adjustment through education follows, industry may be referred to as the independent variable, and education as the dependent variable.[24]

This state of affairs may go on for years and is usually looked upon as "one of those things," just an unfortunate upset in social and business life.

Without doubt, machines are the major factor in what is called industrial progress; they turn out the gadgets, small and large, which give to society its ever-increasing comforts. This remarkable performance is due, in part, to the complex interrelation between machines and the distribution of materials, a combination controlled by conveyors under electric power. Some of these devices perform not one, but dozens of tasks; they have been developed to save time and cut costs. This transfer of work from skilled hands to countless machines has given to the world what is known as *automation*. This operation is causing great concern—that is, How can an industrial shock like this be overcome? It could easily lead to social and economic disaster—really, a second industrial revolution.

Wives and daughters will suffer under this change in industry: (a) women working in factories will face a certain amount of unemployment; (b) women clerking in large retail establishments will find the demand for their services growing less; (c) women em-

[24] Ogburn, William Fielding. *Social Change*. The Viking Press. New York. 1950. p. 201.

ployed with a small number of workers will have a fair chance of sustained employment. It is certain that manufacturers will make every effort to reduce costs.

Although the Trades Union Congress is concerned over the spread of mechanical forces, it declines to accept the theory that change will lead to social distress. Wishful thinking often holds up the morale of individuals faced with troublesome problems. A hopeful attitude is reflected in a report presented at a meeting in Brighton, England, in 1956:

> Noting that automation has come to mean many things to many people, the council said that for some it was an evil force bringing mass unemployment and social upheaval; for others . . . it has been the key to Utopia and with nuclear energy would bring an age of plenty.[25]

What the council would like to see is a development of automation so gradual as to lessen the chance of labor distress. Although no one can foresee the future, it is fairly obvious that industry will undergo considerable transformation in the coming decades.

Social dislocation will surely come to the communities losing old-time companies. To prevent a major catastrophe, the Government will have to co-operate with labor leaders, a group not always sensitive to both sides of a question. More than likely, some kind of guaranteed wage will be introduced in one of the large industrial plants, and this move will form the pattern for companies less influential in the business world. It will be the old familiar story: management will bear the brunt of worry from beginning to end. But there is considerable hope in the new development, for automation may introduce greater strength in industry by stabilizing factors long uncertain. For instance:

> Piecemeal investment will not be possible. Long-range and total planning will become an industrial pattern. The labor force will be permanent, for it will require long training and precision skills to keep automotive units going.[26]

[25] The New York *Times*. U.S.A. August 21, 1956.
[26] The New York *Times*. U.S.A. June 28, 1956.

Possibly the use of displacement insurance might give manufacturers additional incentive to go ahead with technological improvements without fear of bankruptcy. For mechanical changes do not make a one-way street; both capital and labor will have to do their part in overcoming the inevitable confusion in business.

The impact of these developments will be felt in other fields. Parents have long faced the fact that many boys and girls dislike arithmetic—really a handmaiden of engineering. With this thought in mind, a research project was undertaken at Teachers College, Columbia University, New York City, to determine just what effect a calculating machine would have on the ability of children in the first grades of school work. To give publicity to the experiment, a group of young people appeared on television. A small girl was selected for the demonstration; she seated herself before a calculating machine, and with all the aplomb of a professional operator solved the following problem in a matter of seconds: 326 multiplied by 58 equals 18,908.[27]

While it is too early to form a definite conclusion about such an experiment, there is some indication that children in these special classes are taking more interest in arithmetic, and that they have less fear of a long line of figures. Then too, pupils in the elementary schools are being taught to do sums automatically, not to eliminate brain work, but to speed the solution of difficult problems. So it is that the machine age is changing educational methods for the smaller members of society.

A similar condition exists in England, mathematics being too much of a hurdle for many children. Quite a few adults—now middle-aged employees—say that they were not given "enough mathematics at school."[28] Civilization is on the march. It may be that it is more important to reckon than to read in this second half of the twentieth century. Be that as it may, the Government should perhaps

[27] Station WLW (8 A.M.). Cincinnati, Ohio. U.S.A. January 31, 1957.
[28] *The Times Educational Supplement*. London. March 29, 1957.

look into the methods used in teaching mathematics, and make sure that the program is suitable for pupils struggling along with little or no help at home. Crowded classes do not make for a satisfactory atmosphere, either for the students or for the teachers. The wonder is not why some children fail, but how so many make a passing grade.

As for engineering, educators more or less agree that there are two main stumbling blocks: the first is a desire to leave school at an early age and make "big money" in the business world; the second concerns the large number of boys and girls who fail the day to day requirements in both the lower and upper grades of school work. Further, the inflationary process in England since World War II has not helped the general situation, for it takes four or more years of formal study before a student can qualify for a university degree. Practical experience is also desirable. Small wonder that young people hesitate to take up engineering. Then, as a profession, it is not especially lucrative—£1,500 being a fairly good income after ten years of self-directed practice. The exceptional individual might provide a different set of figures—personality, more often than not, being the deciding factor.

The pay-advantage so long enjoyed by the graduate engineer has disappeared in recent years. Strangely enough, a salesman with a university degree has risen from far down the line to first position in the economic race.[29] This was a time of course when agents could sell almost anything from shoe-laces to motorcars. The writer talked to a man in London who had bought a large, expensive kitchen range "on time," although he lived alone in one back room, and had no use for such a luxury. But this individual—far along in years—was not dissatisfied, and described his purchase with considerable pride.

During the past decade, semi-professional training has been offered women in England; it has to do with the various branches of heating and ventilation. But the movement has been too limited for the needs

[29] *United States News and World Report*. Dayton, Ohio, U.S.A. January 4, 1957.

of families generally. This is a good field for women, as it brings into use a great deal that has been learned in the home. However, applicants must be well-grounded in physics, chemistry, and mathematics. The preparatory work covers many subjects and may be broadly divided under the following heads:

(a) That concerned with the health and comfort of normal people. This includes ventilation, heating, hot-water supply, etc., in houses, flats, offices, hospital wards, lecture rooms, cinemas, churches, etc.

(b) Specialized health as in the exact control of conditions such as warmth and humidity in operating theatres, and incubators for prematurely born babies.

(c) Industrial conditions in which both the product and the worker have to be considered. Temperature, humidity, dust removal and fume extraction often have to be exactly controlled. The ventilation of mines is an example of difficult work for the Heating and Ventilating engineer.[30]

In addition to being well-grounded in basic knowledge, the man or woman entering this branch of engineering should be able to work from first principles, as no two contracts are alike in this fairly new and precise field of technology.

Women in England also do well in chemical engineering and in applied chemistry. It is now possible for them to go straight from technical school to factory, as the calls for workers are more or less constant from oil, food, and sugar industries. Further, manufacturers of alkalis are interested in improving their product through research. These openings are ready-made jobs for women, really carry-overs from the family kitchen—scales, boiling pots, and other forms of household equipment. Products such as penicillin, modern plastics, dye-stuffs, and fertilizers require men and women of the greatest skill. Then too, there is enormous scope for the chemical engineer in artificial textiles such as the nylons now so widely used.

In spite of these advantages, recent reports indicate that many girls in England beyond the average intellectually, are leaving school

[30] *The Woman Engineer*. London. Autumn, 1956.

because of servant shortages. Unfortunately, many parents who live in rural districts, "so far from believing in further education for their daughters, will not even allow them to take up a grammar school place when it is offered."[31] These are the people who are not only blind to the advantages of study, but who are quick to recognize any real or imaginary disadvantage in routine instruction. Such an attitude is a sad commentary on parental wisdom, and this remark does not refer to lower-class families, but to the well-to-do middle class, often called the backbone of English society. Evidently, the only way to utilize the reserve talent among girls is to further the movement for adult training. For it is a short-sighted policy to deny any group the right to receive a good education.

Far too often the needs of women are discussed by educators and then put aside as material for thought at some future date. So it was when representatives of twelve countries met in UNESCO on June 26, 1950. They deliberated on a number of subjects, but were unable to form any definite conclusion concerning women in technological society. It is all very well to talk about educational parity between boys and girls, but it is something else entirely to offer equal opportunities to young people of both sexes. Indeed,

> The fact that relatively few women have so far pursued certain careers must not be permitted to sway the educational administration's judgement unduly. This failure to pursue a certain type of occupation in the past may well have been due to a lack of suitable educational opportunity or to prejudice and not to any inherent unsuitability of women for the careers themselves.[32]

Now that women are found so frequently in the double role of home-maker and wage-earner, something should be done to train them for a way-of-life which grows heavier, rather than lighter year by year. Women can no longer stand on the side-lines waiting for something to happen.

[31] *The Woman Engineer*. London. Spring, 1957.
[32] *The Woman Engineer*. London. Autumn, 1953.

With the development of radio and aeronautics, the application of electricity attracts more and more women, and they dream up bits of fantasy now and then. So it was that Elsie E. Edwards presented the advantages of electricity in the following lines:

> She's like a fairy on the hearth
> And though her years be few
> You'll find there's hardly anything
> This clever child can't do.[33]

Among the smaller conveniences, the electric iron probably takes first place. Imagine standing near a hot stove for hours on end just to keep a string of irons hot. Yet this was the method used in laundry operations up to thirty or forty years ago. The writer has been told that many large households in England retained the old-style flat irons up to World War II—electrical equipment being confined to upper floors. It was no doubt a matter of timing—people being slow to spend money for essentials far down in the basement.

In all fields of engineering, women have made progress by taking the most menial of jobs. But when war came there was no effort to sort workers; it was just a task of filling vacancies as soon as possible. Strangely enough, this untrained group of workers displayed a high degree of efficiency, many becoming skilled artisans. Employment brought a shift of habits for hundreds of wives and daughters: a walk in the cool air of morning, a bit of conversation with co-workers on the way home at night.

At the close of World War I, women workers were replaced by sailors and soldiers ready to take their accustomed place in civilian life. This move brought resentment of no mean order, for women had been tasting freedom, and carrying full purses for the first time in their lives. Why go back to cooking and scrubbing? Unrest brought changes quite revolutionary in character. For one thing, the Women's

[33] *The Electrical Age.* London. April, 1934.

Engineering Society was established in 1919 for the purpose of protecting "technical women." The following objectives were listed:

1. To permit the training and employment of women in engineering and allied trades.

2. To work for the admission of women to all schools of engineering and technical colleges.

3. To give special attention to the future of women who have attained some degree of skill in engineering and allied trades and professions, and who wish to continue their work.

4. To work for the admission of women to membership of all suitable institutes of engineers.

5. To enable technical women to meet and to correspond, and to facilitate the interchange of ideas respecting openings in various branches of technical and mechanical science by the circulating of information in such places.[34]

It is apparent from the Prospectus that the term *Engineering* was used in a broad sense; referring to anybody who looked after machinery. This is of course an incorrect terminology—only college-trained individuals having the right to be called engineers.

The admission of women to schools of engineering and technical colleges—one of the chief goals of the Women's Engineering Society—was accomplished in due time. Another step forward was this: the Society undertook the publication of a magazine, *The Woman Engineer*.[35] Within a short time, the Civil Engineers, the Mechanical Engineers, and the Automotive Engineers all signified their willingness to admit women to membership. The college course leading to a B.Sc. degree covers a three-year period. Women take the program in stride, many finishing in the top third of their class.

Consultative work, the branch of engineering most highly esteemed, demands considerable capital, as office rent and salaries run into hundreds of pounds each year. Another drawback is that the engineer cannot hide really serious mistakes. A misfit of any kind

[34] *The Prospectus of the Women's Engineering Society.* 1920. p. 1.

[35] This magazine is a very reliable publication, even circulating during the difficult post-war years.

must be adjusted at the expense of the office. Further, to produce satisfactory work is the only permissible form of advertising. The consulting engineer should make a wide circle of friends, for work is secured almost entirely through personal contacts. Of course he or she must have ability, and show a willingness to spend plenty of time with office obligations, starting the day at eight or nine o'clock in the morning. Then too, this group must maintain a high degree of integrity in order to inspire confidence among associates. The temptations are many and varied. In her student days, the writer knew a young engineer who was offered a tailor-made suit of "fine wool" if he would install equipment not specified in the original contract.[36] It goes without saying that the interest of the client must always come first. At the present time, there is a tendency for local authorities to employ their own engineers, an approach which interferes to some extent with private practice.

Apparently, a firm bond exists between women in the engineering profession. They do, of course, share similar hardships, similar advantages—a good reason for close understanding. So it was that in 1926 a group of engineers, all women, established Atlanta, Ltd. The idea was to help sister workers in their search for employment. The plan worked very well. As one observer remarked, "The girls got a lot of good jobs." In another operation, three women began to install electrical devices in different parts of England—Miss Caroline Hazlett, Miss Margaret Partridge, and Mrs. Laura Wilson were the pioneers. Others joined them and succeeded in wiring many homes and shops—often it is said, "for a doubting clientele."

Although many girls have been trained in the technical schools, this fact has made little impression on public understanding. Consider the case of an electrical engineer in Devonshire: this woman was chased by a London policeman across the roof of a building in Picadilly Circus. "Actually, she was fixing one of those neon signs,

---

[36] The offer was refused on the ground that "it is best to pay one's own way."

which was not, of course, a thing the policeman was likely to think of, nor to believe."[37] This little episode is just a reminder of how difficult it is for women to obtain practical experience as technical experts. However, more of them are employed in electrical work than in any other branch of engineering. To the credit of men in this industry, they have seldom objected to women workers—certainly, no organized resistance. Women graduates do well in their home-towns; in some cases, they have added sales-work as a temporary side line.

In a way, women have a special advantage in dealing with problems which arise in the home. The housewife in a small village, for instance, is none too sure about electrical gadgets. It may be that she is more outspoken with a woman that she would be with a man. Margaret Partridge in her book, *Memories at Random*, tells of one client who said, "Do please come in and tell me. If I have an electric light in this hall, which is very draughty, will it blow out? Both the young men I have seen say it won't, but you know what men are."[38] Another client, equally perturbed, said, "The young lady who came yesterday said she'd put a lamp in the middle of the ceiling; but how be I get up to light him?"[38]

In spite of skepticism and other difficulties, the "starting up" arrangements were always worth watching—something like the rehearsal of a new play. For everything had to be in perfect order. The neighbors assembled in the streets, talking, laughing, and of course joking about the new undertaking. Then, as the hour of darkness approached, a strange stillness fell over the crowd. Suddenly, lights flashed from all directions—it was one more triumph for electrical engineering.

Changes, both social and economic, come so slowly that it is difficult for the average person to grasp what is taking place. It was a shock to the citizens of Cambridge, that staid university town, when

[37] *The Woman Engineer*. London. Winter, 1956.
[38] *Ibid*. Spring, 1956.

the first woman-electrician got down on the floor of Ely Cathedral—dragging a bag of tools behind her. Said the old sexton to the writer, "Women can do as they please, but it hardly seems decent to me." But everything must have a beginning. It took time for people to learn that sex had nothing to do with efficiency in electrical work.

In 1930, Miss Winifred Hackett of Birmingham University received a grant from the Institution of Electrical Engineers: she worked under a Thanksgiving Education and Research Fund with the important light-current phase of electrical engineering. Some time later, further recognition of woman's ability in this field was given when Miss Jeanie Dicks was placed in charge of installing electric light and heating in Winchester Cathedral. Make no mistake, there is something innately tough about the English woman. This attribute, or whatever it is, may be the secret of her success in the professions.

While men carry on debate about psychological and physiological differences, women have been going ahead steadily and quietly in almost every field of activity. Of course they are better suited to some tasks than to others. As for electronic technicians—keeping in motion the mechanical equipment of today—employers say that women are more patient, more reliable than men over a long stretch of time. Perhaps this is one reason why women give way to verbal explosions —relieving nervous tension in this way. Consider the young mother leading five active children to a train in Victoria Railway Station who said, "Well, I never would have married, had I known this job was ahead of me."

A certain amount of passivity is needed in other branches of engineering. Take the remodelling of old houses—these contracts being listed in the minds of engineers as "nuisance cases." Most certainly they require something more than book-learning. Illumination is another task which requires more than ordinary skill. To some extent, this assignment is a *natural* for women, as even small girls know what is good, and what is bad in lighting effects—lowering the shades half-way for strangers, and letting them fly ceiling-high for family reunions. Yes, there is plenty of work in the world—just making vision possible in darkness, will call upon the genius of many men and women now engaged in scientific studies.

Among women engineers, the most famous is Amy Johnson—the first English woman to take a serious interest in aviation. It is possible that her courage and ability spurred other women to daring feats in the air. It should be understood that Miss Johnson was no upstart in her chosen career. She had prepared herself quite unknowingly for engineering—taking courses in science at Sheffield University. Like thousands of girls, Amy spent her early life in a small suburban town, in an "ugly suburban street." She was fortunate in that her parents were sensible folk, going about their tasks in the quiet British way, the mother cooking and sewing, the father working day after day in an effort to support his family.

As far as engineering is concerned, Amy Johnson had what is still considered the best study-program for a girl; she went first to a private school, then to a secondary institution, and later attended regular courses in a university. She was an apt pupil but lacked the urge to study. This unfortunate state of affairs was due in part to a faulty school system. In *Myself When Young*, Amy Johnson gives an account of her difficulties in entering a secondary school.

It was the first day of term and activity was intense. Waiting along with many other new girls I took stock of my surroundings. . . . We were the last, and almost never got there at all as, apparently we were unexpected.

Our entrance form had been mislaid or lost, . . . my name was not on the list, and it looked as though I should have to go home again. My mother rightly indignant that all her work and expense in acquiring my outfit (the school uniform) should go wasted, insisted that I should be taken. Eventually, she won the day. But it was found that I should have to go into a class with girls younger than myself, as there was not room in the class of my own age and standard.[39]

[39] *Myself When Young*. (Edited by the Countess of Oxford and Asquith). Frederick Muller, Ltd. London. 1938. p. 136.

As might have been expected, Amy had an easy time and developed lazy habits. During the next few years, she had a medley of interests: trapeze work, hockey, cricket, and lastly, more study in scientific subjects. It is clear that this young woman was moving with sure steps—and in a given direction.

There were other forces at work in Amy's life; she belonged to that group of girls who were growing up when the dreaded Zeppelins were soaring over the home-land. She tells of,

Air-raids on our town, which, to the children were grand fun as we could stay up and play games and have hot chocolate in the early hours of the morning when we ought to be in bed. Two of the highlights of the air-raids are of my father chasing me when I escaped outside, because I wanted to see the Zeppelins and, as I ran hastily indoors again, my sister—frightened at the noise—collapsed into the coal bucket in the darkness of the cellar in which the family were sheltering. I shall never forget the scare this clattering gave us all, with nerves strained as they were to breaking point after a raid every night for a week.[40]

It cannot be said that a Zeppelin raid caused any woman to take up flying, but it is quite possible that an experience of this kind made an observing child air-conscious. Furthermore, Amy Johnson would get more of a thrill out of war-happenings than the average child, for she had sprung from adventurous stock; her grandfather was a Dane, who traveled the seas as a boy, and her father was one of those devil-may-care men who took part in the Klondike gold rush.

In her choice of a university, Amy Johnson was fortunate, for Sheffield offers a mild form of the "sandwich method," a plan by which students working for a degree are required to spend some time in the shops of engineering companies. In this way she gained practical experience. After a somewhat varied career—beginning as an office worker in London—Amy started out on the course which not only brought her fame, but paved the way for other women in a new,

[40] *Myself When Young.* (Edited by the Countess of Oxford and Asquith). Frederick Muller, Ltd. London. 1938. p. 139.

and somewhat hazardous profession. As she says, "The most important milestone in my life was the decision to take flying lessons at the moderate fee of £1 each."

After learning the fundamentals of aviation then current, Amy Johnson undertook a solo flight to Australia in May, 1930. She knew little about navigation, but managed to reach her goal in spite of several mishaps. The daring young visitor was warmly received by the "Aussies," a people who understand the fine points of hospitality.[41] She was invited to Canberra, the new seat of authority, and introduced to officials high in Government service. In tribute to Miss Johnson's achievement, the Australian Limited arranged for the flyer to go from Brisbane to Sydney as their guest. This was another turning point in Amy's career, for it was on this trip that she met her future husband, James Allan Mollison, an Australian pilot.

Back home again, Miss Johnson, still using her maiden name, received not only a special award from King George V, but a substantial gift of money from the London *Daily Mail*. By now she had decided to give her life to aviation. In 1933, the Mollisons, as a team, flew across the Atlantic hoping to land in New York; they touched Newfoundland, Nova Scotia, Maine, and Massachusetts, but were forced down in Connecticut, just thirty miles short of their destination.

World War II came, and this woman-flyer volunteered her aeronautical skill for the cause of freedom. It was a tragic moment, for this move was the beginning of the end. In 1941, Amy Johnson died in the service of her country. A group of English women decided, almost at once, that a tribute of some kind was in order. The lead was taken by the Women's Engineering Society, an organization which had been very dear to Miss Johnson's heart. She had acted as president of this organization from 1934 to 1937. Before plans could be carried out, hostilities ceased, flooding the aviation field with war-

[41] In 1956, a taxi-driver in Sydney, Australia, invited the writer to his home for dinner, because, as he explained, "You were all so kind to me when I was in the United States."

time pilots in search of work. The money which had been collected for a scholarship was invested in national bonds, and more than a decade passed before the Amy Johnson award became a reality. There were precise requirements. A few are listed here:

(a) The Scholarship will be awarded by a Selection Committee whose decision will be final and binding. The Committee will include representatives of the Royal Aero Club, the Association of British Aero Clubs, the Guild of Air Pilots and Air Navigators and the Women's Engineering Society.

(b) Candidates must be British subjects by birth, under the age of 30 on 30th September, 1954, and be able to furnish satisfactory evidence of their physical fitness.

(c) The successful candidate may choose, subject to the approval of the Committee, where she wishes to carry out an approved course of flying training.[42]

Considerable publicity was given to the competition. Twenty-six young women, all of whom had had some experience in flying, applied for the scholarship. The Committee made their decision—Miss Dorothy White of Runcorn, Cheshire, was selected as "the holder of the first Amy Johnson Flying Scholarship." This young woman was a bank cashier with a fine record of achievement as an air pilot. She had long been a member of the Women's Junior Air Corps, and had won a flying scholarship in 1947. In addition, she had been a pilot in the Women's Royal Air Force Volunteer Reserve for three years before it disbanded. Through this mark of honor, the work of Amy Johnson will continue to live in the minds and hearts of the English people.

Another prominent engineer was Miss Gertrude Entwisle, A.M.I.-E.E.; she stands as "the very first retirement in Great Britain of a woman who had had a complete career in industry as an employed professional design engineer."[43] It was by the merest chance that Gertrude became a "Lady Engineer," as she had attended—for no special reason—courses in engineering at the University of Man-

[42] *The Woman Engineer*. London. Spring, 1955.
[43] *Ibid*.

chester. Then in 1915, a request came to college authorities for a woman-worker who had had some technical training. This request brought out a telling fact: ". . . the firm had just successfully tried the tremendous experiment of employing an office girl so why should it not try to find some female technical staff."[44] The outcome of the matter was that Miss Entwisle decided to take a chance at engineering.

The position had been offered by the "British Westinghouse," as the Metropolitan Vickers Company was then called. In much the same way that she had surprised men-students in an engineering class—making good grades—so Miss Entwisle surprised top officials in an industrial plant. For, within a few months, this woman-engineer was taking special training "Under the excellent system of half-a-day in the shops, and half-a-day in the office, although the foreman of the Motor Test Department had threatened to leave his job rather than suffer the indignity of a female on the test bed."[45] But stings of bitterness were ignored. It is said that Miss Entwisle's fine example brought many other women into war work.

It is clear, as this study progresses, that women are very frank, very honest about passing on first-hand experiences. This truth is illustrated in an article written by Lt. Gwendolen Sergant, W.R.A.C., an officer serving with the R.E.M.E. She says, "The best way to become a successful engineer is to be born into a family whose members live and think engineering."[46] Lt. Sergant, like so many girls of today, learned to drive an automobile while living in the country. Under such circumstances, there was space for all maneuvers.

As she grew older, Gwendolen accepted a position in the family engineering works where she spent time over "blacksmithing, oxyacetylene welding, and the maintenance of refrigeration equip-

[44] *The Woman Engineer*. London. Spring, 1955.
[45] *Ibid*. Autumn, 1954.
[46] *Ibid*. Autumn, 1954.

ment, as well as general automobile repairs."[47] After a few years of study at Loughborough College, this young woman started out quite independently. She was not particular about the kind of work offered, accepting almost anything that came along. Some time was given to the study of fluorescent lighting, and at a later period, Miss Sergant was able to work on illumination for the Festival of Great Britain and the Rhodes Centenary Celebration.

In July, 1933, Miss Sergant joined the Woman's Royal Army Corps on a Short Service Commission. This meant some basic training, first at the Depot at Guildford and later at the W.R.A.C. School of Instruction. The following year she spent on assignments in various places and finally landed in the Army Workshop where guns, tanks and all kinds of vehicles were dumped for repair. In the the words of Lt. Sergant, women do very well in "the overhaul and repair of tanks and their engines . . . the final assembly line in the tank Engine Bay is manned 100 per cent by women fitters and their work is of a very high standard."[48] By quietly demonstrating their competence, women are gradually taking their place in occupations once closed to them.

A problem to be faced is this: the engineer must depend upon skilled helpers in order to attain success. Such a state of affairs is unfortunate. Not long ago, Miss Kathleen M. Cook, a mechanical engineer, specializing in production, had this to say:

> If one is in a position to pay thousands of pounds for a machine, one cannot buy a person to work it. The secret of success of the individual is the ability to occupy one's self in the work for which one is particularly suited and interested. The success of every establishment lies in the ability of the Management to select the most available persons for the different tasks. Every employer should have the gift of diplomacy, psychology and understanding.[49]

[47] *The Woman Engineer*. London. Winter, 1955.
[48] *Ibid.*
[49] *Ibid.*

This statement may explain, in part, why so many people steer clear of engineering—only 387 women being fully qualified operators in the year 1951. However, at that time, 12,251 girls and older women were working over drawing-boards in widely scattered districts of England—the last figure indicating formal training of some kind.

Many engineering companies recognize the suitability of women for certain jobs. But there are obstacles to be overcome. This is especially true of large manufacturing plants. At least two barriers might be mentioned: (1) parents do not like to have their daughters do rough work in factories; (2) parents do not like to have their daughters work in districts where proper lodging is not available. The matter of prestige also enters the picture, as office work is considered more genteel than factory work—even in this day of free thinking.

In regard to training, educators agree that while a girl of sixteen is more mature than a boy of the same age, it is desirable that she remain in school longer—that is, taking up professional duties at a higher level where the opposition is less, and the need greater. Every move from this time on will be experimental, with a great deal depending on the character and ability of the average woman-student. Indeed, the matter of ability looms large all along the line of professional work.

Perhaps it should be mentioned that there are unlimited opportunities open to girls who wish to earn their living in a foreign country. The only requirements are: (1) a small amount of ready cash; (2) a degree from some reputable institution; (3) a reliable foreign contact. It is well to bear in mind that there is more prejudice against the employment of women in some countries than in others. As to the prospect of a job, it may be said that at the present time there is such a demand for university graduates that no one with an engineering or scientific degree should have difficulty in obtaining employment.

However, a warning is in order: many employers are anxious to obtain technical experts, but are not at all concerned with the workers' future prospects. It is for the woman to insist upon getting workshop experience. This is the only way to become an all-round engineer.

The position of women up to World War II was something like that of an understudy to a famous actress. For many had prepared themselves for special roles with little or no assurance that opportunity would ever come their way. But after countless prophecies about "peace in our time," war was declared on a Sunday, in the autumn of 1939. As a matter of fact, bomb-shelters[50] had been built and extra men had been called into defence work some weeks before. All this was a signal for approach: women who had long watched from the side-lines, took their places in office and factory with all the confidence of finished performers.

With little discussion, almost a studied silence, women were called into the National Service. Government officials were forced to employ women or send thousands of men to their graves. How this new group of workers lived up to their responsibilities stands as a revealing sketch of life in war-torn England.

There were of course ludicrous moments in the employment of women, a group that had been conditioned to home obligations since the world began. Consider Bessie, a circus performer, who was "directed into munitions,"

In no time at all, complications arose: Bessie's father announced that he was leaving for a fortnight, and that some member of the family would have to stay home and take care of the pet lion. The request made sense to a dutiful daughter, so she applied for a leave of absence, giving full details of the problem. But the idea was turned down with little or no ceremony. But Bessie was not to be outdone

[50] The writer recalls sitting in her Chelsea studio, and hearing Mr. Chamberlain's tired voice announce over the radio: "There is nothing more I can do to prevent war — that is why we are digging trenches in Hyde Park tonight."

in any such manner. She took 'French leave,' and to the delight of her fellow-workers exercised the lion in a field near the factory. The employers would stand for no such nonsense, and reported the case to the National Service Officer. Bessie was ordered to 'go back to work immediately.' She paid no attention to the summons—the lion taking his exercise as usual. As a result, the refractory war-worker was dismissed. Then of all things—independent spirit that she was—Bessie put a red bow in her hair, and returned to work as though nothing had happened. The management took council—and looked the other way.[51]

While the war opened many doors to women, the majority of graduates in engineering still find that practical experience is difficult to obtain. It is a well-known fact that a girl must at times rely on chance and be ready to grasp any opportunities which come her way. It is often wise to seek employment with a large engineering company—entering a department in which technical training is a specified requirement.

Other positions open to women without financial resources are to be found in Government service; but these posts are limited—a few being offered in the Woolwich Arsenal. Women are also employed, (1) as Assistant Examiners in the Patent Office; (2) as factory inspectors in the Home Office. Then at times, unexpected opportunities arise. Thus, in October, 1934, Mrs. I. M. Bolton was asked to represent the London County Council on the London and Home Counties Joint Electricity Authority.

Further evidence of women's expanding place in engineering is shown in the career of Miss L. S. Souter, who belongs to a well-known engineering family. This young woman obtained the practical part of her training by working first in her father's plant, and later with the General Electric Company at Wembley. Further, there were specialized operations which had to do with heating and cooking problems—also, fluorescent lighting. Such a beginning led to more important assignments. Between 1944 and 1949, this young en-

[51] *The Woman Engineer.* London. Spring, 1956.

gineer was working on technical problems of small components for electro-medical equipment. It was because of this work

Involving, increasing contact with fundamental physics, that she came to join the solid physics group in their research into the physical properties of semi-conductors—the class of materials used for crystal rectifiers.[52]

Time was given also to a special project: work on the properties of germanium, the applications of which are of importance in radar and television. Miss Souter joined the Women's Engineering Society in 1937 and was made a full member in 1940. She is also an associate member of the Institution of Electrical Engineers.

But it took Mrs. Maria Killick to stagger the imagination of English people everywhere. For she invented a special sapphire stylus-type phonograph needle which is now being used in many parts of the world, but—and here the story hinges—without anyone paying anything in the way of royalties. This subterfuge led to a legal skirmish which dragged on for ten years, a British Court finally ruling in Mrs. Killick's favor. As a result of this decision, accountants were pressed into service; they worked for many months trying to unravel what amounted to a delicate money-tangle. The sum is even now close to £1,000,000, with additional windfalls rolling in each year.

Amazingly enough, this new-found fortune is tax-free as it is paid in the form of damages—a loophole which prevents England's Internal Revenue Department from claiming any surtax. This phase of the case puts Mrs. Killick in a rare class of millionaries—an income flowing in without any of it flowing out again.

The question arises as to how this mother and her four children adjusted themselves to their new-found wealth. Being a sensible person, Mrs. Killick gave considerable thought to the future. She settled large sums of money on her immediate family. In addition, Mrs.

[52] *The Woman Engineer*. London. Spring, 1951.

Killick purchased a beautiful country home, a property which in-cludes a swimming-pool, a garage for three cars, and several acres of ground. Now that prosperity has come—and the Killicks have known what it is to pawn valuables—this middle-aged widow is planning to take flying lessons. It would not be surprising if Mrs. Killick started an air-line of her own. The story of her unusual ex-perience has all the overtones of a medieval drama. Miracles do occur of course—the trick being to profit by a god-like gift.

Some people believe that it is possible to remove one of the causes of war—the unequal distribution of wealth—by utilizing modern machines, and newly created forms of energy. This plan might be feasible if refined understanding could overtake scientific achieve-ment. Let this chapter end then with a ray of hope—the inventions of today leading to a better way-of-life tomorrow.

VIII. The Church

THE origin of Christianity in Britain is more or less a matter of speculation, as no piece of writing remains to give even a hint of what the church was like in the long ago. The Gospel may have followed the footsteps of countless Roman soldiers, a suggestion made by Tertullian and other early apologists. It is not to be questioned that the people had places of worship, for the Bishops of Britain were included in the list of invitations sent out by Constantine the Great to the first Ecumenical Council of Nicaea.[1]

However, by the sixth century, religious activity had all but vanished from sparsely populated regions of the island. This fact was due in part to the long contests between small groups of natives, and roving bands of invaders. Many people at this time were reduced to a state bordering on slavery, especially in the South, and more central parts of the country. All of this happened in the dawn of history when life for the average person was little more than a rugged experience, just one violent change after another.

Pagan influence was strong in those days. In fact, an idea prevailed that the world was coming to an end in the year 1000. For several centuries before that date, it had been the custom in some communities to begin a legal document with these words: "In view of the approaching end of the world." This leaning towards superstitious beliefs is still widespread among the lower classes of England—a fact often ignored by historians. The hymn, *Dies Irae*, sums up a common approach towards the future:

> '*Day of wrath, that day of burning,*
> *All shall melt, to ashes turning;*
> *When the Judge shall come in Splendor,*
> *Strict to mark and just to render.*'

[1] A.D. 325.

But the material world survived, and with the new lease on life came faith, hope, and charity.

Another period of darkness followed. Then, a monk by the name of Gregory visited a marketplace in Rome—the Rome that was no longer the seat of a great empire. He saw a group of slaves with fair skin and light-colored hair being put on an auction block. These young men had probably been purchased from Southern tribes—really pawns of battle. Gregory questioned the dealer at some length, and was told that they were Angles from Northumbria. "They have an angelic mien," said Gregory, and should be "coheirs with the angels in Heaven." It was such a man who planned to convert the English people. He could not undertake the long, hazardous journey himself, but saw to it that a band of priests under the guidance of Augustine should visit Britain.

Ethelbert, the powerful King of Kent, received the missionaries as casual callers, greeting the newcomers far out in the fields.[2] He feared most probably that these visitors might exert an evil influence over his home. The priests approached Ethelbert carrying a silver cross and singing the *Litany* in high pitched voices. The King was not impressed by this outward show of fervency; however, he was polite, allowing the strangers to remain in Canterbury, and carry on religious services to suit themselves. The efforts of these early churchmen were not without results, Britain taking her place with the Christian countries of Europe along in the eighth century.

The next step forward was by way of a building program—the people of England erecting many beautiful abbeys, cathedrals, and monasteries. These projects were a demonstration, not only of pride, but of an awakening in matters spiritual. As a rule, religious institutions were conducted in a business-like manner, and commanded the respect of men and women everywhere. Church workers stood for a holy way-of-life in an age of crudity—their kindness and help in

[2] A.D. 597.

isolated communities being a real blessing to many families. Perhaps Chaucer's satire sounded a sensitive note: the average churchman was "full, fat, and in good point." But make no mistake, class feeling was very strong in God-fearing circles. It followed that the status of this mixed multitude of religious houses ". . . varied infinitely. In sum, social considerations had some weight; parents might find it difficult to gain admission to a rich and famous monastery for a son who would be welcome in a less-conspicuous house."[3]

Conditions did not differ much for a daughter who wished to follow a holy way-of-life. The importance of class, or social distinction, was the main consideration in church agreements. A woman, for instance, seldom became a social worker—that is, an abbess or prioress—unless she belonged to a family that was both wealthy and aristocratic. It was only by means of a generous gift that a young girl could ". . . enter a religious order at all. For in spite of protests from church authorities, the custom of seeking a dowry from girls desiring to enter a convent became so universal as to amount to a rule."[4] These organizations were self-sufficient in every way. Thus, women who did religious work became an important part of the national economy.

It is said that "maidens of the Church" did not necessarily have strong religious views, they often entered the cloisters as an outlet from family restrictions or to avoid the unhappiness of a loveless marriage. These groups were carefully supervised, as no breath of scandal could be tolerated on consecrated property. To this end, dignitaries of the Church made regular visits to the convents, seeing to it that all was well in the Kingdom of Christ.

The nuns in England, as is the custom today, went about with one or more companions; they were supposed to look neither to the right

[3] Watson, Edward William. *The Church of England.* Williams & Norgate. London. 1914. p. 59.
[4] Royden, A. Maude. *The Church and Women.* James Clark & Co., Limited. London. N.D. 1924. p. 75.

nor left, and to get on quickly with the business at hand. It was a dull life, with almost no diversions from the daily round of work and prayer. Possibly, the good ladies looked out of the windows now and then to watch a group of strolling players (the writer saw such a pleasing picture in England back in 1931). It should be mentioned that the inmates of these institutions did not always take kindly to the rules and regulations set up for them by the Church. The instructions for nuns differed widely from those prepared for priests, both in matters of diet and general behavior. Prayers the nuns made in plenty: Matins, Mass, Vespers. Further, every sister was expected to attend daily services, unless "hindered by sickness or other reasonable cause."[5] Taking everything together, it was an occupation well-suited to an ambitious girl, especially at a time when opportunities for useful work were so few, in fact almost non-existent.

The country was on the verge of a disturbance of some significance. For now comes the story of Henry VIII (1509–1547), an English ruler who was extremely self-centered, even tyrannical. After tiring of his wife—the first of six—he began to look for ways to get a divorce, pretending to be worried over the fact that he had no son. The authorities in Rome ignored such a plea. Not to be outdone, Henry married Anne Boleyn in a small church on the outskirts of London. All Parliament could do was set aside the rights of the Pope. Then, in 1535, the famous "Act of Supremacy" was passed—Henry becoming head of the Church of England. Although this monarch ruled with an iron hand, he became very popular with men and women in the street. He had brought wealth to the country by confiscating church property.

From this time forward, the Church was looked upon as a national institution, with the Bible standing as the highest authority in matters of faith. The "Holy Writ" was treated as a legal document, and interpreted according to rigid formula. The primary idea in Chris-

[5] Phillips, M. and Tompkinson, W. S. *English Women in Life and Letters.* Oxford University Press. Humphrey Milford. 1927. pp. 6–8.

tianity had been all but lost by the end of the sixteenth century. Then a spiritual frenzy developed, really a quickening of religious feeling that had lain dormant for a number of years. It is quite likely that this church revival was possible because a few unemotional church-men had kept the altar candles burning (as priests in Russia are doing at this time),[6] and carried on with missionary work, and fervent prayer.

The Anglican clergy were known for their learning all through the seventeenth century. But this group of church men, with all of their attainments,

Did not leaven the nation as the Roman Church had done by works of charity and benevolence. It was remarkably indifferent to social work and religious propagandism, outside the doors of the church. The traditions of the Roman Church were not carried out by the Protestants, who probably felt a repugnance to any methods adopted by their enemies, the Papists.[7]

There was a great deal to be said against the old system of alms-giving at the convent gates—but nothing was offered to take its place. In retrospect, it is clear that Anglican parishes lost control of their members by way of indifference—that is, a refusal to help the weak and distressed. To leave such duties to the State, was to leave them to an uncertain foster-mother.

A timely subject arose, now and then, among clergymen: should women be allowed to preach the Gospel on the same terms as men? It was a shocking idea put aside in a hurry. As usual, a Quaker writer sensed part of the difficulty in these words (an undated *Dissertation*):

There is yet another strong prejudice against women's preaching . . . and this no less than the united interest of the whole body of men called clergymen. For if, say they, the pastoral function may be exercised by laymen and even women, then we shall be deemed no longer necessary, nay, perhaps down goes our trade, our pomp and revenues. And, indeed, it is hardly credible to me that these men would

[6] In 1931, the writer visited a church in Russia that had three worshippers kneeling in the nave, and twelve candles burning on the altar.

[7] Hill, Georgiana. *Women in English Life*. Vol. I. Richard Bentley & Son. New Burlington Street. London. MDCCCXCVI. p. 250.

have ever made the opposition that some of them have done to a women's preaching Jesus in a sensible manner, if preaching were a profession which there was nothing to be got by.[8]

Here was food for thought—one religious group daring to bring out the weak point of another—an adversary. But conditions in church life had become too notorious not to be observed.

Some time after the Tudors, a movement was started (1729) in the town of Oxford to widen religious practices. The program was fostered by John Wesley—founder of Methodism—who felt his heart "strangely warmed" one night while reading Luther's preface to the Epistle (to the Romans). Social movements go along in a peculiar manner. A few decades later, the French Revolution made an indelible mark on Church history. The English people were shocked at the Godless propaganda endorsed by the revolutionists; they turned as one large family to the religious observances offered by their churches. For, it was argued, how could a system hallowed by the reverence of generations be thus lightly cast aside?

Many churches in sparsely populated districts were handicapped by family rule. That is, it often happened that a wealthy family received special attention in return for large contributions. One writer describes what went on in a village church as late as the nineteenth century (c.1845):

We had got pretty well on in the service when the Vicar—old Dr. Bracken—made a solemn pause; this continued, and on turning round I saw Lord and Lady Downe followed by a footman carrying an array of prayerbooks and other comforts, walking with slow and stately pace up the aisle. As they approached the pulpit, the Vicar made a profound bow, which was most politely returned by Lord Downe, who then entered the family pew and reverently placed his face, as was then the custom, within his hat; then having comfortably seated themselves and calmly found the places in their books, the service, which had been completely

---

[8] Hill, Georgiana. *Women in English Life.* Vol. I. Richard Bentley & Son. New Burlington Street. London. MDCCCXCVI. p. 249.

suspended, was allowed to proceed. This seemed to excite no surprise in the congregation, and I was told afterwards that it was a thing of ordinary occurence.[9]

The same respectful demeanor was observed when important people left the church; the congregation waiting until a dignified exit had been made. This aloofness in spiritual matters still persists to some extent in England. There is, to the writer's knowledge, one English family still clinging to its ancient screened pew, built behind the choir stalls—a secluded spot where seeing or hearing is well-nigh impossible.

Wealth and family prestige blinded the people to what was really worthwhile in life. Social distinctions do not lead to a healthy society, for they are bound to affect entire communities with vague conceptions of real worth. The reason is this: the privileged groups can prove their merits by way of education, while the less privileged groups have no way of gauging their capacities (it sometimes takes a war to stress the importance of ability over prestige). Small wonder that English women could make little headway, denied as they were all but the most menial jobs in church work. But from polishing brass candle-sticks, to placing clean linen and fresh flowers on the altar, to putting together steak and kidney pies for church suppers, they did make their way into religious circles. An early, and very important role was that of Deaconess—an occupation especially suited to the inborn talents of women.

The Sisterhood movement in England has won its way into the good graces of the Church because, for one thing, the Sisters have performed so many outstanding deeds of mercy. The highest position to which a woman may aspire in the Church of England is that of Deaconess. An applicant should be between twenty-five and thirty years of age when offering her services; further, she must

[9] Stirling, A. M. W. *The Letter-Bag of Lady Elizabeth Spencer Stanhope Compiled from the Cannon Hall Papers, 1806–1873*. Volume Two. John Lane, The Bodley Head. London. MCMXIII. pp. 71–72.

satisfy the Bishop of a given diocese as to general fitness for this type of work. Any deaconess who holds a university degree may be sent out as a teacher or lecturer,[10] and she will receive a higher salary than the worker who holds a position of minor importance. These women are summoned at times by Chaplains for hospital work; they are often kept busy ministering to patients in the wards of public institutions. Then too, homes for defective children provide another type of employment. In addition, many well-to-do churches have at least one woman on their payroll. In a parish of this character, the Deaconess devotes herself to the problems of women and children exclusively. This is also a set policy in manufacturing centers. Clergymen, as a group, are not blind to the parochial work being done by their assistants; however, they are reluctant to express appreciation in any form having objective reality. In the nineteen-thirties there were fewer than three hundred Deaconesses in active church work. But, by now, the number has probably increased as social problems had become more urgent.

The deaconess comes, as a rule, from a home in the country; she often takes up religious work by way of domestic service, for the occupations dove-tail to some extent, the deaconess needing a subservient approach to many of her problems. The training of recruits differs with denominations, some laying stress on hospital training, others like the Anglican, concentrating on pastoral preparation. For this reason,

It is utterly impossible to tell the tale of work being done by trained women with the support of volunteer groups who give both money and time. It covers every imaginable kind of social work and much of it is local and may not even be known to the headquarters group to which the local group is affiliated. . . . The

[10] "The canonical restoration of the order in the Church of England in 1923 and 1925 has now been followed by the provision for the same ministry in the Church of India and in the Church of China. Deaconesses are now working in a number of dioceses in the Church overseas as well as in the Church at home. Admitted by ordination to a life-long service in the Ministry of the Church, they work in every case under Episcopal authority." *Careers and Vocational Training.* The Women's Employment Publishing Co., Ltd. London. c. 1934. p. 58.

number and variety of these local pieces of work is past description and compu-
tation.[11]

The duties change with social progress, very little now being heard
about help for old people, and a great deal being heard about help for
young people, especially those in the under-twenty group.

The work of the deaconess has a religious bias, with some emphasis
on social responsibilities. For example, girls go great distances from
home these days in order to earn a livelihood in some well-paid occupation, and most of them have had very little experience outside
the home. The need for special care and attention cannot be overlooked. Consider the call for a deaconess (a replacement) to go up
and down the coast of England with girls of the herring fleet, a group
ever searching for the shoals of fish so plentiful in these Northern
waters. It is a delicate situation. While men have roved the sea for
centuries quite unprotected, no such lack of supervision could be allowed the fisher-girls.

The question of giving the deaconess wider training comes up in
committee meetings more or less regularly, the fact being that social
services have not kept up with the improvements in communication
and transportation. But with wars, and their aftermath of sorrow and
dislocation, speedy progress is not always possible in work of this
character.

At this point, it should be mentioned that women did not meet in
public groups until well along in the nineteenth century (c.1885).
The movement started when a few church women formed a helping-
hand society—the idea being to earn money for missionary work.
This is . . .

The only women's organization of the Anglican Church in England and in
many dioceses overseas, except for the Girl's Friendly Society. Of the two the
Mother's Union comes nearer to performing the functions of the typical 'overall'

[11] Bliss, Kathleen. *The Service and Status of Women in the Churches*. S. C. M. Press, Ltd.
London. 1952. p. 40.

women's organisation in the parish, where a branch may only be started with the permission of the minister.[12]

Further, the home-society promotes various activities in districts outside of England:

> From Headquarters in London 32 workers are supported in most of the colonial dioceses of the British Empire, to work under the bishops in close touch with any Anglican missionary society in the field.[13]

This group of pioneers undoubtedly set the pattern for church groups in other parts of the world (a movement of this kind being very strong in the United States). These societies have high standards of conduct—the women reading prayers each day to their families and performing various charitable deeds in the community. It is clear that a whole denominational movement has crystallized around a religious group consisting of half-a-million women. What a force to be reckoned with, if wrong opposed right on a national question!

The churches prefer highly-trained women for administrative work. This is not a plan to supplant the recognized employee—the trained deaconess, the Sister of Mercy—but to bring individuals with social experience and spiritual consciousness into the service of the Church. Criticism has arisen of course, many people feeling that only a well-qualified person should undertake religious duties. It is a reasonable argument, for a weak staff is at a disadvantage, especially where parochial psychology is an item in the balance sheet. At times, university women discuss the subject of "Women in Holy Orders," but usually they stop just short of making any drastic suggestions. It is about all they can do at the present time. For the old argument of "insufficient strength" and "family obligations" still plays a definite part in public opinion.

---

[12] Bliss, Kathleen. *The Service and Status of Women in the Churches*. S. C. M. Press, Ltd. London. 1952. p. 54.

[13] *Ibid*. p. 54.

Churchmen as a group understand their own weakness; they know very well that what the church needs is more ministers. The question of sex should not enter the discussion at all. Consider the following remarks made by two different ministers: (a) "Women should know their place is in the home as wife and mother." (b) "Women will lose the modesty and restraint which is their real beauty if they try to do men's work." These comments savor of the long ago when women wore crinolines, and seldom raised their eyes above a man's collar-button. It will be difficult for present-day readers to grasp the meaning of such ideas, apparently put forward in *good* faith by *good* men. Dean Inge, world-renowned minister, favored the idea of women in the ministry.

How much better it would be, [he said] if women could bring their troubles to an experienced member of their own sex, invested with whatever authority ordination to the priesthood can confer! I know that cynics may say that women never would confess anything to another woman. If so, they had much better not confess at all; spiritual flirtations are abominable. But I do not think it is true.[14]

This particular Man of God was always far ahead of his colleagues in matters of a social nature.

The younger group of scholars are more and more seeking professions which offer better salaries than the Church can provide. In 1914 . . .

There were more than 20,000 clergymen at work in England, and even then the supply was said to be not equal to the demand. Now there are but a few more than 15,000, though the population has grown during the interval, and even if this number is to be maintained at least 500 men must be ordained every year. Since the War [World War I], this number has never been reached, and the average for the last five years is 390.[15]

It is evident that some change must be made in Church policy. Possibly more money should be spent on personnel, and less on elaborate building structures.

[14] *The Evening Standard.* London. May 7, 1930.
[15] *The Times.* London. September 15, 1930.

It is worth noting that the Baptists and Congregationalists have long favored women in the ministry. However, the matter of preparation has become something of a problem in both denominations: the Lancashire Independent College, an institution training all applicants for the ministry, closed its doors to girl students in the nineteen-thirties. The following reason was given: "peculiar difficulties" in food and lodging arrangements. Problems will arise in situations of this kind. In truth, an educated girl will almost surely attract a coterie of men friends; and she may in the natural course of events give some thought to matrimony. These facts can easily be exaggerated to the disadvantage of women. Consider this report given out by A. J. Grieve in 1938:

> Out of six women trained here [The Lancashire College] four have married and three of them are no longer in pastoral work. Three of the six had difficulty in finding pastorates and there is no demand for women ministers.[16]

This is rather a discouraging account. However, the girl who has her mind set on a special career does not turn back in the face of unfavorable reports.

Students who take up ministerial work in England still face a long, hard pull, for the subject matter is said to be "pretty tough." Further, if a course is failed—Greek for instance—all instruction comes to a sudden stop. There is one jump which appeals to young people: the liberal arts course is skipped, and theological studies are substituted. This arrangement is supposed to be somewhat commensurate to an average three-year course in other fields.

Candidates for the ministry do not slip in easily; they must meet the Central Advisory Committee on Training and answer a long list of questions, which hinge fortunately on factual material previously covered in the classroom. No doubt luck plays some part in the final decision, for if all hands are raised in the committee meeting, the ap-

---

[16] *Letter* to the writer (from A. J. Grieve). March 5, 1938.

plicant is "in," but if one hand is not raised, the applicant is "out." The diocesan Bishop has a word of course, but his vote is apt to be favorable, so flexible are the rules for admittance. The Church of England pays for the theological training of its ministerial candidates, quite a blessing for people who are proud, and have suffered financial reverses.

Members of the Methodist Church deserve considerable credit, for they have done especially well in pushing women forward — seldom if ever, holding them back. But just moral support is not enough. At the close of the nineteen-thirties, official figures showed a peculiar trend in Methodist affairs, . . .

The total number of male preachers, both fully accredited and on trial, [was] 30,431, compared with 2,478 women. Indeed, in 1944, the number of men had fallen to 29,668, whilst the women had increased to 2,649.[17]

Of course, there were disturbing social forces at work, which might account for a part of this fluctuation.

Few people realize how badly preachers are needed in England, many churches offering sermons by an ordained minister only once in three months. The shortage of personnel is one reason why the deaconess is so often in demand, her services being most useful when the head of the local church is ill or away from home. The Methodist Church is very strong in the United States. As for deaconesses, there are more than five hundred in active service, a large number being affiliated with church institutions.

The Church of England is being forced, in a way, to take a long step forward, then a short step backward, in an effort to keep up with new ideas, and still please the more conservative members of a given congregation. This change in religious practices will hover for years to come between the spirit of innovation and the demands of conservatism, some people accepting the change, others watching

[17] Bacon, F. D. *Women in the Church.* Lutterworth Press. London. 1946. p. 138.

the transformation with apprehension. But the grievances of long ago, those which excited the nonconformists[18] for instance, have not been duplicated in recent years. Changes of all kinds must be accepted in the light of *what must be will be* in a world changing so fast. It seems only yesterday (October 5, 1957), the first man-made moon was set speeding around the heavens!

Many young girls still look upon the ministry as an ideal career. Fortunately, the theological schools allow women to take the B.D. and D.D. degrees. But unlike other professional institutions, the authorities cannot provide openings for this class of graduates. The thinning ranks of clergymen—an item often mentioned in this chapter—may be attributed in part to a weakening in parental control. To be more specific, it is no longer possible to force half-grown boys and girls into occupations that are distasteful to them. Facts must be faced.

Junior clergymen are in a position that is far from enviable—that is, they must make their way in a parish that is dominated by an older man, usually a much-beloved personality. Family life is out of the question, as a rule, until after the thirtieth birthday. This is an unfortunate situation. Indeed, only a few churchmen today lead the life of a "second squire." A suggestion had been made that young, unmarried clergymen, especially those stationed in large cities, live with a group of colleagues in well-organized social centers. But such an innovation would mean a great loss—the homes of clergymen having long been the nucleus of parish activities, and an ever-present refuge for those in need of spiritual help. This regular habit was never more noticeable than during the trying months before World War II—men and women flocking to their rector for heart-to-heart talks. Again the English people were quietly seeking solace in religion.

[18] The term, "nonconformist" was first applied to clergymen who refused to accept the "Act of Supremacy" in 1662.

Foreigners are apt to mistake this British piety for innate weakness or lack of spirit. Hitler was misled by such an assumption; he thought these peace-loving people would be a "push-over" in any real conflict. But when Germany threatened her freedom, England never faltered in the method of procedure. She turned to God—the Archbishop of York calling his clergy together and arranging for daily prayers—and thousands of church people made their way to various places of worship. It became the thing to do. In London, the usual greeting between friends was, "Have you been to the Abbey today?" Unbelievers were adrift, so to speak, in a social set-up that had been turned topsy-turvy within the space of a few months.

It is clear that as women grow older, the sphere of their influence tends to widen, be they spinsters, or married women. This fact was brought out quite clearly when the late Queen Mary, with her strong will and great ability, swayed the thinking of countless British subjects. There is nothing incongruous or psychologically unsound in the belief that women can do well in the ministry or in any post requiring brains and common sense. However, young people of both sexes should lean toward a calling for which they have some special talent. How often a really good sermon has been spoiled by the muffle of words, and an almost inaudible gasp at the end of each sentence.[19] Ability is a two-sided proposition, with women having their own place in church life, just as they have in all other branches of society.

Strangely enough, the statements of Jesus Christ are often passed over as being unsuited to present-day thinking. But this is a questionable assumption, for the

All-knowing Teacher felt that men and women were alike as members of the same spiritual kingdom, as children of God's family and as possessors of the same spiritual capacities. Women were freely accepted as our Lord's disciples and

[19] In large educational institutions with classes for adults, Catholic priests, rather than Protestant clergymen, predominate in classes given over to public speaking.

ministry in the Christian community was assured, and it remained, and indeed still remains necessary to discover and determine how they may best share in religious activities. The fact that one large section of the Church must forever be ministered to and forever barred from any possibility of ministering cannot fail to impoverish the Church as a whole.[20]

Unfortunately, many centuries had to pass before Christ's ideas became deeply rooted in society. It is the old story: social reforms take time.[21]

What might be called a true *Christian Movement*—the Salvation Army—was started in 1865 by William Booth, a Methodist minister, who became famous by holding religious services in an unused graveyard in London. This organization stood for many years almost alone in trying to help poverty-stricken individuals, especially those who had no church connections. The Army has always been a fifty-fifty group, women doing half the labor, whether it be nursing in the homes, or preaching in the streets. It was a peculiar development in religious practices. These workers try to keep in touch with what is going on around them. They employ native converts in foreign countries—people who are familiar with living conditions in their own employment centers. This is, of course, the sensible approach to missionary work, for no individual cares to follow the advice of strangers, particularly in matters of a personal nature.

The work of the Army has excited some curiosity among far-seeing Bishops in the Anglican Church, and an effort was made in the last century to amalgamate

The Army in the Church of England, or at all events of co-operating with it. Booth was willing for the two organizations to run side by side, like banks of a river, with bridges thrown across over which the members could mutually pass and repass.[22]

---

[20] *The Times*. London. April 22, 1930.

[21] There have always been a few outspoken British Churchmen in the House of Lords — Dr. Herbert Hensley Henson being a good example.

[22] Irvine, St. John. *God's Soldier. General William Booth*. Vol. I. William Heinemann, Ltd. London. 1934. p. 608.

But the methods of the Army were not acceptable to churchmen as a group. For one thing, the Church opposed female ministry. Amalgamation would have meant the dismissal of all women-officers in the Army. Countless other obstacles prevented the union of the Salvation Army and the Church of England.

An account of the church would not be complete without some mention of Evangeline Booth, who stood head and shoulders over the crowd, as she pushed on with rehabilitation work all through the last quarter of the nineteenth century and well on into the decades that followed. This remarkable woman was the fourth daughter of General William Booth, the founder of the Salvation Army. She was born in London on Christmas Day, 1865. The little "Eva" was very much impressed with life around her, and listened with childish wonder as her mother read aloud the Scriptures and told the story of Christmas. At the age of ten she was "preaching" to her dolls, and her scrawny dogs and cats that she had rescued from the gutter. Her father, listening to her from the stairs, took notes, and at the bottom of the page he wrote, "Eva will be a real orator."

It is not surprising to hear that this young woman began preaching in the main streets of London before her eighteenth birthday. Evangeline was given greater responsibilities as the Army expanded; in fact, she was appointed Captain of a Corps located in the worst part of London—the troublesome West End. Naturally, there was a struggle to overcome the prejudice that had long prevailed against women in public life. But in the end, the girl-preacher found herself with a bodyguard of self-appointed ruffians. It was a beginning significant in many ways.

There was at this time no religious organization giving undivided attention to those who were without food and shelter, to say nothing of medical care. In other words, the people who listened to the words of the Gospel had nice manners and lived in nice houses; they were, to speak plainly, a thoughtless, somewhat selfish group of first-class citizens. But the Army workers changed this, feeling that religion was for the poor, as well as the rich. This new philosophy was accepted readily by the unfortunate and downtrodden inhabitants in the dark spots of the great city.

It is clear that Army workers needed plenty of courage. As for Miss Booth, she was never afraid to go out and fight for "her soldiers." Disturbances of some kind occurred almost daily. Drivers would complain that crowds frightened their horses; merchants would complain that crowds blocked the entrance to their shops. Miss Booth would rush to trouble-spots—places where indignant citizens had gathered—and offer words of encouragement to her followers—all of whom would be nervous, and somewhat perplexed. For after all, serving the Almighty was an honorable occupation. She would appear later before a magistrate, and plead for her people without benefit of help from headquarters.

The whole controversy was placed before the House of Lords in 1888. This august body went over the situation most carefully, and decided that the Salvation Army was innocent of "any breaches of the peace." At last, praying in the streets was a lawful vocation.

Evangeline Booth was appointed to any number of offices in the Army before her twenty-fifth birthday. She was known as "Field Commissioner" in those days. But this was only a novitiate for more strenuous work in the new world. The Salvation Army in Canada was in need of a better organizing force, and without much ado, Evangeline was sent across the Atlantic to take over this responsibility. The Army is organized on a quasi-military basis, and its members never question orders any more than a regular military man would do. Miss Booth spent nine years in Canada; she performed a service there which was fruitful in many ways. During the mad rush to the Klondike, a Nursing Corps was taken to that desolate spot—Army workers sharing all the toil and danger of a somewhat perilous journey.

In 1904, Miss Booth moved on to the United States where she became national leader of a religious body that differed widely in ancestry. This was a formidable task. As a rule people in the States are quick to detect real worth, be it in social or business affairs. An undated pamphlet of the Army records that Commander Booth ". . . endeared herself to all sections of the nation by her simplicity of purpose and her devotion to the ideals set out so vividly in her public addresses." The extension and consolidation of the Salvation Army's work during this period bears testimony to Miss Booth's administrative abilities. Faced at the onset with overwhelming problems of money and personnel, she established the new organization on a sound financial basis.

The "lassies" became familiar figures in cities, towns, and even country cross-roads; they carried tambourines, and wore navy-blue uniforms with bonnets to match, a bright red ribbon stretched across the brim. This was an odd idea in religious life, catching the interest of people young and old, many of whom had been born into poverty, and had never been able to improve their station in life.

In retrospect, it is amazing that these strangers dared to preach the value of fresh air to a group of new settlers who were sleeping the "European way" behind closed doors and windows. The Salvation Army went further in its health campaign, attacking the problem of under-nourishment. For where great poverty exists, poor families are apt to subsist for the most part on bread and potatoes. A strong social force was getting under way—the Gospel of a good life for everybody.

Then came the news that a war was in the making (1913)—possibly a struggle which might bring distress to many families. The question of procedure arose, and Evangeline Booth found the answer. Strangely enough, she had no idea that her "humble services" would one day receive wide-spread attention. The responsibility of raising money for an expedition abroad fell upon the shoulders of Commander Booth. She borrowed twenty-five thousand dollars from different banks and began to make preparations for war work. It was a gamble, so to speak, for no one knew exactly what was to be done; but when the call came, the Salvation Army was ready. There was a touching appeal in the short talk which Evangeline gave to her "lassies" the day before they left for France.

> She called the little company of pioneer workers together in a quiet place. . . . She looked down into the eyes of the young maidens and bade them put utterly away from them the arts and coqueteries of youth, and remember that they were sent forth to help and save and love the souls of men as God loved them; and that self must be forgotten or their work would be in vain.[23]

Miss Booth also said that if any worker felt the assignment too difficult, he or she should turn back, even at the last minute. It was made clear that the undertaking might be one of hardship.

The real issue back of the Army's doughnut-canteens has been overlooked by more than a few people who have gone over the records of World War I. The Salvation Army workers went to France to save the soldiers from themselves,[24] not just to mix batter and fry little circles of dough in hot fat. The serving of food was only a clever, rather subtle approach to a well-organized plan of mission work.

And who could point out the merits of this operation better than "Scoop." He was a soldier, a drunkard and a gambler. But there was something about the Salvation Army huts that appealed to this young man, and he got into the habit of dropping in at odd moments for a friendly chat with the attendants. Before anyone realized what was happening the

> Consecrated men and girls began to work in his heart and conscience and speak to him of better things that might even be for him.

[23] Booth, Evangeline and Hill, Grace Livingston. *The War Romance of the Salvation Army.* J. B. Lippincott Company. Philadelphia, Pa. 1919. p. 53.

[24] The average soldier becomes very homesick in a foreign country, especially during periods when mail is delayed.

When he felt the desire for drink or gambling coming on he gave his money to the girls to keep for him.

On the last pay-day before he was sent to another location he took a paint-brush and some paint and made a little sign which he set up in a prominent place in the hut, his silent testimony to what they had done for him: FOR THE FIRST TIME ON PAY DAY SCOOP IS SOBER![25]

The Salvation Army has become a spiritual force in society for two reasons: (1) the officers work on the principle that any outcast may be restored to society, if that individual shows a desire to mingle with law-abiding groups; (2) the question of sex has no place in the Salvation Army, men and women working together in unanimity for a common cause. Concerning women in the Army, a high official had this to say:

Eliminate the women and the Salvation Army would be less than half what it is; far less, not merely because women officers out-number the men, but because to eliminate them would mean not alone the loss of their influence and work, but the loss of the influence resulting from the combination of men *and* women, which is different from, and more potent than, the influence of either sex by itself. 'Male and female created He them.'[26]

Evangeline Booth was elected General of the Salvation Army in the year 1934, thus becoming the *first woman* to lead an international religious organization. She accepted this last honor merely as a continuance of God's work under another title, and in an inspiring address of dedication, the newly-elected General repeated her Covenant[27] before the High Council of the Army.

This was a dramatic moment in the life of the Salvation Army, one which was to have far-reaching consequences in the years to come. It was the old story: reward coming with competence. What

---

[25] Booth, Evangeline and Hill, Grace Livingston. *The War Romance of the Salvation Army.* J. B. Lippincott Company. Philadelphia, Pa. 1919. p. 124.

[26] Booth, Catherine Bramwell. *Bramwell Booth.* Rich & Cowan. London. 1933. p. 195.

[27] Wilson, P. W. *The General (A Story of Evangeline Booth).* Hodder and Stoughton, Limited. London. 1935. pp. 100–103.

this woman accomplished after taking over the reins of leadership is almost beyond belief.

> She . . . travelled more than 200,000 miles, inspecting the Army's activities and addressing huge public gatherings. In 1936 the General conducted services on the Continent of Europe and in England, including a Motorcade from Land's End to John o'Groats, holding four and five meetings daily for ten days, and reaching 100,000 people.

> From November, 1936, to February, 1937, she was on tour in the Far East, visiting India, Ceylon, Malaya and Java. Campaigns during 1937 included a two months's visit to the United States and Canada, in addition to many great gatherings in the Homeland, ending with a Birthday Party to 1,500 slum children.[28]

How Evangeline Booth took the wear and tear of such a life is beyond understanding, for she was not the rough type. In later years, there were many anxious conferences as to whether she should remain in control of the Army, for while General "Eva" was seventy-three years of age, she was in good health, and possessed remarkable vitality. In a fitful moment of mirth, she once challenged Lord Abedare, Chairman of the National Fitness Council, to a duel at driving, riding and hurdling. This remarkable woman's whole life had been dedicated to the uplifting and betterment of mankind. But all journeys must end. She passed to the "Fortress of God" in New York City on July 17, 1952.

Maude Royden, the daughter of Sir Thomas Royden of Frankby Hall, grew up in a society that was somewhat backward in social matters; but despite this handicap, she developed advanced ideas concerning people in different classes of society. As for education, there were lessons at home, and further instruction in private schools. Maude studied for a time at the Ladies College, Cheltenham, and then went on to do more advanced work at Lady Margaret Hall, Oxford University.[29] She left Oxford before graduation. The

---

[28] International Headquarters of the Salvation Army. *The "Transcript Particulars" of Miss Booth's Career.* London. E.C.A. February 15, 1939.

[29] *Letter* in the writer's file. October, 1938.

Royden family belonged to the established church, an institution very close to their hearts. However, "a daughter was frozen out" of church life in a grossly stupid manner.

At the Victoria Women's Settlement, Liverpool, in 1901, Miss Royden began a really active career. The more time she spent in depressed areas, the more she felt that social questions should be settled in the Christian way. Evidently this particular churchwoman was open-minded in religious matters, for she was attracted to the Roman Catholic faith for a short spell, because of its emphasis on Christian formula, including prayers at all hours of the day. It was not that Maude Royden failed to find Christian principles set forth in Anglican churches, but that she sometimes found them set forth in a make-believe manner. For instance, having left a parcel in an Anglican church, Miss Royden asked a friend to call for it the following day. The Verger looked suspiciously at his caller and said: "What was the lady doing here?" At another time, she attempted to say her prayers at Westminster Abbey. She said:

> To begin with, I found that I was expected to seek a dark and dank little corner called St. Faith's Chapel before I could pray without exciting the curiosity and even consternation of passers-by. Having found it, I had hardly fallen on my knees when a loud voice announced that the chapel was about to be closed. This was the middle of the afternoon. I emerged and reflecting that, after all, nobody's curiosity need prevent me from saying my prayers. I knelt down in the nave, and when I rose to go, found that I had become encircled in a crimson cord and was apparently regarded as an essential part of evensong, for, when I tried to leap over or crawl under the crimson cord, the Verger was greatly annoyed with me.[30]

These experiences naturally impressed the mind of a woman whose thoughts had turned toward church work as a full-time occupation. These few lines present the story of an independent spirit making adjustments with life, working here, and worshiping there in an effort to sift values in the great strainer of experience.

[30] The Countess of Oxford and Asquith. *Myself When Young*. Frederick Muller, Ltd. London. 1938. p. 374.

Maude Royden could not be called an *extremist*. She liked animals, but according to friends was never silly about them. She owned dogs at different times, but Rufus, a "rascal cairn," was the only one who established himself with any degree of success in the Royden household. Interests for this woman lay in scholarly pursuits. She produced several worthwhile books: *Sex and Common Sense* (1922); *I Believe in God* (1927); *Women's Partnership in the New World* (1941). Miss Royden wrote as well as preached on subjects touching life at many angles. Her sermons contained no nonsense, no attempt to gloss over facts in the face of truth. Indeed, men and women—both the young and the old—sat spellbound at this daring approach to religious teaching. In retrospect, it is amusing to learn just how an English rector would introduce a woman preacher. There were songs, there were prayers, after which came the announcement: "The service is at an end. Miss Royden will now talk."[31]

It seems the turning point of Maude Royden's career was her association with the church of Luffenham in Northamptonshire. It was here that she spent one year as a quasi-curate. From all reports, the scripture lessons became a hilarious event, ". . . peals of laughter, hitherto unknown, used to echo from her classroom through the house, making it like Charles Kingsley's rectory at Eversley, the house of gayety."[32] Laughter and gayety bespeak contentment; a young woman, not stereotyped in character, was finding herself.

Possibly, Miss Royden's real opportunity came with her temporary appointment as preacher to a large congregation at the City Temple.[33] She became a vogue for churchgoers in and around the great city on the Thames. Some worshipers may have attended the services out of curiosity; they returned to hear the messages of the Bible presented in simple, straightforward English.

[31] *Time* (Magazine). 540 North Michigan Avenue, Chicago, Ill. (U.S.A.). January 18, 1937.
[32] Courtney, Janet E. *The Women of My Time.* Lovat Dickson, Limited. London. 1934. p. 208.
[33] The City Temple in London is sometimes called the "Cathedral of British Noncomformity."

Within two years, the question arose as to what Maude Royden would do next. That she had preaching ability, friends and the public at large did not doubt. Then, assisted by her parish priest, Miss Royden started "fellowship services," but she saw to it that the hours of worship did not conflict in any way with those of the established church. The first meeting was held in Kensington Town Hall. By 1920, more suitable quarters were secured in the Guildhouse on Eccleston Square, not far from Victoria Station.[34]

The meetings were very informal in character, and attracted large groups of young people. The preparatory activities, such as arranging flowers and distributing hymnals, were carried on almost entirely by teen-age boys and girls.[35] When conducting services, Miss Royden wore a dark blue gown and small beret of the same color; she brought a kind of theatrical quality to the pulpit, restrained, yet most compelling. She always observed a period of silence both before and after the sermon. A unique part of the church-hour was this: Miss Royden answered questions after the final prayer, and even sought advice on subjects of importance. It was natural for a spirit of fellowship to develop.

Like many other women, Maude Royden felt herself forced into the Suffrage movement. She is reported to have said, "How could I do anything, if I had not the elementary rights of a citizen? And whose position needed changing so much as women's."[36] In time, she became a member of the National Union of Women's Suffrage Societies; but she avoided all militant activities, such as window breaking and various other destructive operations.

This woman-preacher, so far-seeing in other matters, really thought that men would give the vote to women without being

---

[34] Miss Royden gave up her ministerial work in 1936 with the idea of giving lectures on *Peace*.

[35] The writer's diary. 1933.

[36] The Countess of Oxford and Asquith. *Myself When Young*. Frederick Muller, Ltd. London. 1938. p. 374.

bullied and frightened into such a pronouncement. There are many ways of serving society during a life time; one is showing what can be accomplished that has not been accomplished before. Maude Royden belongs in this particular category of pioneers.

A career means just so much to the average woman, and then possibly she begins to give serious thought to the years ahead. Miss Royden did not consider wedlock apparently until she was well along in the sixties. Then she married a friend of long standing, the Reverend G. W. Hudson Shaw, who had but recently retired from the vicarage of St. Botolph's, Bishops Gate. As so often happens when a couple have reached three score and more, the marriage ties were soon broken by Mr. Shaw's death. This turn of events was most unfortunate for Mrs. Shaw, but she stayed on in London "among her books and flowers" for twelve years. Her death occurred on July 29, 1956.

In looking back, it is a joyous thought to recall Maude Royden in the heyday of her success, crowds of people making their way on a Sunday to the Guildhouse on Eccleston Square. England was sorely in need of spiritual remedies in the nineteen-thirties. It was a period of faint hope, and considerable discouragement—a state of affairs especially bad for the under-thirty group. Miss Royden made every effort to reach these individuals, and succeeded beyond the fondest dreams of friends and acquaintances.

Dorothy F. Wilson was the daughter of Sir Courthope Wilson, a prominent resident of Liverpool. Miss Wilson prepared herself for the ministry at Mansfield College,[37] Oxford University, one of the few theological colleges then open to women. She gained experience as a minister by going from place to place while still a very young woman. In January, 1928, Miss Wilson was appointed assistant pastor of Carr's-Lane Church, Birmingham, one of the foremost Congregational Churches in England. Later on, she widened her

---

[37] Dorothy Wilson was the first woman to be awarded the Oxford Diploma in Theology with Distinction.

vision by traveling and delivering sermons abroad. She was chaplain and lecturer on religion for a time at Mills College in California, U.S.A. Miss Wilson had set ideas about handling everyday problems, but she never strayed far from the simple lessons taught by the Master nineteen hundred years ago.

In 1938, shortly after her affiliation with the City Temple in London, Miss Wilson preached to a crowded congregation at the Union Church in Brighton. The young minister wore a flowing black gown and a small pointed cap, the costume being both becoming and appropriate. The press reported that the services by the seashore left nothing to be desired. Miss Wilson was said to think straight, and to present her material in a clear, forceful manner.

The Reverend Dorothy Wilson was especially blessed in her chosen profession, having a voice that was not only musical but well modulated. However, her career as a minister ended sadly in a way, being cut short by an attack of spinal arthritis, a disease that has long baffled medical science. Miss Wilson understood the nature of her problem, and in effect, the perils of her homeland with its constant rains and chilling winds. She began a series of ocean voyages in search of a new home, settling first in the West Indies, and later moving further south to the Province of Natal in South Africa. Apparently, this woman, once so active in religious circles, found some degree of comfort in her final years of retirement, staying on in the colorful city of Dunbar until her death in the autumn of 1956. She had followed closely in the footsteps of Maude Royden.

The women who made a name for themselves in the preaching field stayed away from matrimony during their creative years. Possibly, women do their best development work when not tied down with the responsibilities of family life. In the long ago, the Council of Chalcedon considered the problems of women engaged in church work, laying down the rule that they "must be at least forty years of age." Of course, it would have been neither seemly, nor practicable, for a young mother to go about the country ministering to strangers while the care of her own household was being undertaken by servants. But the evidence submitted thus far would indicate that women who are interested in preaching the Gospel have little concern for the everyday chores of housekeeping. On the other hand, few women in England have shown any desire for the self-effacing duties of church work. This situation brings to mind the idea stressed again and again in this book, that women, as well as men, should select a career for which they possess a natural aptitude.

The City Temple of London sustained its reputation for "free thought," and called the Reverend Marjorie Inkster to its staff as assistant minister. This new-comer to church ranks is an experienced social worker, having specialized in psychiatry. The treatment of disease has gone a long way by means of mental influence. It was on May 3, 1959,[38] that Miss Inkster preached her first sermon, dwelling on the fact that all things must be started "the right way round," if success is to be achieved in even the smallest undertaking. The young speaker wore an academic robe and a stiff, white cravat, which added both a formal note and a touch of style. This latest recruit to church work got along without any head-covering, a somewhat odd departure from established custom. St. Paul spoke with some authority on this subject, but his words have apparently faded through the centuries to a weak whisper.

The writer has found very little material concerning the elevation of women to prominent positions in the Presbyterian Church in England. But apparently, without much ado, these churches have been keeping abreast of the times. For the news has come that Miss A. I. Gordon ". . . is to become the first woman minister of the Presbyterian Church of England. Her application to be received into the ministry was considered in private yesterday by the general assembly of the Church, who decided to grant it."[39] Miss Gordon is

---

[38] *The News Chronicle.* London. May 4, 1959.
[39] *The Times.* London. May 11, 1956.

not a new-comer to duties such as these, having been very active in missionary work for the Church of Scotland for more than a decade. This service involved travel to distant lands — India and Manchuria.

The question arises as to how ministerial work in England compares with that of other countries. Conditions differ somewhat from place to place. The clergymen in England cannot afford motor cars; they must either walk or ride bicycles on their daily round of duties. Few parishes cover anything like the acreage of assignments abroad. The Church of England, through the Church Commission, looks after the ministers' yearly stipend, the amount depending upon the paying ability of a given community. English clergymen are not favored over other professional groups in money matters; they must pay taxes along with neighbors up and down the street — the "juicy bit" being the new pound notes which are slipped under a parsonage door at Easter, or, as so often happens, on Christmas Eve. There is a certain charm about this custom, for the average parishioner is willing to make gifts, but dislikes the idea of paying out precious cash for repairing a roof, or rebuilding a chimney on church property.

The British equivalent of an American parish pastor will be a salary of $1,500 to $3,000 a year, plus his house. But an assistant, for maybe five years, will receive a minimum of only $700 to $900.[40]

Then there is the matter of social prestige so dear to the British heart. A clergyman in the States will rank with a well-respected business man, while in England, a man with the same training will move along with the chosen few in a given parish. This difference may not be deep-seated, but it has a quality which is very real to an outsider sipping tea in the garden of an old manor house.[41] The Church of England does fairly well for a Bishop, allowing him a stipend that is close to ten thousand dollars each year, and a house that is superior to other structures in the neighborhood. Many of the

[40] The Cincinnati *Times Star*. Cincinnati, Ohio (U.S.A.). August 17, 1957.
[41] The writer's diary, July, 1931.

church properties are on low ground, and they often adjoin, or are close to, village cemeteries. This is especially true of the older parsonages, many of which were put up in the last century when unemployment was rife, and civic projects almost a necessity.

There may be another consideration in ministerial work: It is said that women can sense hidden sorrows or difficult situations more quickly than men.[42] This communication may be called "mental penetration," "immediate insight," or other term to denote *intuition*. Ray Strachey, an English writer, says of women:

> [They] do seem to look at life and its problems from an angle slightly different from that of men. Either by nature, or by the normal circumstances of their lives and personal experiences, their scales of values are just a little different. They do seem to attach more importance to people than to things, and to be, in an emergency, more realistic.[43]

This may be a questionable assumption. Yet it is worth a little thought in a day when everything in life is being held up for inquiry — even discovery.

What about the Church of England in the twentieth century? It has developed some—not a great deal—in the way of insight into human affairs. Consider the different forms of worship: (1) there is the High Church—sometimes called the Anglo-Catholic; (2) there is the Low Church—sometimes called the Anglican; (3) there is the Broad Church—sometimes called the Modernist. This last group is particularly interested in social problems. A small boy said to the writer not long ago, "Oh, my church isn't much for looks. But I like it because we do more eating than praying—with hardly any Jesus Christ stuff." Possibly, the younger generation is moving away from church ritual—clinging more to the mundane things of life.

There is no doubt but that women-ministers are needed today as

[42] Hartman claims that woman is closer to the Unconscious, that is, closer to the ultimate ground of existence than man. (See Hartman, E. von. *Philosophie des Unbewustens.* Zweite vermehrte Auflage. Berlin. Altenburg. 1870).

[43] *The British Civil Servant.* Edited by William A. Robson. George Allen & Unwin, Ltd. London. 1937. p. 189.

never before in history. For many boys and girls have not been subjected to any kind of religious teaching; they drift from home to
school picking up what is good or bad on the way. Indeed, the time
has come to alter the managerial technique of church work now that
early marriages are accepted quite generally, especially among
lower-class families. The law gives some protection to this group,
the consent of both parents being required before wedlock can be
undertaken. But there is another side to this problem, one which calls
for spiritual help. It is this, ". . . 23,386 of the 97,601 brides under the
age of 21 were already pregnant on their wedding day. . . . Doubts
are inevitably aroused as to the moral, material, and physical preparedness of these young people for their responsibilities towards each
other and for home making."[44] Then, there are individuals who
purposely or otherwise take on the responsibility of parenthood
without marriage. In these cases, the girl is often immature, not
quite sure of her responsibility, and anxious to be popular with the
boys in her immediate circle. What these youngsters need is not a
gloss-over of facts, but some down-to-earth comments on what happens to the wayward, especially girls, in a society bound by traditional decency.

There is still another problem. Many half-grown boys and girls
have but one thought: how to get ahead with a well-paid job. They
are not at all enthusiastic about a faith that will make them strong
and self-sufficient in the years ahead. Unfortunately, few young
people, with the exception of Roman Catholic groups, go to church
nowadays—standing in front of many churches on Sunday will
verify this statement. Yet the average individual, both young and
old, places great value on religious activities. The difficulty lies perhaps in a lazy approach to anything requiring mental effort. For
spiritual insight does not come through chance; it requires—except
in very special cases—many years of work in various fields of study.

Social workers report that children, as a group, seldom seek the

[44] *The Times Educational Supplement.* London. March 1, 1957.

counsel of older people when faced with unforeseen difficulties. On a holiday in Brighton in 1937, the writer asked three young friends if they ever went to a minister of their faith with personal problems. An account of this interview follows: (a) first girl, age 12, offered a blank look; (b) second girl, age 14, gave a non-commital reply; (c) third girl, age 15, provided a challenging idea; she said, "Oh, that old man!"

Progress in the ministry can be reported in some quarters, women now being welcomed in all lay offices in the Baptist, Methodist and Congregational Churches. The Church of England still remains aloof. Of the different denominations, it is quite impossible to tell from the published reports just how many women have been rejected because of hard-set ideas—prejudice if you like—in a particular community. This angle of religious policy seldom meets the light of public discussion. One difficulty—always kept under cover—has been the selfishness of men in religious circles—bad enough in England, but to some extent, worse in other countries. In Italy, as late as 1950, a woman's name could not appear on a list of subscribers to a Protestant church fund—that mark of respect being reserved for the "lady's husband." In this case, the church was following a rule introduced in times long past; such a policy does not reflect either present-day thinking, or present-day trends in social matters.

All through this period of church quibbling, women have quietly preached the Gospel of Jesus Christ, and thus enlarged their sphere of usefulness, not only in England, but in far-away countries. They have carried on quite unselfishly, neither receiving, nor expecting any special attention. A situation such as this leads quite naturally to speculation—many people being convinced that women will be admitted to Holy Orders within the present century. It is no secret that a few, forward-looking clergymen feel deep down in their hearts that women as well as men should be invested with the right to give spiritual guidance to all who have weakened in the social struggle.

IX. Law

A SHORT review of England's legal system will be given at this
point—the opening of a new chapter—for what happened
yesterday, may condition what happens today. English law is em-
bedded deep-down into national life—that is, it reflects the everyday experiences of many common folks. And truly, society was not
far removed from barbarism in the long ago—women, slaves, sheep,
and cattle being placed on the same footing in legal documents. On
the whole, there are too many debatable questions to go much further with this phase of history. Suffice to say, there has been evolved
the marvelous idea of selecting twelve men to settle disputes by way
of discussion.

This plan is known as *trial by jury*—the famous common law in
the making. It is amusing to note that juries—like the men called up
900 years ago in England—were never intended to be tools of freedom, but rather instruments of oppression. As it came about, William
the Conqueror contrived the scheme of forcing a group of workers
—under oath—to make out a concise record of neighborhood possessions.[1] It was a sound bit of reasoning: no acre of land, no head of
stock, could escape taxation. This undertaking is fully described in
the *Domesday Book* of 1086, a work describing England's first tax
structure.

A legal system that could be helpful to a powerful group, could
also be helpful to a less-powerful group—that is, land-owners were
quick to see that a jury of close neighbors could be used to advantage
against a body of autocratic Norman nobles. It followed that during
the next one hundred years, the right of *trial by jury* was wrested
from King John, a monarch who was much-disliked by his subjects.
Thus, the *Magna Charta* of 1215 carried this promise of justice: "No

[1] The custom of prying into neighborhood affairs is still followed by insurance companies in
many parts of the world—senior residents being interviewed.

free man shall be imprisoned or outlawed or banished or in any way destroyed except by the legal judgment of his peers or by the law of the land." This was a strange twist in legal procedure. It all goes to show how social trends *can*, and *do*, upset national affairs. Incidentally, to attain justice is far more difficult than to attain order. For justice, as the world understands the term, is "to give every man his own" (*suum cuique tribuere*). But in all trials there are circumstances which may interfere with justice.[2]

There were problems of course, as local authorities did not like to take part in disputes of any kind. In the natural order of events, a really serious fracas might develop. Then it was that elders of the community would hold a meeting, and cautiously—very cautiously, it is said—"toss about a few unpleasant facts." If the accused refused to talk, or had been caught red-handed, he would receive a fine, accompanied by a stiff lecture from the Chairman. It frequently happened that friends or relatives would come forward with help—either by pledges, or with gifts of goods. But, as might have been expected, the day came when royal officials approached court procedure from the profit-angle—old records mentioning special sums for "disobedience to the King." This short review indicates that the legal pattern had shaped up rather well by the fifteenth century. A point to remember is this: English law was colored by Roman law.

Over a long period of time, it was all England could do to keep the jury system in working order. Many forces were at play against justice. There was the case of William Penn (1670), the Quaker who preached to crowds in the streets—the Meeting House having been closed by soldiers. This pioneer social worker was arrested, and imprisoned for disturbing the peace. It was a delicate subject. Realizing that the right of free speech was involved, a group of *non-Quakers* gave a speedy verdict of acquittal. But the presiding judge objected to these findings, and had the jurors locked up for three days without

---

[2] In a "cruelty to animals" case not too long ago, the writer was told by a juror, "I'm sorry, lady, but I had to vote with the crowd, as my business is suffering." (The trial involved a coal company that changed drivers, but not horses, day after day, and night after night.)

food, water, or even a few creature comforts. It followed that all twelve men were given prison sentences. Members of the highly-respected bar were horrified; they appealed to the Court of Common Pleas for help. This body voted to set the jurors free—the only lawful thing to do. It is clear that England was fighting every step of the way in order to establish what is today a near-perfect legal system.

In reviewing jury cases, let one fact be understood: a verdict of *"not guilty" cannot be set aside*. Favoritism in court procedure has always been illegal. Certain abuses of the jury system have come to light from time to time. There was, for example, the daring move of James II (1633–1701) in the Trial of the Seven Bishops. This Monarch "packed" a jury to suit himself—even calling in his own brewer. This individual was so perked up with his new duties that he talked freely of a possible acquittal. For otherwise, he said, there would be "no more beer" sold at the Palace. Finally, the Revolution of 1689 brought the Bill of Rights with its strict provision against the coercing of jurors. Fortunately, the habit of accepting a judgement by peer and neighbor was seldom questioned in the New World. Those early settlers were fighting for a new way-of-life; they had no intention of giving up rights of any kind to despotic rulers, be they domestic or foreign.

This was one reason why the Stamp Act of 1765 was so unpopular in the colonies. Signs of danger were on all sides. Yet the ministers of George III

Placed enforcements in the hands of admiralty courts, with no juries and with judges who served only at the King's pleasure. It was this flagrant denial of trial by jury, added to the indignity of taxation without representation, that forced even the hesitant among the colonists into the ever greater resistance that culminated in the War of the Revolution.[3]

The English people have never been able to get over the shock—American students hearing the story over and over again in English

[3] Maisel, Albert Q. "The Right to Trial by Jury." *Newsweek Magazine* (U.S.A.). January, 1963. p. 123.

universities. This subject is treated quite casually in American institutions of learning—just another awkward political disturbance.[4]

It is clear that men and women in the Colonies had great faith in the jury system. And there is some data to support the idea that an average jury can decide a court case quite as well as a group of scholarly judges. A study of this subject was made in the United States—and in a most painstaking manner. The following question was considered: Can juries made up of individuals without legal training decide cases as fairly and wisely as skilled, experienced judges?

Strong evidence that they can comes from about 700 state and federal court judges co-operating with the Jury Study Project of the University of Chicago Law School. In some 4,000 criminal cases, these trial judges set down the verdicts they would themselves have rendered if a jury trial had been waived. When these hypothetical verdicts were compared with the actual jury decisions, it was found that in 80 per cent of all cases judge and jury were in complete agreement. For almost all of the remainder, the judges conceded that the juries' decisions were not miscarriages of justice but justifiably different evaluations of the evidence.[5]

Most significant is the fact that in nine out of every ten instances where judge and jury disagreed, it was a case where the jury voted to acquit. For, in criminal cases, juries work under a special rule: they must not convict a defendant unless the evidence convinces them of his guilt *beyond a reasonable doubt*. A concept of justice is based upon the premise that it is far better that some guilty men go free than that any innocent man should ever wrongfully lose his liberty.[6]

No one would care to deny that there are weak links in the jury system. But through the centuries, it has been the only way to come even close to handing out justice. Jesus Christ selected "twelve ordinary men" as assistants. Is it that wisdom springs from life itself?

It is evident that adults in England are given a fairly good deal in the courts. But what about children, the really helpless members of

---

[4] A generous treaty of peace was signed in Paris in 1783 and the independence of the Colonies was specifically recognized by the mother country.

[5] Maisel, Albert Q. "The Right to Trial by Jury." *Newsweek Magazine*. (U.S.A.). January, 1963. p. 124.

[6] *Ibid*. pp. 124–125.

society? There are many angles to criminal responsibility. And a court case is a serious matter, for conviction may be a handicap later on in life—especially in the matter of employment. However, the age of recognition (of wrong-doing) was raised from seven[7] to eight years by the Children's and Young Person's Act of 1933. The law is specific:

> To obtain a conviction in the case of a defendant between the ages of eight and fourteen the prosecution must prove not only that the child committed the crime but also, on evidence which is clear and beyond all probability of doubt, that he had guilty knowledge that he was doing wrong. Where evil intention is an essential ingredient of the offence a child is protected by a legal presumption that he has not sufficient capacity to know that what he did was wrong. This presumption may, however, be rebutted by evidence concerning his behavior in relation to the alleged offence, as for example that on seeing the police officer the child took to his heels and, when caught, denied having the stolen articles which were afterwards found on him.[8]

Fortunately, the Committee left a loop-hole in its recommendation —there being a vague promise of special consideration for less-mature individuals. The main idea back of this legislation is to keep little folks away from ordinary courts of justice.

Welfare workers try to shield children who are in trouble—that is, keep them from the glare of publicity. For after being cited for minor offences, boys and girls—a few at least—are apt to conclude that they are very special individuals. This is one reason why juvenile trials are held in buildings especially set aside for the purpose— some distance from quarters given over to adults. Further, no person shall be present except:

(a) Members and officers of the court;

(b) Parties to the case before the court, their solicitors and counsel, and witnesses and other persons directly concerned in that case;

[7] The age of criminal responsibility had stood at the age of seven for hundreds of years—an incredible situation.

[8] Cavenagh, Mrs. W. E. *The Child and the Court.* Victor Gallancz, Ltd. London, 1959. p. 73.

(c) Bona fide representatives of newspapers or news agencies;

(d) Such other persons as the court may specially authorize to be present.[9]

There are restrictions as to what may be published about children. Thus, the strong protect the weak.

A number of women have done good work as magistrates; they succeed remarkably well with children, persuading young offenders "to tell it all to me now." The office of magistrate is usually a good-will assignment (unsalaried). The number of women doing this type of work is increasing year by year—now reaching into the thousands.

The life of a woman justice is replete with interest, each day's work bringing unforeseen experiences. A small furore was caused in 1926 when a woman magistrate in Colchester Police Court refused to leave the Bench during the hearing of a case that brought blushes to the cheeks of a fellow magistrate. The newspapers warmly applauded the woman's resistance in the matter—one pointing out that "a false feeling of delicacy is getting out-of-date, and while it does credit to our sentiment, it does not increase respect for our judgement.[10] So much for common sense in a changing world.

Without question, legal practices in England were evolved over the centuries, by way of trial and error.

The use of lands was, originally, a device for enjoying the benefits of land-ownership without incurring any of its legal responsibilities. As we have seen, one of the fundamental principles of tenure is, that the position (the *status* or 'estate') of the tenant is burdened with various services and 'incidents of tenure.' Regarded as a means of achieving certain political objects, these liabilities were essential. Regarded as a condition of the enjoyment of the profits of the land, they were mere encumbrances, to be got rid of if possible. Moreover, they were liabilities which, in many cases, could not actually be performed by certain classes of persons. Thus, a child, a woman, or a religious house, could not in person perform military service; though, doubtless, in such cases, a substitute could be sent. On the other

---

[9] Jiles, F. T. *Children and the Law.* (Pelican Books). England. p. 23.

[10] *The Westminster Gazette.* London. November 8, 1926.

hand, a certain class of person was only too liable to commit treason or felony, and thus incur a forfeiture of his estate, or to run into debt, and have his land seized by his creditors under the new remedy of Elgit provided by the Statute of Westminster the Second [1285]. Finally, the desire to extend to land the power of testamentary disposition which, as we have seen, had been acquired for chattels in the twelfth and thirteenth centuries, grew stronger with each generation.[11]

To some extent, the easy transfer of land had been started by mendicant friars who came to England in the first half of the thirteenth century with the idea of establishing churches, schools, and hospitals. These holy men had no idea of purchasing ground, for they had taken vows of poverty for all time. Unfortunately, by the fourteenth and fifteenth centuries, there were imitators a plenty — groups who took over "squatter rights." Indeed, to "alienate land" for almost any purpose became an established custom in England.

As long as legal authorities borrowed quite at random from foreign records in the earlier stages, there could be no uniform system of law for trying court cases in England. From time to time, Rules and Orders were made by the Chancellor and Justices on their own responsibility. Later, these findings were published for general use. However, the material was compiled so far back that the original source is not recorded.

Among the oldest are the General Orders (as distinct from decrees affecting only particular cases) made by the Chancellors for the regulation of Chancery procedure; and it may have been that, until this example of prerogative legislation had been set by the holders of the Great Seal, the judges of the Common Law courts did not venture to exercise similar powers. At any rate, while the known Chancery Orders go back to 1388, the oldest Common Law Rules (viz. those of the Common Pleas) date only from 1457; but the oldest of these latter refers clearly to still older Rules, which seem to have disappeared. The oldest published Rules of the King's Bench appear to be of 1604; but it is more than probable that these are not in fact the first made. The oldest Exchequer (Plea) Rules known to

[11] Jenks, Edward. *A Short History of English Law*. Methuen & Co., Ltd. London. 1938. pp. 95–96.

the writer date from 1571; but these were issued by the Lord Privy Seal, not by the Barons.[12]

However, the royal officials of the twelfth and thirteenth centuries accomplished the chief part of establishing order and justice in the land, and prepared the way for drawing nearly all causes to the King's courts, thus strengthening the authority and revenue of their master, and preparing the way for one uniform system of law.

Judgement is an important intellectual exercise—for to think, is to judge. And this faculty implies the power to balance facts, and to reach conclusions that are not only fair, but preferable, or deserving preference. This last statement is a gentle reminder that the English people have long been conscious of their responsibility to children, enacting stringent legislation in their behalf.[13] This is one of the main reasons why such care is taken in selecting men and women for the Judiciary. Superior judges are named by the Crown; they are allowed to carry on for life—the demise of a Sovereign having no effect on the appointment. These guardians of justice were long addressed as Mr. Justice Brown, or Chief Baron Brown, or Lord Chancellor Brown, according to the courts over which they presided —these titles being reserved for the more formal duties of court life. As for a Judge Ordinary, this description would fit only the Judge of the Divorce and Probate Court.[14] The way of a judge is far from smooth, as questions of jurisdiction arise more or less regularly in a society where people have their own ideas as to what is right, and what is wrong.

Legal reforms got well under way by the nineteenth century. Indeed, Common Law Judges (including the three chiefs) were

[12] Jenks, Edward. *A Short History of English Law.* Metheun & Co., Ltd. London. 1938. p. 191.

[13] In 1958, "Criminal Statistics" for England showed that only one child under two years of age had been abandoned in 27 years.

[14] By 1960, the nomenclature had changed: Judges in the higher courts are now addressed as, "My Lord" or "Your Lordship"—in the County Courts as, "Your Honour."

allowed to make rules for court procedure on a wide scale. Then, additional rulings were incorporated into Common Law Procedure Acts (1852 and 1854), and meanwhile in the Chancery Amendment Act of 1850.

> The Chancellor, with the concurrence of the Master of the Rolls and one of the Vice-Chancellors, [was empowered] to make General Rules and Orders for carrying out the objects of the Act. In the Chancery Amendment Act of 1858, this power was extended to cover virtually the whole procedure of the Court; the Rule-making body being enlarged to include the newly-created Lords Justices of Appeal in Chancery. Under this power, the great consolidated Orders of 1860 were issued; and thus the way made easier for the reform undertaken by the Judicature Act of 1873.[15]

These standards of control have affected court work to this day. But far too many suggestions were based on facts of the past, and with little or no consideration for needs of the future. So it was that Judicature Acts took on the character of the *Civil Retis* of ancient times. But the changes helped to establish uniform procedure in the courts, and it became much easier to handle complaints in an impartial manner.

It is clear that reform was in the air. There were the so-called "sloppy sentimentalists" who concerned themselves chiefly with juvenile problems; but it was Charles Dickens, a down-to-earth writer, who brought the movement to public notice. He described Fang (the real name was Lang) as a powerful magistrate who made life miserable for any boy or girl brought into his court. Indeed, without much ado, these children would be branded as ruffians. Note the experience of Oliver Twist after being thrown into prison: the boy found himself

> In a small cell, something like an area cellar, only not so light. It was most intolerably dirty; for it was Monday morning; and it had been tenanted by six drunken people who had been locked up since Saturday night. But this is little. In

---

[15] Jenks, Edward. *A Short History of English Law*. Methuen & Co., Ltd. London. 1938. p. 192.

our station houses, men and women are every night confined on the most trivial charges in dungeons compared with which, those in Newgate, occupied by the most atrocious felons, tried, found guilty and under sentence of death, are palaces.[16]

Old registers show adults and juveniles on the same report waiting for their turn in court—on a single morning, there was a burglar, a bigamist, three prostitutes, and a young boy who had been caught stealing from a warehouse. So much trouble in the old days centered around those dingy, unguarded structures along the Thames.

Children whose only playground is the street get a poor start in life. From earliest years, this group has a fear of the law—really a constant dread of being "put away" either alone, or with school friends. Fortunately, few of the hapless fall from grace before the age of eight.[17] But if trouble arises, even weak laws offer fairly good protection—little being left to chance. Consider the small boy who robbed a store; he came before the Bench and was questioned as to what took place:

Chairman: 'What do you call a person who takes things belonging to other people?'
Boy: 'A thief, sir.'
Chairman: 'Is that what you are, then?'
Boy: 'No sir, . . . I just wanted the pencils.'[18]

These few lines give a vivid picture of childish reaction to man-made laws. The situation was clear—fear being confused with fact and feeling. Boys under arrest start with what is called a "reflect handicap"—boy-criminals outnumbering girl-criminals.

It is possible that "Prediction Charts" (what a given background suggests) may one day prove useful in cases which involve anti-social behavior among children. As matters stand, authorities differ greatly

[16] Dickens, Charles. *Oliver Twist.* Belford, Clarke, and Company. New York (undated). p. 75.

[17] In 1960, a Government committee recommended that the age of criminal liability be raised from 8 to 12.

[18] Cavenagh, Mrs. W. E. *The Child and the Court.* Victor Gallancz, Ltd. London. 1959. p. 135.

as to the best method of handling juvenile delinquents—that is, should they be fined, sent to an approved home, or just dismissed with a lecture on deportment. There is, of course, a close connection between a poor home—too much discipline, too little affection—and the first public complaint of unruly behavior. Indeed, the unhappy child has long been known as a "social risk."

Perhaps some device could be set up to catch semi-erratic pupils in nursery schools—unusual traits of character showing up very clearly in play activities. Why not hand out punishment before a half-grown boy or girl becomes a menace to society? Then too, the law is not above reproach, as witness what Mrs. Cavenagh had to say in her book, *The Child and the Court:* "England, Ireland, and Scotland are the only European countries that still bring school children before a court of criminal jurisdiction."[19]

Leaving a few unfortunates, there are always boys and girls in England who receive the most careful upbringing. Certainly, the schools and universities do their part. As for the Law Society, it is very co-operative, giving credit for work which has been covered in the universities. The law examination is not difficult, but on the other hand, it is not easy. So it is that students who dwaddle along, often fail to make a passing grade, or even a grade good enough to justify further effort and expense.

The few who reach the Bar should begin at once to study in either the Common Chancery or the Criminal Law Chamber, for in this way students may learn the intricacies of court procedure. The fee for such service is £200 per year. The average person should consider well before selecting a chamber. Timidity, for example, is fatal in any branch of law requiring lengthy debates. In such cases, a wise choice would be the Chancery Bar,* where much of the really important work is scholastic in character. The Government provides openings for a number of legal experts. The requirements differ, the

[19] Cavenagh, Mrs. W. E. *The Child and the Court.* Victor Gallancz, Ltd. London. 1959. p.237.
* The Chancery Bar deals with the rights of property, wills, land, trusts, etc.

best posts going to the man or woman who has secured a university degree.

For many years, the Bar Examination has consisted of the following subjects:

PART I

(1) Roman Law.
(2) Constitutional Law.
(3) The Elements of Contracts and Tort.
(4) The Elements of Real Property.

PART II

(1) Criminal Law and Procedure.
(2) Common Law.
(3) The General Principles of Equity.
(4) Company Law.
(5) Evidence and Civil Procedure.
(6) A general paper in two parts:

(a) Common

and

(b) Equity.

Law, in its various branches, is a pleasant way to earn a living. Possibly, this is one reason why so many women are drifting into the profession. However, the expense angle will no doubt deter a great many ambitious students. For instance, few girls have parents who could pay one thousand guineas, this sum being demanded quite recently by a firm in London, just for the right to become a clerk in a solicitor's office. This system of premiums might have been practical in times past, but it does not fit into the budgeted schemes of today—the average family listing income and expense down to the last penny. It is clear that this question was back

Of the first National Conference of Solicitor's Articled Clerk's Societies held recently in London. The members were unanimous in their recommendation that a clerk should begin his articles at £2 a week, increasing by £1 a year for each year of service. Thus, in the last year he would receive about £6 a week. Graduates would start at the third year rate.[20]

The Law Society favors practical experience; but such training can only be obtained in the regular routine of office work. So it is that many beginners stand in an awkward position. This arrangement has all the overtones of a fairy tale, but it has flourished these many years under the veil of custom.

At this point, the important matter of personality enters the picture, for success or failure in law may hinge on a question like this: Have you, or have you not, that distinctive something which sets you apart from other people? It is said that friendliness, and an unassuming manner make up what is known as "a distinctive character." This subject is frequently discussed, but seldom understood. Sir Ernest Wild in giving hints to barristers put it this way:

He should maintain an unruffled demeanour and smiling face; in a word, if he 'plays the game,' the great brotherhood of the Bar will eventually welcome his intrusion as inevitable. Then too, cultivate other friendships and other activities than the confines of the Inns of Court provide. Spend your vacation for choice with laymen. The bigger your world the more a man of the world will you become. This can be done without in any way severing your life from the pulsating life of your glorious profession. Never bore your wife with 'shop,' but consult her when you want a sound judgment upon matters of fact.[21]

Sir Ernest Wild goes on to say that it is well to ". . . place in the forefront of your aspiration the single-minded desire to do your small part" in upholding the present standard of British justice.

Possibly more details concerning Solicitors and Barristers[22] should be given at this point. To begin, the payment for services differ—the solicitor taking almost anything from a bank note, to a plot of ground

[20] *The Times Educational Supplement.* London. June 7, 1957.

[21] Cairns, J. A. R. *The Problem of a Career.* Arrowsmith. London. 1926. pp. 139–140.

[22] The business and reputation of individual barristers depends very often on favors handed out by solicitors—a fact seldomed mentioned in legal circles.

in the country; the barrister holding aloof from anything but cash, or a promise of payment in the near future. To some extent, it is a story of supply and demand—just a few practitioners in a given community will mean higher charges for services. Then there is a special group—the handicapped for example. These men and women often take up legal training because they can stay at home, and earn a good living. This idea appeals to the individual who dislikes crowds, or who has other interests—agriculture fitting in admirably, with some knowledge of the law. Starting out as a law student is not altogether difficult—a boy or girl asking a family friend, preferably a lawyer, to write a letter of recommendation. However, applicants should be sure that they have stamina, and more than average brain power. All in all, this is a formidable undertaking—a career for the few, rather than the many.

Now about the qualifications for a solicitor: a university degree is said to be extremely useful—almost a necessity. There has long been a tendency in England to place an eldest son, be he a good or bad student, into the exacting field of law. It cannot be denied that such a move carries prestige, so much in fact, that any number of men and women study law as background knowledge so necessary in positions in present-day corporate business, or public life—that is, they have no idea of doing serious work in any branch of the legal profession. But fortunately, there are studious individuals who have in the past, and will in the future, do credit to the Bar. David Lloyd George, for instance, made his way against countless obstacles in an effort to become a solicitor. He finally reached the top rung of the ladder as Prime Minister of Great Britain.

It is not generally understood that the advisory branch of law covers about everything in human relationships: births, deaths, and marriages, occurring with clock-like regularity. This is where trust enters the picture—a solicitor must have a flawless reputation.

In considering the barrister, opinions differ as to the proper method of training. Many people in England now believe that courses as given at the universities are not really of great importance. Even Latin, except elementary courses, is under some question. Not long ago a prominent barrister expressed the opinion that it is a mistake to provide

Too much adjustment of general education to meet the needs of professional training. Sometimes it might be a drawback to have studied at the university, because, as an advocate, the approach to law is different from that of an academic lawyer . . . the important fact to remember was the necessity for the best trained mind possible.[23]

The theory is that proficiency in the field of law can best be acquired by reading the subject in which the student has shown marked ability. A helpful plan might be to study law while in Chambers. These suggestions are based on the fact that many successful advocates have not received a formal education, but have been brought up in homes or communities having good libraries. This program would be especially suited to the man or woman who senses his or her own potentiality—and then moves in a particular direction.

Many famous barristers have been accused of self-centered conduct in court proceedings—completely ignoring social changes, to say nothing of other derangements in national affairs. As a group, the English people seldom direct criticism towards men and women highly placed in professional life. But the outside world is not so considerate, as witness what the *New Statesman* (April 1917—U.S.A.) had to say concerning an investigation of legal methods in Great Britain. This article stressed the fact that there is

Undisguised contempt in which both solicitor and barrister, notably those who have attained success in their professions and control its organization, hold, and have always held, not only all scholarship or academic learning of a professional kind, but also any theoretic or philosophical or scientific treatment of law.

It may be that judges, as a group, need the common touch—that is, more leisure for contacts in the market-place. Marcus Aurelius set a

[23] Women's Employment Federation Career School. London. 1957.

good pattern by declaring that no one should go on trial "during the harvest season."

A weak link in the judicial system of England is that which regulates divorce. Unfortunately, the problem touches many people who have little knowledge of legal procedure. The plea of cruelty is frequently offered, because on the whole, it offends good taste the least. But the word, cruel, is difficult to define, as there are so many angles to abuse, say nothing of torment.[24] A judge would have to be something of a mind-reader to sift the truth from what often amounts to a jumble of biased evidence. Not long ago, a law suit of this type attracted wide attention:

> In London, Edward George Carter, 39, testified that his wife had slapped him in the presence of his step-mother, left him in the middle of a dance-floor, smacked him on the head with a potted-plant, and hidden the family supply of tea; the judge dismissed the divorce suit on the grounds that such incidents amount to 'a case of ordinary wear and tear of married life.'[25]

Law, as interpreted in English courts, is often a puzzle to outsiders. For instance, people in the United States may speak of a particular law as "precious," meaning something that is admirable, but not quite understandable. A legal opinion of this kind in England made international news in 1960: a baker of Little Hulton, England, showed great originality by making an oval, well-turned-out loaf of bread instead of the roughcast product so familiar to housewives. It was just a slight variation, but it got one man into no end of trouble. The judge said that while he appreciated the impulse to turn out artistic merchandise, it must be understood that it is illegal to manufacture "overweight loaves." In substance, the kneaders of dough must submerge any urge to be artistic, and pay more attention to the rules which cover business life in England today.

As a student, the writer heard a professor at the University of

[24] In a definition of legal cruelty, Halsbury (3d Ed. 1955) adds the qualifying adjectives "bodily" and "mental" to the word *health*.

[25] *Time* (Magazine). 540 North Michigan Avenue, Chicago, Illinois, U.S.A. April 11, 1960.

London say, "Laws in England are made to be broken." This statement sounded too radical to be true. Yet, on second thought, these people are independent; further, they do have a keen sense of justice —and to tell them what to do might be risky business. Further, complications arise with great regularity. State officials are rarely intimidated — that is, they think first and last of the greatest good for the greatest number of people. But this is not an easy undertaking.

Consider the case of Richard (Dick) Davies, a Cockney pushcart peddler; he challenged the authority of Scotland Yard, and an entire city council. The trouble started when Dick was asked to get his cart out of Olde Worlde Shepherd's Market, so that parking meters could be installed. The man explained the situation thus, "They said I'm causing a bloomin' obstruction, . . . But I've been 'ere 15 years and I ain't moving if I don't 'ave to." This remark caused a commotion of no mean order, for the British are ever ready to defend tradition—say nothing of the underdog. So it was that Lady Hilda Salisbury-Jones, wife of the marshal of the diplomatic corps, wrote from her apartment in St. James Palace: she said quite frankly that "This beautiful, well-run stall is a great feature in Shepherd's Market and it interferes with nobody."[26] But legal tangles take time to unravel. This particular "barrow boy" may stay in his old place for quite some time.

These idiosyncrasies make life in England truly delightful. Perhaps, this slow approach to new ideas explains why women were kept in the background for so many years. As late as 1903 —the present century—a woman was denied the right to practice law on the ground of sex. Ten years later (1913), four more women, all with high university qualifications, applied to the Law Society for permission to enter the preliminary legal examination.

They based their claim on a clause in the Solicitor's Act of 1843, which set forth that 'every word importing the masculine gender only shall extend and be

[26] The Cincinnati *Enquirer*. Cincinnati, Ohio (U.S.A.). July 4, 1961.

applied to a female as well as a male, unless it be otherwise specially provided or there be something in the subject or context repugnant to such construction.'[27]

It was quite easy for the Law Society to find something "repugnant" in the attempt of the four young females to become barristers.

The next attack on this purely masculine stronghold came through the introduction of a bill in Parliament, which was intended to give women the right to engage in any branch of the legal profession. There was considerable opposition to such a radical proposal. Lord Haldane said,

> Just the fact that the Prime Minister and the Law Officers of the Crown are in favour of the principle of allowing women to practice as solicitors may encourage the Committee for the Admission of Women to the Solicitor's profession to believe that a successful end to their labours is at hand. But they should clearly understand at once that before such a measure becomes law it will have to contend against the opposition of those most intimately concerned in the matter, the Law Society and admitted solicitors.[28]

The Law Society fought the proposed legislation with determination; they pursued shabby, really underhanded tactics. The matter was shelved for a time. This was a discouraging situation. Then the news spread that business firms throughout England were favoring the idea of having women-solicitors. But prejudice was still raising its ugly head. Both men and women began to write letters to the newspapers, most of the correspondents taking the stand that solicitors were making only a fair living—that the entrance of women into the profession would make conditions intolerable.

As a rule, the men who advanced reasons why women should not practice law lacked not only vision, but a high-souled approach to social problems. For example, when the third reading of the Solicitors (Qualification of Women) Bill was formally moved in the House of Lords on March 19, 1918, the Earl of Halsbury moved the rejection of the Bill.[29] He said, in substance, that in a great measure

[27] Lang, Elsie M. *British Women in the Twentieth Century*. T. Werner Laurie, Ltd. London. 1929. p. 147.
[28] *The Times*. London. June 2, 1914.

he objected to it because he thought it extremely inopportune at the present moment seeing that the persons most concerned in the matter —solicitors and attorneys—had not been consulted. Many of them were now and had been for a long time serving their country in the field. He had great sympathy with a great deal of what had been said. His principal, and in one sense his only, objection to permitting women to be solicitors or attorneys was the fact that a great deal depended in the first instance, before litigation was actually commenced, upon the conduct of proceedings between the parties. One objection, and he was very sorry to take what appeared to be a sex objection, appeared to him to be that a woman had no recognition of any side but her own. In spite of his intervention, the Bill passed the House of Lords by a majority of 47 to 19. In all fairness, let it be said, that this well-respected Earl was ninety-two years of age, and had lived through five reigns of give and take in national affairs. Naturally, it was difficult for the elder members of Parliament to adjust themselves to a new social order. To them, a woman's place was in the home—ever ready to serve tea in the late afternoon.

A war changes the prospective of all things economic, and in due time, lawyers were forced to accept women on their payrolls as clerks, and research workers. Even then, the Law Society and the Benchers begrudged women the opportunity thrown in their way by providence. It is clear that the movement for sex equality was not popular with the public at large. The press reported facts in as few words as possible. Here is a typical news item: ". . . recently a woman applied for admission to Gray's Inn. The members refused to admit her on the ground of sex, and the judges on appeal agreed with their decision."[30] The only reason for excluding women was the "uninterrupted usage of centuries," a basis on which a number of rights rested. Thus, the conflict raged!

In the closing years of World War I, prejudice lost some of its

[29] For a complete report of the Earl of Halsbury's speech on March 19, 1918, see, The Fawcett Library (Parliamentary File). 27 Wilfred Street, London, S.W. 1.

[30] *The Times*. London. March 2, 1918.

old-time driving force. In fact, without warning of any kind, two speakers struck out on their own, and offered a few kind words concerning the women's movement.

Mr. Holford Knight, speaking at the annual general meeting of the Bar, asked that the question [of women in business and professional life] be reconsidered in the light of the further experience which had been gained during the War of the extraordinary capacity shown by women in many spheres of activity. Women were now occupying responsible positions requiring mental qualities, integrity, dignity and civic responsibility. . . . In the situation in which we were likely to find ourselves after the War, the nation would have to mobilize all the intelligence and capacity which it could discover, and in making all the energy which could be brought to carry on the nation's work, regard must be had to capacity and not to sex. . . . The legal profession had attracted the finest intellects in this and every civilized community, and there were in this country women who were fit to join that company, and had shown by their talents and character their fitness to serve the State in the capacity of members of the Bar.[31]

Another member drew attention to women lawyers in other countries. In France women had had the right to practise since 1900; in Sweden they might practise as either barristers or solicitors if unmarried; they had practised as lawyers in Denmark since 1906, in some of the cantons of Switzerland, in Finland, Norway, the Netherlands, the Argentine Republic, New Zealand, parts of Canada, throughout the greater part of Australia, in the United States of America, except Georgia, Arkansas and Virginia; even in Russia, four women had been admitted to the Bar.[32]

The gentlemen who opposed the movement had little to say; they really had no ground for a straightforward debate. When a vote was taken, the women had twenty-two supporters out of two hundred members present. Men in the legal profession had decided to go on fighting for what they must have known was a lost cause.

But far-sighted barristers must have known that women would one day be admitted to an Inn, and most likely to the Bar. For at that

[31] Lang, Elsie M. *British Women in the Twentieth Century*. T. Werner Laurie, Ltd. London. 1929. pp. 156–157.
[32] *Ibid.* p. 157.

particular time the movement for sex equality was going ahead quite rapidly. However, English groups resist anything which savors of change; they use delay tactics, not to clear up difficult situations, but to postpone any definite line of action.

English women were determined to take up the study of law—prejudice or no prejudice. They persevered in their efforts until they had won their objective. The Sex Disqualification (Removal) Bill, having passed both Houses of Parliament, became law on December 24, 1919. The first female barrister was called to the Bar in 1921.

The casual observer really missed one of the main reasons why men did not want women to practice law. It all amounted to this: barristers had established off-duty customs which were not altogether praiseworthy—that is, they had taken to amusements somewhat beneath a group of learned men. For the "good old days" of traveling circuits had produced many deep-rooted habits. All in all, it was felt that

'Full-blooded hilarity' which had so often attended the meetings of the Bar, would be inconsistent with admittance to the Bar mess of gentlewomankind. And yet it is frankly conceded by most members of the Bar that to exclude them entirely would be a denial of right to privileges which are common to all . . . the main body, it would appear, are favorable to a middle course, a sort of compromise, mainly, full right of admission for all purpose save dining and participation in the subsequent exercises . . . and while the ladies would share in all the strictly professional benefits, the men would preserve to themselves the sanctity of the recreation to which they had grown accustomed and regard as a very special heritage.[33]

Thus, a few unvarnished truths came to light.

Everyday living is something of a puzzle now that customs are changing so rapidly. Consider a social event in the early nineteen-twenties: a group of solicitors and barristers acted like spoiled school-boys, sitting in complete silence the day women dined in

[33] *The Daily Telegraph*. London. December 30, 1922.

Inner Temple for the first time. What a lack of chivalry! But in the natural order of events, these same men could not stay aloof forever; they began to agitate over the problem of "ladies dress." Consequently, in April 1923,

A Committee of Judges and Benchers of the Inns of Court considered the question and expressed the wish that women barristers should conform to the following rules: — (1) Ordinary barrister's wigs should be worn, and should completely cover the hair. (2) Ordinary barrister's gowns should be worn. (3) Dresses should be plain, black or very dark, high to the neck, with long sleeves, and not shorter than the gown, with high plain white collar and barrister's bands; or plain coats and skirts may be worn, black or very dark, not shorter than the gown, with plain white shirts and high collars and barrister's bands.[34]

As luck would have it, the ensemble was most becoming. How much help was given by wives or sisters will never be known. But with all of this effort toward regimentation, the women stood quite alone in wigs that had been washed white as snow. As a well-known Bencher said, "We never thought of washing wigs in all our years of contented wear."

The effect of this dictum on dress was felt several years later. *The Daily Telegraph* of London, September 16, 1932, reported that:

Two prisoners who asked for 'dock briefs' at the Old Bailey yesterday were surprised to find that the Counsel they had selected were women. The men walked from the dock to make their choice from a large number of barristers in wig and gown. 'I'll have that gentleman with the glasses,' said the first man, pointing to Miss Venetia Stephenson. 'That is not a gentleman, but a lady, and a very efficient one,' commented the Recorder, Sir Ernest Wild, K.C. His companion then made his choice. 'I'll have that man,' he said, and there was much laughter when he pointed to Miss Helena Normanton, 'You have both made a wise choice,' said the Recorder.

As students, girls often take up the study of law because the training is helpful in research work. Consider the office of an average barrister or solicitor—no one knows the part played by women behind

[34] *The Woman's Leader.* London. April 27, 1923.

the scenes. It took the all-seeing eye of Charles Lamb to grasp even one story:

> There was once a Mr. S. who had the reputation of being a very clever man, and of excellent discernment in the chamber practice of the law. I suspect his knowledge did not amount to much. When a case of difficult disposition of money, testamentary or otherwise, came before him, he ordinarily handed it over with a few instructions to his man Lovel, who was a quick little fellow, and would dispatch it out of hand by the light of natural understanding, of which he had an uncommon share. It was incredible what repute for talent S. enjoyed.[35]

Just so long as there are legal questions to be settled, just so long will there be "Lovels" employed in law offices.

There is no doubt but that law is an attractive, even a fascinating profession. For one thing, women, as well as men, like the thought of wearing a white wig, . . .

> To be *ipso facto* learned! The duel appeal of apparel and nomenclature accounts for a high percentage of the failures—placed as high as 70 per cent by some authorities. Therefore, at the outset, let the aspirant for forensic success denude himself of both apparel and nomenclature. These are but the trappings and the suits of potential disaster. At the Bar, as in every other walk of life, It is the human being, with all his possibilities, his capabilities, his limitations, that alone counts. Not that I would abolish the garb or the epithet; both are of value as helps to strenuous endeavour—in themselves they are nothing. But it cannot too strongly be impressed upon the youth that he must examine himself, prepare himself, before embarking upon the perilous adventure of a Call to the Bar.[36]

According to this account, a lawyer must be a super-man, always in good temper, always co-operating with the presiding judge or magistrate. And really, it is a tense moment when the judge puts on his eye-glasses, and leans forward to find out whether he is being hoodwinked or not.[37]

The well-educated English woman has a capable, somewhat sub-

---

[35] *The Essays of Elia*. Edited by Charles Kent. George Routledge & Sons, Limited. London. 1894. p. 153.

[36] Cairns, J. A. R. *The Problems of a Career*. Arrowsmith. London. 1926. p. 133.

[37] The writer's diary. (Class assignment, London School of Economics, 1933).

missive manner that is admired both at home, and abroad. These characteristics may account for one fact: the woman-barrister has suffered little from prejudice—judges, and attendants in the courts being most co-operative. When a woman is trying a case, no one tries to make a witty or caustic remark—this being a method used in English courts to upset a barrister who is pleading a dubious case. Famous jurists like the late Lord Darling have left behind them a reputation for wit. It is good to know that women have been spared such harassment.

In general, the public hears little about the uphill road traveled by women in law—that is, how they are inhibited at every turn of the way. Consider the first year after graduation—what then? There are men in every direction, the group for whom society has put forth its best efforts. All a woman can do is stand aside, relying on a streak of good luck to pick up her spirit. Here are some facts:

> A young student having eaten her last dinner and been called to the Bar may frequent the Courts and devil for a senior; but the Judges, the King's Counsellors, the Lord Chancellor, the Attorney General, and, as a rule, the senior for whom she devils, are not women, and it is still impossible for many able women to make a bare living from the law.[38]

An unfortunate part of the story is this: the movement for sex equality was so slow that the general public did not realize what was happening. Even a well-known bookshop in London was caught off-guard, promising to send the writer a "list of books on English women in law." All that came—indicating empty shelves—was a polite note of regret."[39]

It seems that the woman-lawyer is far down the list when it comes to matrimony. There are not many men in England, or elsewhere, who would make congenial companions for this group. It is the price

[38] Holtby, Winifred. *Women (and a Changing Civilization)*. John Lane, The Bodley Head. London. 1936. p. 100.
[39] *Letter* in the writer's file. November 26, 1959.

a few highly-trained women must pay for their knowledge. English girls who work for law certificates—as a professor at the University of London said to the writer—are above the average in good looks. But truths cannot be ignored, and maritally speaking, it has been shown (the 1951 Census of Population) that "ladies of the law" are not doing too well. The question was this: How many English women in a group of 100 have husbands? A separate report is not available. Here are some figures: "religion 15%; law 25%; accountancy 26%; medical and dental services 29%; education 35%; other professions 31%; average, all professions 31%."[40]

In discussions among undergraduate groups of women, it is conceded that men-lawyers "are difficult socially," and in courtship, they often resort to cross-examination, a habit acquired in the practice of their profession. Fortunately, the women-lawyers are enjoying a good income at the present time, and this fact may affect the marriage rate—money often being a deciding factor in plans for wedlock.

As for special benefits, in the past women were overlooked almost entirely. Consider the report from *Whittaker's Almanac:* "Spinsters leave money for the education of young men—seldom for young women." This is a sad commentary on the reading habits of a particular group, as the need for educated women has been preached by the press for over fifty years. However, under the present system of Government scholarships and allowances for college and professional study, no keen-minded girl has to give up study when she is ready and anxious to take up work at university level. But to practice what has been learned requires capital. It would help a great deal to have money, possibly a loan at low interest, just to provide the proper background—that is, first-class office quarters. This support could easily make the difference between success and failure. Indeed, one writer gets down to hard facts and says,

[40] *The Status of Women* (submitted by the R.I.B.A.). London. June 12, 1958.

If the woman barrister is spending her Saturday afternoons washing camisoles, and answering her letters, instead of sending the former to a laundry, dictating the latter to a secretary, and motoring out to glean briefs on Sunningdale golf links — whose fault is it that her male colleagues collect the business?[41]

That question may remain unanswered for some time to come.

Unfortunately, many women are forced to stand behind an economic drop-curtain. But there have been a few exceptions. Helena Florence Normanton will always be associated with a group of English women who first established a good law practice. She was born in Kensington, a well-kept residential section of London. It was a chance remark which turned Helena's mind toward the legal profession. For, as a young girl, she had gone with her mother to visit the family lawyer on a complicated business matter, and ". . . the solicitor discovered that the daughter understood the subject far more easily than her mother did, and remarked 'she is quite a little lawyer.'"[42]

As for education, Helena had lessons at home, and then followed the usual pattern of going to schools in the neighborhood. More formal training led to first-class honours in modern history at the University of London and a diploma in French, History, and Literature at Dijon University in France. All in all, Miss Normanton was by this time a well-educated woman. It is not surprising to hear that she was admitted to the Middle Temple within hours after the Sex Disqualification (Removal) Act had been passed (1919); a call to the Bar came in 1922.

By middle age, Miss Normanton was living in Beckenham, an outer suburb of London. Her practice was, at this point, quite varied —everything from divorce to murder. It is worthy of remark that this able lawyer believed in the abolition of the death penalty at one time; however, she changed her mind completely after dealing with

[41] Holtby, Winifred. *Women (and a Changing Civilization)*. John Lane, The Bodley Head. London. 1936. p. 90.
[42] *Manchester Guardian*. Manchester. October 16, 1957.

a number of under-world characters, defending some, prosecuting others. In the meantime, Helena had married Mr. Gavin B. W. Clark. It was his death in 1948 which publicised the fact that English women had gained the right to use their maiden names for professional purposes. This was a pet idea with Miss Normanton; she went so far as to argue a right-of-name case for women in the United States.

Helena Normanton contributed the following publications: (1) *Everyday Law for Women*; (2) *The Trials of Norman Thorne*; (3) *A. A. Rouse (Notable Trial Series)*; and (4) *Sex Differences in Salary*. There was also a contribution to the *Encyclopaedia Brittanica* (13th edition). This busy lawyer also acted as president of the Married Woman's Association until April, 1952. Then it was that members of that body criticised their very able leader for what was called an "anti-man" policy. This was a cowardly approach to two social problems—marriage and divorce. It was not Miss Normanton's way to give up what she knew was right—actually honest. She formed a break-away organization known as, The Council of Married Women. Miss Normanton continued reform work even after retirement.

The writer recalls Miss Normanton as a woman who wore eye-glasses, had rather large features, and was altogether the wholesome type. She was what is known in professional circles as a "person of parts," finding the time for walking, swimming, and studying Shakespeare at odd moments. She contributed a learned article for the press when *Twelfth Night* was given in Middle Temple Hall on February 2, 1951. To add to the glamour of that occasion, Queen Elizabeth and the Queen Mother attended the performance. She also took great interest in cooking, and may be remembered by some as, the Acting Junior Secretary of the Bar Mess at the Old Bailey; and she put this business venture on a sound financial basis. In addition, this gifted woman was not only "Associate Grand Dame" for the International Society of Woman Lawyers, but also a lecturer to post-graduate students at both the University of Glasgow and the University of London. She usually presided over meetings of the International Society of Business and Professional Women. There is little more to say, except that few women have accomplished so much in so short a period of time. Helena Normanton died in a nursing home in 1957.

One English woman, really a pioneer, has made a worthy name for herself in law—Ethel Bright Ashford, who has given most of her adult life to legal activities. In speaking of her profession, Miss Ashford said, "It is a very pleasant way of gaining knowledge."[43] Ethel was born in London, and lived, as a child, only a short distance from the Crystal Palace. Her father, Henry Bright Ashford, was a well-known merchant in the wholesale district—a trade pattern that was wiped out during two world wars. Indeed, the warehouses along the Thames have almost disappeared.[44]

Ethel attended private schools until the age of thirteen, and then went to Croyden High School—traveling by train or bicycle. She then took up a more formal study program, receiving a Bachelor's degree from the University of London. A short period of time was given over to graduate work. After that it was but a step to the Middle Temple (1922). This woman-lawyer was made welcome into local Government chambers; she "never had anything but pleasant associations" with barristers and solicitors in day-to-day business activities.[45] In due time, Miss Ashford began to write, and lecture on legal subjects, finally becoming a Counsellor at St. Magdalene (one of the West-end boroughs of London). Miss Ashford still finds plenty to do, and is active in various types of social work.

A knowledge of law can be very helpful in all walks of life. This fact was brought out in a vignette of Margaret Delina Kennedy, who

[43] *Letter* in the writer's file. July 22, 1960.

[44] Miss Ashford explained the situation thus: "Everything has changed with regard to business in the city, for now all is ready-made direct from factory to shop."

[45] *Letter* in the writer's file. July 22, 1960.

started legal training after she had become Bursar of Newnham College, Cambridge. In the natural course of events, day-to-day business brought widespread responsibilities. Margaret was born in Plaistow, in 1895. She describes this town as "a run-down suburb on the fringe of the 'East End.'" Her father, Angus Endicott Kennedy was a medical practitioner whose ". . . forebears had been doctors in this part of London for five generations.[46] Margaret attended the West Ham High School for Girls (an ordinary grammar school), and then went on to study at the West Ham Technical College, followed by a year at Newnham College, Cambridge. Graduate work in mathematics was covered at the University of Munich (Germany). As fate would have it, the study of law came after the age of forty—once known as the "lace cap period" for women.

One of the most successful barristers in England is Sybil Campbell (Mrs. N. J. Lane). She was born on October 9, 1889. Her father, Neill Graeme Campbell, was a planter in Ceylon, a lovely island in the Indian Ocean. Miss Campbell described her old home to the writer, as a "tea estate."[47] It was a part of those well-kept white settlements perched high on the mountain slopes—a never-to-be-forgotten sight for tourists. The intrinsic merit of tea-drinking has been paraphrased (from the Bible) as follows: "Tea is better than wine, for it leadeth not into intoxication; it is better than water, for it does not carry disease."

So much for the environment of a little girl who was to have the benefits of an education abroad—a school in North Berwick, Haddingstonshire, Scotland, where she completed both elementary and secondary school work. With such a sound foundation, it is not surprising that Sybil entered Girton College, Cambridge, majoring in Natural Science, Part I, and Economics, Part II. She became, in due time, an Investigating Officer under the Trade Boards Act, an occupation which offered splendid experience in "case work" in actual

[46] *Letter* in the writer's file. August 23, 1960.
[47] *Letter* in the writer's file. July 13, 1960.

situations in society. In this work, law took on a special value, and when the legal profession was opened to women, Sybil began to read in the office of H. H. Joy, K.C. There she earned the right to carry on as a full-fledged barrister, practicing first on the Midland Circuit. Friends insist that,

> It is, no doubt, to her legal training that Sybil Campbell owes that exceptional ability in marshalling essential facts, in presenting a reasoned case and in coming to an unbiased decision which characterizes all she undertakes.[48]

Miss Campbell played a part in the building of Crosby Hall, that delightful meeting-place for university women in London. In retrospect, it is amusing to note a bit of conversation which preceded the great building venture: Miss Campbell said, "Who is going to do the work?" And the reply came sharply, "You are." The story of how stones for Crosby Hall were carted one by one—each stone being numbered—from downtown London to Chelsea has been told many times. Suffice to say, this dear-bought material was set up on a plot of ground facing the Thames. The movement was sponsored by the Crosby Association, Ltd., an organization devoted to the welfare of university women. One of the main objects was to provide a residence hall for students who wished to carry on advanced work in England.

It was understood from the first that the hall would be open to college women from all parts of the world. To quote a leaflet on the subject, "Possibly no other group of women have the privilege of dining daily in a beautiful 15th century Banqueting Hall. And this fact is justly prized by those in the Commonwealth and the United States of America."

The undertaking served its purpose well until after World War II. Then with great foresight, this small band of English women—at a time when pangs of hunger[49] were being felt by almost everyone

---

[48] *University Women's Review.* (An article by Margaret Gladstone). London. July, 1950.

[49] Sandwiches made with tomato catsup (a gift from Canada) were the usual tidbits at teatime.

—extended a helping hand to sister graduates on the Continent. It followed that many forlorn guests arrived—often at night—clutching their few shabby belongings. Overcrowding resulted—cots being placed at times in rooms that were occupied. Miss Campbell and her associates sensed an emergency, and put forward the idea of an addition to Crosby Hall. The new building has been finished, and is occupied, no doubt, by a group of highly cultivated women.

With such unusual ability, it is not surprising to learn that Miss Campbell has a flair for cooking and house-furnishings. She does a great deal of entertaining in her cottage at Bletchingly, Surrey. But professional duties have never been neglected, as witness the following:

From 1930 to 1939 this woman-lawyer was a Metropolitan Chairman of Courts of Referees; from 1929 to 1930 she was organizer of the Girton College Building Fund; from 1930 to 1939 she was the first Secretary of the Cambridge University Appointments Board—a post in which she opened up many worthwhile avenues of employment for university women.[50]

During World War II Sybil Campbell was made Assistant Divisional Food Officer (Enforcement) for the London Division of the Ministry of Food, a service for which she was later awarded an O.B.E.[51] In 1945, Miss Campbell became the *first woman* stipendiary magistrate in the country—these duties being carried out at the Tower Bridge Magistrates Court. It may be said that this woman-lawyer stands above the crowd as far as service to her country is concerned.

Another English woman very active in legal practice is Dorothy Knight Dix (Mrs. Bentley H. Waddy), the second daughter of William Knight Dix, a prominent English barrister. This young woman attended St. Christopher's School, Hampstead, and later

[50] *University Women's Review.* (An article by Margaret Gladstone). London. July 1950.
[51] The Order of the British Empire (O.B.E.) is given by a Sovereign for work of national importance.

went to University College, London—receiving a degree from that institution (the Honours School of English, 1931). After three more years of study, Dorothy was called to the Inner Temple Bar. At the present time she is a member of the South-East Circuit, and Kent Sessions.

A fortunate opening came for Miss Dix in 1946 when Mr. Christmas Humphreys left England to take part in the War Trials in Tokyo. For then she was asked to take over substitute duties, becoming the first woman barrister to sit as a Recorder (*i.e.*, a Judge of a Borough Court of Sessions). This Recordership gave to an English woman—for the first time—the power to sum up a jury and to inflict a maximum sentence (penal servitude for life). Without doubt, wars have been a liberating influence for English women. Miss Dix, Q.C., has written *The Law Relating to Competitive Trading* (1938), and (with G. Evelyn Miles) *In the Eyes of the Law* (1937).

Although Miss Dix has covered a great deal of ground, she has managed to keep out of public notice. Nevertheless, on July 16, 1946, the *Manchester Guardian* reported a trial of some interest. This woman-lawyer was pleading for a man from Sidcup, Kent, knowing full well that he had a police record—a situation which often leads to complications. Miss Dix was quite equal to the task, saying, "If I unwittingly give any indication of my own opinion, you must disregard it, because you are the ones to decide whether this man is guilty or not guilty." A statement of this kind requires a lot of courage, for who wants to lose a case after all the bother of obtaining evidence? However, on this occasion, an honest pronouncement paid off—the jury declared the man guilty. But the Court was lenient—only six months' imprisonment for a man who had shown little respect for the law.

Miss Rose Heilbron, Q.C., made international news recently when she was appointed Recorder of Burley. To go back to an earlier day, the woman thus honored, was born in Liverpool in 1914. She was educated in neighboring institutions, going first to a girl's public school, and then to Liverpool University where she received the degree of LL.B. with first-class honors in 1935, and the higher degree of LL.M in 1937. Two years later, Miss Heilbron moved ahead to accept the Lord Chief Justice Holker Scholarship at Gray's Inn. She was called to the Bar that same year and met the challenge of brilliant legal minds throughout England. But possibly it is in criminal law that Miss Heilbron has made her mark—the Jack Comer case was one that drew considerable publicity. On being acquitted of a stabbing charge in Soho, Jack called out to members of the press, "If you want something to write about, don't write about me, but about Rose Heilbron, the greatest lawyer in history." As the work of a Borough Judge will take only part of Miss Heilbron's time, she will be able to carry on almost as usual with private practice.[52]

One by one the names of professional women are recorded in the pages of this book; and now we come to another, Mary Elizabeth Barber, who was born in Winchester, that lovely cathedral city in Hampshire. She grew up with the thought of having a legal career. In a way, it was a natural decision, for Mary's father, Frederic Viccars Barber, was a solicitor by profession. In addition to private work, he held the post of Clerk to the Hampshire County Council. As a young girl, Mary attended St. Swithins, a school within walking distance of the Barber home. Later, she matriculated in Somerville College, Oxford University. The next step was admission to Gray's Inn in 1935.

In summing up her impressions of women in the legal profession, Miss Barber says that they do best in "out of court activities." She also offers this suggestion, "non-legal experience is very valuable in addition to legal qualifications."[53] This comment brings to mind the educational program favored for young men in the last century: extended travel, coupled with social contacts at a high level.

[52] From notes provided by The Fawcett Society, 27 Wilfred Street, London, S.W. 1. 1960.
[53] *Letter* in the writer's file. July 28, 1960.

As for women who have taken up law in recent years, it is said that they are doing very well. The way had been paved for this group—that is, prejudice now plays but a small part in day-to-day activities. But there is an unfortunate angle to legal practice: the general public hears very little about the court cases handled each year by women, and no protests have ever been heard from the fair sex. However, The London *News Chronicle* of February 3, 1959, printed a few lines—far too few—about Nemone Lethbridge, a young barrister, only twenty-six years of age, who had done a splendid job defending a woman known in newspaper circles as the "Black Orchid." Miss Lethbridge stood up in court and ". . . argued for almost an hour before three Appeal Court judges headed by the Lord Chief Justice." It was a trying case for any barrister. Finally, Miss Lethbridge had the satisfaction of seeing her client hurry from the court room—free, and homeward bound.

Mrs. Elizabeth Kathleen Lane, Q.C.—born in 1905—has become a county court judge. She is the *first English woman* to have civil jurisdiction of this kind—a remarkable achievement. Reporters found the "Lady Judge" somewhat difficult to interview, all personal questions such as, "Does needlework [a hobby] help you to relax?" or "What feminine qualities can you bring to the bench?" being dismissed with a smile and four words, "That is too personal." One reporter did break down the legal barriers enough to say, "Mrs. Lane wore . . . a wig, robes of deep purple and light mauve (pale purple), and a starched white stole."[54] It was a rare bit of description for a man—and most court reporters are men. Mrs. Lane has been assigned to the Edmonson circuit, and will be addressed as "My Lord" in the Divorce Courts. She will be known as "Her Honour Judge Elizabeth Lane, Q.C." at other times.

It may be that grave acts are treated too lightly in England. It is certain that as women gain ground in community affairs, offenses

[54] *The Evening Standard.* London. October 2, 1962.

against women and children will diminish. College graduates in over-the-teacups discussions make it plain that they favor severe penalties for sex offenses. Women in the role of judges most certainly will see to it that habitual criminals do not roam the streets. The gentler members of society may prove to be harsher than their male counterparts when it comes to dealing out punishment. It has been reported that Lord Parker, Great Britain's austere Lord Chief Justice, thinks that women have a keen sense of what is right and what is wrong. In Oxford not long ago, he told a meeting of justices that women "... are a tough lot and he wants more of them for the bench. Lord Parker has long favored stiffer penalties. He was the judge who last week handed down jail terms totaling 95 years to five convicted spies."[55] This learned justice ended his talk by saying that women are doing splendid work as "petticoat justices."

England has long had erudite, really shrewd lawyers. But expert counsel means nothing if the public at large lacks the ability to pay for good services. Many law-abiding families get into trouble through no fault of their own—that is, dogs may wander, neighbors may trespass, visitors may misbehave. Any one of these experiences could be hard on a limited budget. Guidance is now available by way of a legal operation—a plan by which help is given free, or at a nominal charge. Such assistance has been a god-send to hundreds of families in middle-class society. What might be called a protective system is not new—the plan having been known to people in small villages for centuries. There is in the United States an organization of this kind which borders on full achievement. The writer recalls a family retainer, an aged Negro, who had a brush with the law over property rights. The American society made short shift of the problem by writing a few letters.

Miss Eulalie Spicer is, at this time, one of England's most active workers in the Legal Aid Scheme. She was trained as a solicitor, and

[55] The Cincinnati *Enquirer*. Cincinnati, Ohio (U.S.A.). March 27, 1961.

is known among lawyers as a women who is "efficient to the point of intimidation."[56] What an asset this could be in cases which involved imaginary grievances. Miss Spicer, like so many professional women, is an inveterate smoker, often punctuating clear-cut remarks with an amber cigarette-holder. Callers are subjected to grave questioning as they sit in that spacious well-furnished office overlooking the chimney-pots of Bloomsbury.

The business operations in Miss Spicer's department are much heavier than the average person realizes. In London alone, the administrative staff numbers close to one hundred, with an additional list of solicitors and barristers on call for emergencies. An oddity is this: damage suits predominate—many of these cases being concerned with personal injuries, and quite a number have to do with medical treatment. All this bespeaks the career of a woman who has gained, not only prestige, but a good livelihood. It has been reported that Miss Spicer earns close to £2,000 each year.[57]

England is keeping up with the movement for legal protection, and recently the work has been extended. A State-financed program has been established to give advice to people whose problems are not serious enough for a court struggle. The service was started on March 2, 1959. It is available for as little as a few shillings—without fee for the very poor. It is evident that this branch of welfare work will one day reach greater proportions. At present, damages obtained in successful actions throughout England and Wales amount to thousands of pounds each year. Human nature being what it is, men and women are much more interested in "going to law," than in "paying the costs."

English women have been moving ahead in a calling that was well-established when Chaucer's "Sargeant of Lawe" rode to Canterbury. Many obstacles have been encountered—not the least of which

[56] *The Evening Standard*. London. February 24, 1959.
[57] *Ibid.*

was prejudice of a stubborn character. But for all that, 677 wives and daughters had become fully qualified lawyers by the time the 1951 Census was taken, and the number has greatly increased during the succeeding years. These newcomers want to be accepted on ability, not on any sentimental notion of sex. In the long run, what is fair has a way of winning out in the race of life. So let it be with women in the legal profession.

X. Conclusion

Duration the past one hundred years there has been a complete reversal in the position of women, not only in England, but throughout the world. The so-called "weaker sex" had accepted a lowly place in society as a matter of course. How could it have been otherwise when strength was a special asset in the labor market? But with the development of new techniques in industry, women found that they could perform difficult tasks quite as well as men. It followed that there was a general awakening among women of all classes.

It had always been thought that refinement in female character depended upon a sheltered life. Naturally, people were distressed when really "nice girls" began to work in large cities. The subject was seldom discussed in exclusive social circles. But finally, Sir Robert Hart (b. 1835) who had been away from London for thirty years, had this to say about change: "The women are now going to business." It was the emergence of womanhood which brought surprise—the girls who hurried to their places of employment each day, and having done a day's work, hurried back to their homes each night. Yet that was the situation in England, the country where anything new is open to question. There was also a decline in good manners during this period—gentle behavior requiring a background of tradition. New methods of transportation had made it easy for people to move from place to place.

Women enjoyed a free way of life even more after their services had been taken for granted, for then they were able to work in offices that were better heated, better lighted, and better furnished—the day of one desk, two chairs, and a faded map having passed into memory. Further, salaries were high enough to pay for decent living quarters.

Then came World War I. Business, especially business in the luxury trades, collapsed almost overnight.[1] This condition dislocated the economic structure, thousands of people being thrown out of employment, but it was soon realized that women could be substituted for men; opportunity was knocking at doors long closed. Women of all classes rushed to the employment bureaus; they signed up for work, work of any kind, in any place.[2] Ability had nothing to do with the movement. Stirring events followed: workers with frail, white hands mended leaking pipes, dug graves, ploughed fields, and gathered crops.

The war period brought out some unknown facts. It was found that women were not only precise—much more so than men—but that they were unusually trustworthy.[3] As for the youth of the country, they enjoyed economic independence to the full, buying this, buying that, going here, going there. But these experiences left a mark not altogether desirable. Girls began to work for a pittance in order to get away from household drudgery—in some cases, the watchful eyes of parents.

Today, daughters are asserting themselves in no uncertain manner. In sum, the average girl wants more spending money; therefore, she makes every effort to secure an office job. However, some parents in upper-class society look upon this new-found freedom as something strange—not quite proper. In a confidential talk, an English mother said to the writer, "After a girl marries, I like to think all this foolishness stops." This is a delicate situation, for an opinion lays claim to truth. It stands to reason that arguments will arise in many families over the right to earn a living.

Too little emphasis has been placed on the fact that married

[1] The crisis of 1938 brought about the same uncertainty; establishments stopping delivery services within a fortnight.

[2] What was called the "Feminine Army" numbered at one time 900,000.

[3] According to Helena Normanton, the English woman-barrister, ". . . there are about eight male criminals to one female." *Good Housekeeping.* New York 19, N.Y. (U.S.A.). January, 1939.

women are the targets for special bias in England, advertisements for "unmarried women" causing little or no comment in social and business circles. This means that the married-woman doctor, the married-woman psychologist, the married-woman alomer may be barred from work for which all of these individuals have been trained. Figures published by the Ministry of Labour indicate that at a time when there was almost no fall in the number of unemployed single women, there was a rise of 6,000 in the number of unemployed married women.

A strong force against women has been the recoil from democracy in what might be called civilized countries. Thus, the International Federation of University Women has taken the following stand:

> We strongly deprecate the tendency increasingly evident in the majority of countries by new regulations to debar women from careers for which they are well qualified, whether on grounds of sex or marriage. We consider that such regulations are inimical to the family which is itself the foundation of society; and desire to affirm our profound conviction that it is only by permitting and encouraging women to play a full and responsible part in the intellectual life of their country that the civilization and the prosperity of future generations may be developed on a sound basis of general understanding and enlightenment.[4]

A business depression always aggravates the employment situation. A study has been made of these trying times—that is, delving into facts which concern earnings, employment, and unfair business practices. Formerly, problems of this kind have been discussed without benefit of reliable data. But along in the nineteen-thirties a questionnaire was sent to a large group of university graduates. The majority responded, giving somewhat detailed accounts of their activities. These experiences covered a ten-year period of good and bad times. The investigation showed that as a rule women work for an employer—only three per cent being on an independent footing. The worst effects of a depression were among those in occupations other than education.

[4] *Journal of the Association of University Women.* Washington, D.C. (U.S.A.). January, 1936.

The drop in number of those whose highest salary in the ten-year period was $2,000 (£400) or more is terrific, being 40 per cent, and the number of those who had received less than $1,500 (£300) as the highest salary in that decade was almost doubled in 1934.[5]

It was distressing to find that 41 per cent of the women in such a body contributed to the support of dependents. This burden was carried by wives and daughters in almost all classes of society. This report suggests that women were suffering from the double handicap of prejudice and responsibility. After all, it is ability, not sex, which should determine what goes on in the business world.

There is a field of activity which awaits women of more than average ability. England needs a large number of technologists. The target is 20,000 of these new scientists by 1966, which would mean almost double of the body of graduates the country produced in the year 1956. It is understood full well that this goal can not be reached without the help of both sexes.

Slipping into old ways of thought, officials argue that the Government trains women, and then gets a poor deal out of the arrangement —the average girl leaving industry for marriage just when her services are the most valuable. But statistics more or less contradict this view, for women by some magic known only to themselves, are not only going in, but staying in, many different fields of employment.

In recent years women have entered all professions in large and small numbers. During World War II and the years since then, women have also entered the new pseudo-professions, all types of business and industry, and the various Government services—including the diverse fields of health and social welfare work. The female labor-market has provided a vast reservoir of brainpower and skill so urgently needed in the country struggling for self-sufficiency. In 1957, over 50 per cent of women in the 20–35 year age group were employed. As previously mentioned, there is still an acute shortage of teachers.

[5] *Journal of the Association of University Women.* Publication Office. Concord, N. H. (U.S.A.). June, 1939.

Some idea of what girl students are doing may be learned from the following set of figures:

In 1951, 16,000 girls passed the G.C.E.[6] in mathematics; in 1955 there were 22,000. In biology in 1951, 12,000; in 1955, there were 20,000. In physics, chemistry and general science in 1951 there were 9,000, and in 1955, there were 12,000.[7]

Without doubt women are holding their own in scholarly pursuits.

No young girl with adequate preparation would have difficulty in entering a university in England at the present time. For with the assistance of Government scholarships and grants-in-aid, countless doors of opportunity have been opened to them. The following table shows the present trend in higher education:

COURSES TAKEN BY FULL-TIME STUDENTS IN UNIVERSITIES, 1960–1961[8]

Arts, including Theology, Fine Art, Law, Music, Commerce, Economics and Education:
    Men. 30,008
    Women 16,378

Pure Science:
    Men. 20,735
    Women 5,718

Medicine:
    Men. 9,315
    Women 2,961

Dentistry:
    Men. 2,461
    Women 625

Technology, including Applied Chemistry, Mining, Metallurgy and Architecture:
    Men. 15,880
    Women 345

Agriculture, including Forestry, Horticulture and Dairy Work:
    Men. 1,806
    Women 216

Veterinary Science:
    Men. 1,125
    Women 126

DEGREES AND DIPLOMAS OBTAINED, 1960–1961[9]

First degrees—honours: Men 11,726
                          Women 3,620

[6] Examination for the General Certificate in Education.

[7] *The Woman Engineer*. London. Autumn, 1957.

[8] *Annual Abstract of Statistics*, No. 99, 1962. Ministry of Education. Her Majesty's Stationery Office. London. p. 100.

[9] *Ibid.* p. 100.

Degrees and Diplomas Obtained, 1960–1961 (*continued*)

First degrees—ordinary:	Men 5,125
	Women 1,955
Higher degrees:	Men 2,994
	Women 279
Diplomas:	Men 5,891
	Women 2,586
Total degrees:	Men 19,845
	Women 5,854

Many appeals for overseas workers are being received by government offices. As for women, conditions are quite favorable—eyebrows no longer being raised when a lone traveler appears at the airport, or steamship dock. Of course British officials make every effort to smooth the way for workers. Mr. Kenneth Lindsay, Parliamentary Secretary to the Board of Education, held forth on the subject of preparedness when he delivered the annual lecture to the Cardiff Guild of Graduates in 1937. He said in substance that, a new synthesis of training and outlook was badly needed. The community demanded men and women with a wide understanding of human problems. Here was a great challenge to the modern university. They must not relax standards one iota or cheapen the value of university education, but, unless universities sent out men and women with gifts of leadership and personality, they were failing in their mission.

The English women who work abroad must have courage of a high order—the duties being arduous, the monetary returns small. But today, men and women often seek careers of this kind with the idea of helping, rather than exploiting, the natives of backward countries. This approach to social service is recognized by all groups, however primitive they may be. The best opportunities are open to well-qualified women between twenty-five and thirty-five years of age.

In 1936, the Society for the Overseas Settlement of British Women

...transplanted 476 women, mostly professional, nurses, governesses, and so on. Nearly 300 went to the Union of South Africa, 85 to Rhodesia, 46 to Australia, 22 to Kenya, 16 to Canada and 4 to New Zealand.[10]

All in all, the fine work that has been done in far-away countries can hardly be estimated. However, the writer found in her travels around the world that partly civilized groups—that is, men and women far down the social scale—over-estimate their own ability for self-improvement and self-government. Foreign posts offer worthwhile opportunities to workers who are trained for a particular type of service. Naturally, individuals with the best credentials obtain the best assignments. To state a fact, men and women in foreign countries are very critical of strangers.

After World War II, overseas re-settlement work was carried on by various area representative agencies with offices in England. Widespread publicity was given to the movement, emphasizing advantages of a gainful nature. Under the careful supervision and assistance of these agencies, thousands of men and women emigrated from the homeland to the British Dominions and South Africa.

The English people face a problem that is very real, but one that is seldom mentioned in polite society—there are many more women than men in England.[11] Therefore, a certain number of girls can not hope to marry, and must adjust themselves to a life in which wifehood plays no part. As might be expected, the question of self-support is uppermost in family discussions. English newspapers, recognizing what amounts to a serious question, present a great deal of material on the subject of employment.

Since life is a series of adjustments, it was only natural that the late nineteen-forties should have brought a number of complex situations to the English people. The writer recalls being surprised when

---

[10] The New York *Times*. February 10, 1937.

[11] According to a Census (England and Wales) taken after World War I, women outnumbered men by more than a million and a half. The figures for the Census taken in 1951 were only slightly less.

she heard a woman's voice call, "Four inside, and the rest up" on a bus going to Piccadilly. In time, the idea of having women collect fares was accepted in all parts of England. But it was not long before a troublesome question arose: how to hold on to bus-jobs. These new workers were clever, in that they solved a serious problem by giving a day's work for a day's pay—this being a feat not only appreciated, but highly valued by all employers. Thus, constancy turned out very well—women-conductors receiving their regular pay envelops despite the clamor of men who had been trained for the same type of employment. In looking back, it is remarkable that such an immature group had so much foresight, considering the average woman-worker was under twenty-five years of age.

The recent past has been something of a testing ground for married people, as nothing brings out real traits of character like war and its aftermath. Consider the men and women in England after World War II; they had to contend with damaged furnishings and crowded quarters just to pick up the old way of life again. On the surface things went along smoothly—that is, Big Ben sounded the hour, swans drifted down the Thames, the "Chelsea Flower Show" opened as usual to the stirring tune of "God Save the King." But it all amounted to a hard pull, as food, clothing, everything was on short rations. But the people had changed; they were more talkative, more enthusiastic, brimming over at times with appreciation of what friends and relations had done in the struggle for existence. This difference was especially noticeable among middle-aged couples. Story after story was told of what "my man did the day after *our* bombing attack." Indeed, the proprietor of a small business establishment said to the writer, "My wife thinks I am the greatest hero in London, seeing how I always opened the shop, and then did my turn as warden at night."

What about the future of English women? Janet Gorham, when a student at the Ladies' College, Cheltenham, said:

Whether an educated woman has either marriage or a career in view, or whether she proposes ultimately to combine the two, there are certain definite ideals and standards to which she will expect to attain.

Her primary aim will doubtless be her own happiness and that of others, but in addition she will have to contend with the practical aspects of life. Having once tasted the fruits of emancipation, women will take an increasingly active part in international relationships, and will expect to have a basic knowledge of politics and economics to enable them to become competent citizens and to take an intelligent interest in the guidance of world affairs.

In the past few years, women have entered nearly every profession and often have not been entirely successful; for this reason, coupled with a growing realization that a woman's primary duty is, after all, to her own family, there will probably be an increasing tendency to revert to the home. From her education then, the average woman will expect to gain these qualifications which will best fit her to play an intelligent and sympathetic part in her community life. The women of today are more experienced and perceptive than they have ever been before; they have also learned the value of ideals, and expect from their training that which will give them breadth of character and a true understanding both of human nature and of spiritual matters. . . .[12]

Now comes a comment that has overtones of distress. A young Oxford graduate is disillusioned with the whole business of living. She says:

The less one does the better. For every time you increase your links with life, you are storing up greater torments for yourself in the future. . . . Of course, you are not still in the intervening nerve-wracking stage when you were eternally puzzled by trying to decide why the world existed. You realize now that all such abstract questions about a non-specified and non-defined world are meaningless, and that you can only talk intelligently about particular and specific aspects of life. And clearly you are happier since you have ceased trying to make a meaningless, non-logical structure into something sensible, unitary, consistent or intelligible. You are no longer perpetually maddened by being unable to decide the purpose of anything, for you see that nothing has any purpose, any aim, any *raison d'etre*. But it is equally clear that there must be aspects of the world which have value for you, or at least a certain likelihood must exist that some will occur in the future, otherwise provided you are logical, you would have committed suicide. . . .

[12] *Letter* in the writer's file (contributed by invitation). London. December 3, 1938.

The problem seems to me insoluble. Either you have got to face the fact that there are usually people being massacred daily in some part of the world, and that it will soon be the turn of yourself and your friends, in which case it seems pointless to continue doing anything.[13]

Is it that the widespread feeling of futility among young people is due to the pagan influence so rampant in schools and colleges? For more than a few in the under-thirty group have discarded the God of their fathers, and placed their faith in an ethical ideal not related in any way to the eternal spirit.

At this point, another group will be considered—that is, the daughters of upper-class families who plan to stay at home, and yet carry on a number of outside activities. Many of the great London balls are now being given for the benefit of charitable institutions.[14] However, the invitation lists are prepared very carefully, just as they have always been for private entertainments. Further, the theme of conversation in home circles the past few decades has been "How shall I occupy my mind?" not "How shall I get a husband?" It all amounts to a new outlook on life. A great deal of credit must go to the half-grown boys and girls of England, for it is they who are largely responsible for this changed ideology. The idea is of course to abolish, or at least to diminish, the evils that have long infiltrated the social structure. In a way, *this will to correct mal-adjustment* in human affairs distinguishes the civilization of today from that of yesterday.

The old saying that a woman can make or break a man was never truer than it is today. For great stress is now being placed on marital status, not only in England, but in many other parts of the world. For instance, a wife comes under scrutiny if her husband is in line for promotion in a large business firm. It is a well-known fact that executives in England seldom send a man abroad unless he is married, and the father of children. Pressure is exerted even further, as one wife

[13] "The Voice of Under Thirty" (from *The Spectator*). London. June 6, 1947. pp. 37–39.
[14] *The Queen*. London. December 16, 1937.

—wealthy in her own right—discovered after moving into a large house in an exclusive neighborhood. Trouble arose almost at once; this particular couple was out-spending all other families in the company. Perhaps the time had come when the wife of an executive was expected in effect, to marry the corporation. Women are rebelling in no uncertain way; they do not like so much emphasis on really personal matters. But this biased approach to employment may as well be accepted—employers having the upper-hand in managerial policy.

Now a few words about the "Suffrage Museum," the smallest in London. A few mementos—all with tragic implications—are displayed in show-cases. Visitors handle rough prison garments with something akin to wonder. However, the item which completely staggers the younger group is a copy of the weird bill, P.T.D.A.[15] which allowed jailors to release a suffragette who had starved herself, and then re-arrest her after a few weeks of rest and care at home. "But the Government never did such a thing," said a girl of sixteen in the writer's presence. She was wrong—evil deeds aplenty having been carried on without *shame*, without any feeling of *incompetence*.

This exhibit brings all kinds of reactions. As for appreciation, some women take their blessings in stride, while others express a feeling of deep gratitude. One English working girl expressed her reactions thus:

Of course I had *read* all I could about the struggle for suffrage. Ever since I was a schoolgirl I devoured every item of information which had come my way; it had mostly been books, because it happened that no one in my immediate circle had been connected with the fight. Later, when I came to London to take up a job I never put a latchkey to my own front door, without the remembrance, conscious or sub-conscious, of what I owed to the women who had got the vote and opened the way to freedom for me and my generation.[16]

Finally, women aspired to seats in the House of Lords. But the

---

[15] Prisoner's Temporary Discharge Act. Passed in 1913.
[16] *Suffragette Fellowship*. "Calling All Women." February, 1947.

general public more or less ignored the debates, thinking the issue would die a natural death. However, the day came when real disparagement was heaped upon women. Lord Ferrere held the spotlight. He said,

> Frankly, I find women in politics highly distasteful. In general, they are organizing, they are pushing and they are commanding. Some of them do not even know where loyalty to their country lies. I disagree with those who say that women in your Lordships' House would cheer up our Benches. If one looks at a cross-section of women already in Parliament, I do not feel that one could say that they are an exciting example of the attractiveness of the opposite sex. . . . It is generally accepted, for better or worse, that a man's judgement is generally more logical and less tempestuous than that of a woman. Why then should we encourage women to eat their way, like acid into metal, into positions of trust and responsibility which previously men have held.[17]

The Lords—a few of them at least—had still to learn that arguments of a serious nature should be carried on without bitterness, without prejudice, certainly without the *cowardly tool of disparagement*.

There were other statesmen who carried on somewhat irregular campaigns—that is, seeing relationships in a confused way. At times the situation resembled the familiar mix-up over "who is taller":

> "Smith is taller than Brown; and
> Jones is shorter than Smith; and therefore
> Jones is shorter than Brown."

It was a simple matter for a speaker to prove to a listless audience that women would be unable to handle Government business in a satisfactory manner. More often than not subtle tactics were used. There would be flowery remarks about England, a word or two in praise of women, then a long list of unrelated facts touched up with a good story that had nothing to do with the situation. The crowd would disperse, well pleased with what they had heard, and in most cases what they wanted to hear. "Speak sweet, I'd have you do it ever."

[17] *The New York Times Magazine.* New York, (U.S.A.). December 15, 1957.

But there were a few men who could, and did do a good job of reasoning. Thus, Lord Mathers stood up in the House, and did himself credit by being not only terse, but honest. The speaker started in an almost apologetic way:

> I must say that I find it difficult to visualize women Peers in this House, but I could not find it possible logically to oppose their entry here, in view of the capacity they have increasingly demonstrated over ever-widening spheres of activity. It is in keeping with modern tendencies to give women the same opportunities that men have, and I think it would be wrong for this House to remain as a sole shelter for men only.[18]

To an outsider thinking only in terms of reason, and completely overlooking age-old sentiment, the important point is not who is going to sit in the House, but who is going to provide the brainpower to direct the affairs of the country in a world beset by confusion—political, economic, and intellectual. War has come to England twice in this century. It could happen again.

There was a strong suspicion that many high officials in England confused social progress with evolution—that is, they believed that vexatious questions would correct themselves. Years passed with more and more confusion, more and more resistance to change. Finally, with patience wearing thin on all sides, the Government broke with a thousand-year-old tradition, and admitted women to the House of Lords.[19] Soon thereafter, the Dowager Marchioness Reading (retitled Baroness Swanborough) was invited to sit in the House. She was introduced with due formality by Viscount Kilmuir, Lord Chancellor, on October 21, 1958. Lady Reading is known for her splendid work in founding the Woman's Volunteer Service.

There are three other women who are now Peers in their own right (1960): Barbara Wootton gained recognition as a sociologist; Baroness Ravensdale shaped the course for a national system of

[18] *The New York Times Magazine.* New York, (U.S.A.). December 15, 1957.

[19] The Life Peerage Bill, by which women were to become eligible to sit in the House of Lords, was finally passed on April 30, 1958, and was given Royal assent on the same day.

girls' clubs; and Katherine Eliot performed special services as a delegate to the United Nations. At a recent session of Parliament, these four ladies appeared before the Queen in a joint assembly of Lords and Commoners in the House of Lords. They were well poised, and becomingly gowned in scarlet robes trimmed with soft white ermine —real peers of the realm. These newcomers are appointed for life only, their titles are not hereditary.

People generally should never under-estimate the courage of a woman. For like a woodchuck defending her burrow, or a town-sparrow protecting her young, she-creatures all display a brand of valor that is past human understanding. It is this fortitude which has so often baffled men in their efforts to subdue members of the opposite sex, especially groups riled to anger. This is a pertinent comment on the struggle for "Women's Rights." The movement was simple enough—a new group of workers going out of their way to establish a social order which would correspond to the economic changes then taking place in society. But this very *sensible plan* ran counter to well-established laws; it was therefore fought stubbornly by high British officials.[20] Strangely enough, after centuries of companionship, English men had not learned a basic truth: women can be *abused* and *intimidated*, but they cannot be *restrained* and *conquered*. Further, like the sweet peas in Mendel's garden, they run more or less true to type.

As time passed, a peculiar situation developed in England between 1925 and 1945. It was during this period that employers began to call for *brain-power* instead of *muscle-power*. Girls who were graduates of the modern Secondary Schools came forward in great numbers. The business world had never known anything like it. Women began to outnumber men in white-collar jobs. Other forces contributed to an economic upheaval: there was the impact of a long depression; there

---

[20] During the suffrage fray, Herbert Henry Asquith was the Prime Minister, and Reginald Mc. Kenna was the Home Secretary—the last official being responsible for enforcing the "Prisoner's Temporary Discharge Act" (The Cat and Mouse Act), which was passed in 1913.

was the tragedy of World War II; there was the slow collapse of class barriers; there was the curious breakdown of religious authority; there was the swift advance in technical knowledge. Thus, it came about that the old dilemma of bondage and marriage or freedom and the market place, resolved itself—wives and daughters carrying on with family duties, and outside obligations simultaneously.

What the future holds will be the creation of human beings yet unborn. May the King of Kings keep watch!

Index